GUCCI

gucci.com

#GucciAria

Spring 2022
Celebrations

Front

Back

Words & Pictures

Front cover:
Will Matsuda, *Kiku #1*, 2021
Courtesy the artist
(See page 128)

Opposite:
**Rinko Kawauchi, *Untitled*,
2021, from the series
*Under the same sky***
Courtesy the artist
(See page 120)

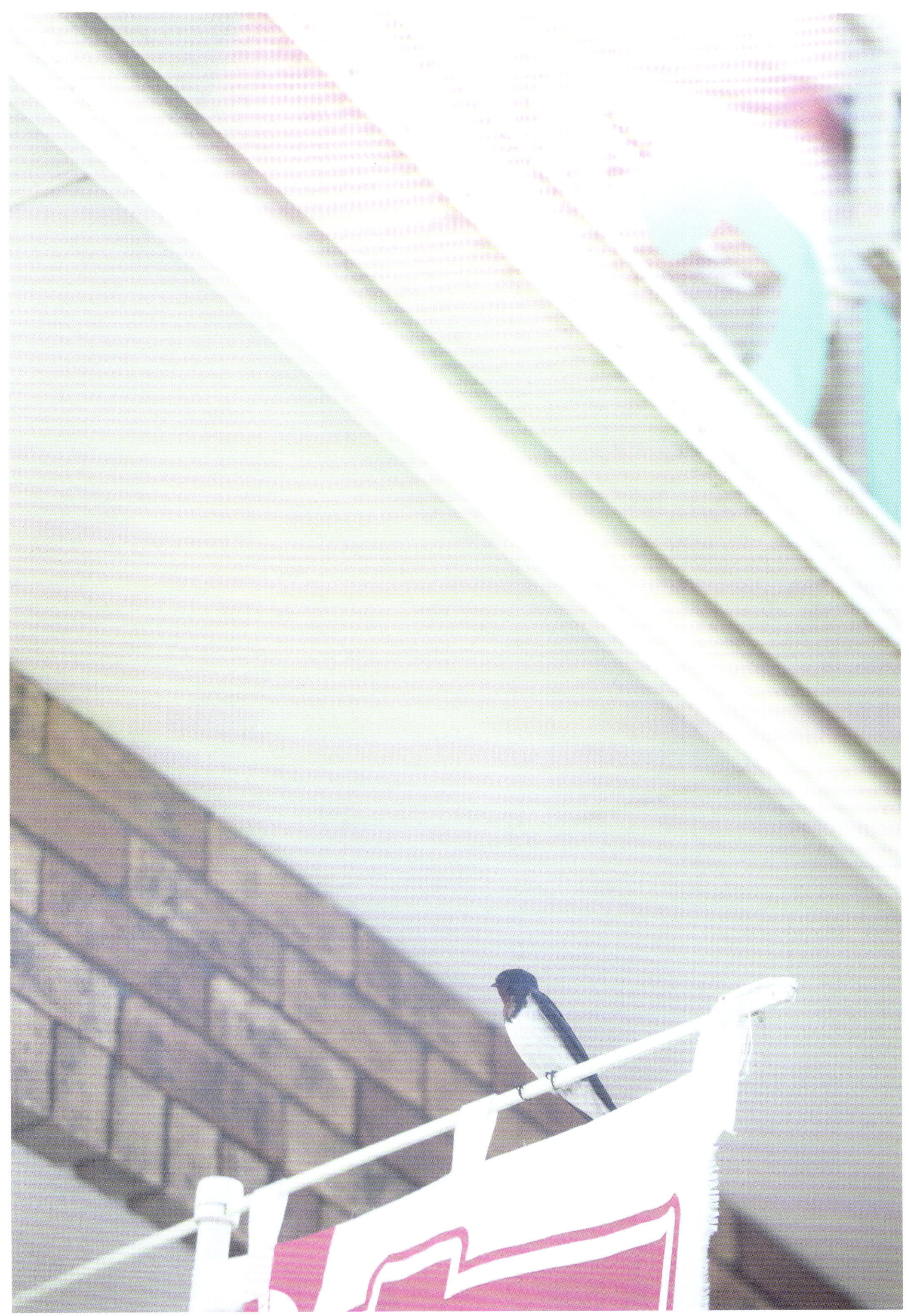

Aperture, a not-for-profit foundation, connects the photo community and its audiences with the most inspiring work, the sharpest ideas, and with each other—in print, in person, and online.

Aperture (ISSN 0003-6420) is published quarterly, in spring, summer, fall, and winter, at 548 West 28th Street, 4th Floor, New York, N.Y. 10001. In the United States, a one-year subscription (four issues) $75; a two-year subscription (eight issues) is $124. In Canada, a one-year subscription is $95. All other international subscriptions are $115 per year. Visit aperture.org to subscribe. Single copies may be purchased at $24.95 for most issues. Subscribe to the *Aperture Digital Archive* at aperture.org/archive. Periodicals postage paid at New York and additional offices. Postmaster: Send address changes to *Aperture*, P.O. Box 3000, Denville, N.J. 07834. Address queries regarding subscriptions, renewals, or gifts to: *Aperture* Subscription Service, 866-457-4603 (U.S. and Canada), or email custsvc_aperture@fulcoinc.com.

Newsstand distribution in the U.S. is handled by CMG. For international distribution, contact Central Books, centralbooks.com. Other inquiries, email orders@aperture.org or call 212-505-5555.

Become a Member of Aperture to take your interest in and knowledge of photography further. With an annual tax-deductible gift of $250, membership includes a complimentary subscription to *Aperture* magazine, discounts on Aperture's award-winning publications, a member-exclusive gift, and more. To join, visit aperture.org/join, or contact membership@aperture.org.

Library of Congress Catalog Card No: 58-30845.

ISBN 978-1-59711-524-7

Printed in Turkey by Ofset Yapimevi

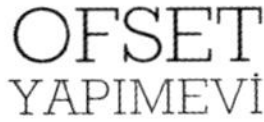

Support has been provided by members of *Aperture*'s Magazine Council: The Kanakia Foundation, Jon Stryker and Slobodan Randjelović, and Susan and Thomas Dunn. Additional support is provided in part by the New York City Department of Cultural Affairs in partnership with the City Council.

Aperture Foundation's programs are made possible in part by the New York State Council on the Arts with the support of the Office of the Governor and the New York State Legislature.

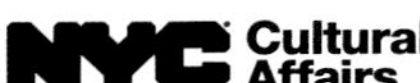
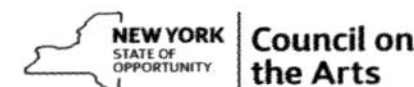

aperture

The Magazine of Photography and Ideas

aperture.org

Statement of Ownership, Management, and Circulation (Required by 39 U.S.C. 3685). 1. Publication Title: Aperture; 2. Publication no.: 0003-6420; 3. Filing Date: October 1, 2021 4. Issue Frequency: Quarterly; 5. No. of Issues Published Annually: 4; 6. Annual Subscription Price: $75.00; 7. Complete Mailing Address of Known Office of Publication: Aperture Foundation, 548 West 28th Street, 4th Floor, New York, NY 10001-5511; Contact Person: Dana Triwush; Telephone: 212-946-7116; 8. Complete Mailing Address of Headquarters or General Business Office of Publisher: Aperture Foundation, 548 West 28th Street, 4th Floor, New York, NY 10001-5511; 9. Full Names and Complete Mailing Addresses of Publisher, Editor, and Managing Editor: Publisher: Dana Triwush, Aperture Foundation, 548 West 28th Street, 4th Floor, New York, NY 10001-5511; Editor: Michael Famighetti, Aperture Foundation, 548 West 28th Street, 4th Floor, New York, NY 10001-5511; Managing Editor: Brendan Embser, Aperture Foundation, 548 West 28th Street, 4th Floor, New York, NY 10001-5511; 10. Owner: Aperture Foundation, Inc., 548 West 28th Street, 4th Fl., New York, NY 10001; 11. Known Bondholders, Mortgagees, and Other Security Holders Owning or Holding 1 Percent or More of Total Amount of Bonds, Mortgages, or Other Securities: None; 12. Tax Status: The purpose, function, and nonprofit status of this organization and the exempt status for federal income tax purposes: Has Not Changed During Preceding 12 Months; 13. Publication Title: Aperture; 14. Issue Date for Circulation Data Below: Summer 2021 #243; 15. Extent and Nature of Circulation (Average No. Copies Each Issue During Preceding 12 Months; No. Copies of Single Issue Published Nearest to Filing Date): a. Total Number of Copies (Net press run): 13,335; 13,667; b. Paid Circulation: (1) Mailed Outside-County Paid Subscriptions Stated on PS Form 3541: 5,586; 5,566; (2) Mailed In-County Paid Subscriptions Stated on PS Form 3541: 0; 0; (3) Paid Distribution Outside the Mails Including Sales Through Dealers and Carriers, Street Vendors, Counter Sales, and Other Paid Distribution Outside USPS: 3,682; 2,915; (4) Paid Distribution by Other Classes of Mail Through the USPS: 10; 10; c. Total Paid Distribution: 9,278; 8,491; d. Free or Nominal Rate Distribution: (1) Free or Nominal Rate Outside-County Copies included on PS Form 3541: 349; 335; (2) Free or Nominal Rate In-County Copies Included on PS Form 3541: 0; 0; (3) Free or Nominal Rate Copies Mailed at Other Classes Through the USPS: 130; 132; (4) Free or Nominal Rate Distribution Outside the Mail: 130; 67; e. Total Free or Nominal Rate Distribution: 608; 534; f. Total Distribution: 9,886; 9,025; g. Copies not Distributed: 3,449; 4,642; h. Total: 13,335; 13,667; i. Percent Paid 93.8%; 94.1%; 16. Electronic Copy Circulation. a. Paid Electronic Copies: 976; 1,089; b. Total Paid Print Copies + Paid Electronic Copies: 10,254; 9,580; c. Total Print Distribution + Paid Electronic Copies: 10,862; 10,114; d. Percent Paid (Both Print & Electronic Copies): 94.4%; 94.7%; I certify that 50% of all my distributed copies (Electronic & Print) are paid above a nominal price. 17. Publication of Statement of Ownership: Will be printed in the Spring 2022 issue of this publication. 18. I certify that all information furnished on this form is true and complete. I understand that anyone who furnishes false or misleading information on this form or who omits material or information requested on the form may be subject to criminal sanctions (including fines and imprisonment) and/or civil sanctions (including civil penalties). Signature and Title of Editor, Publisher, Business Manager, or Owner: Dana Triwush, Publisher, October 1, 2021

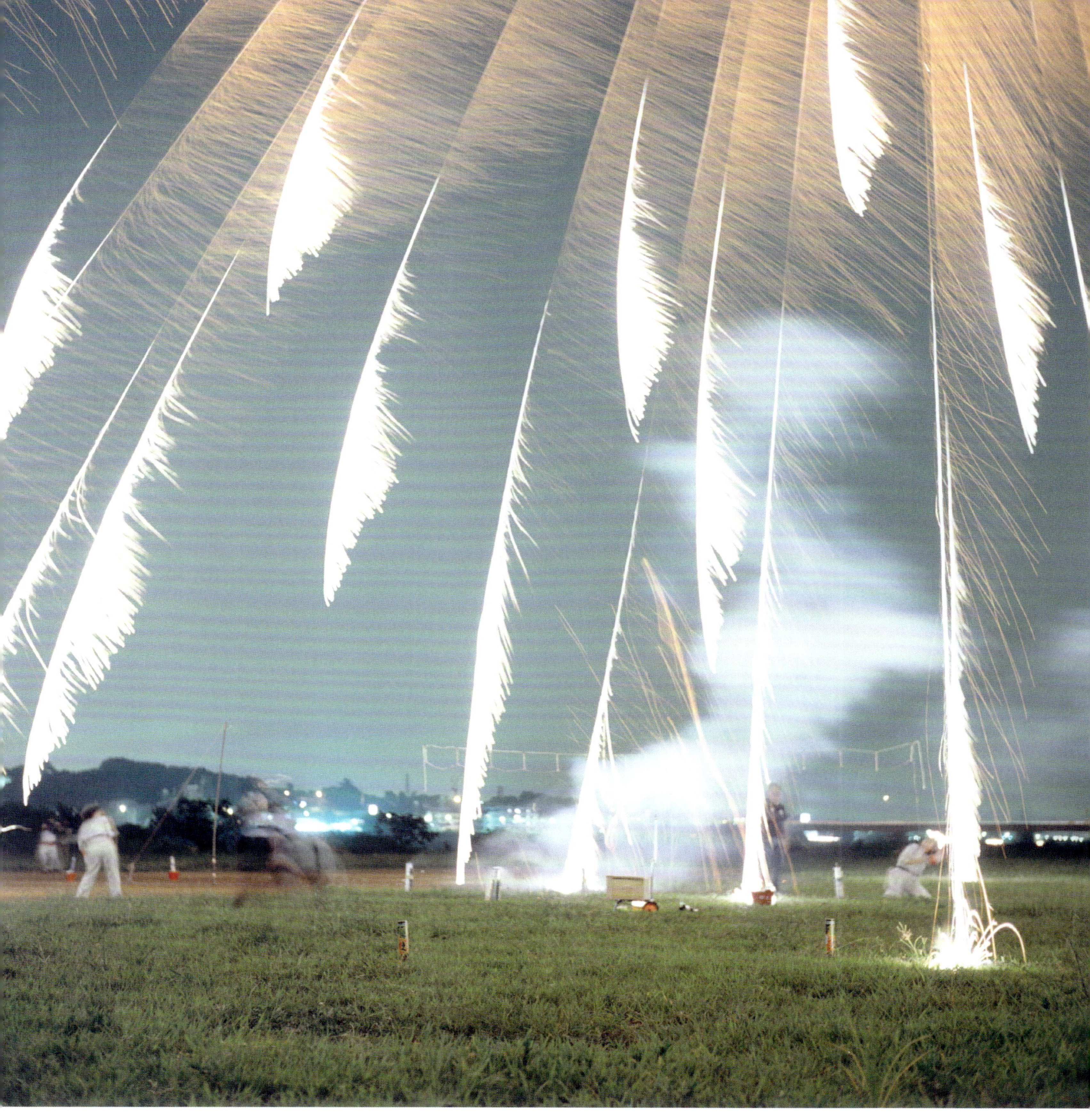

RINKO KAWAUCHI

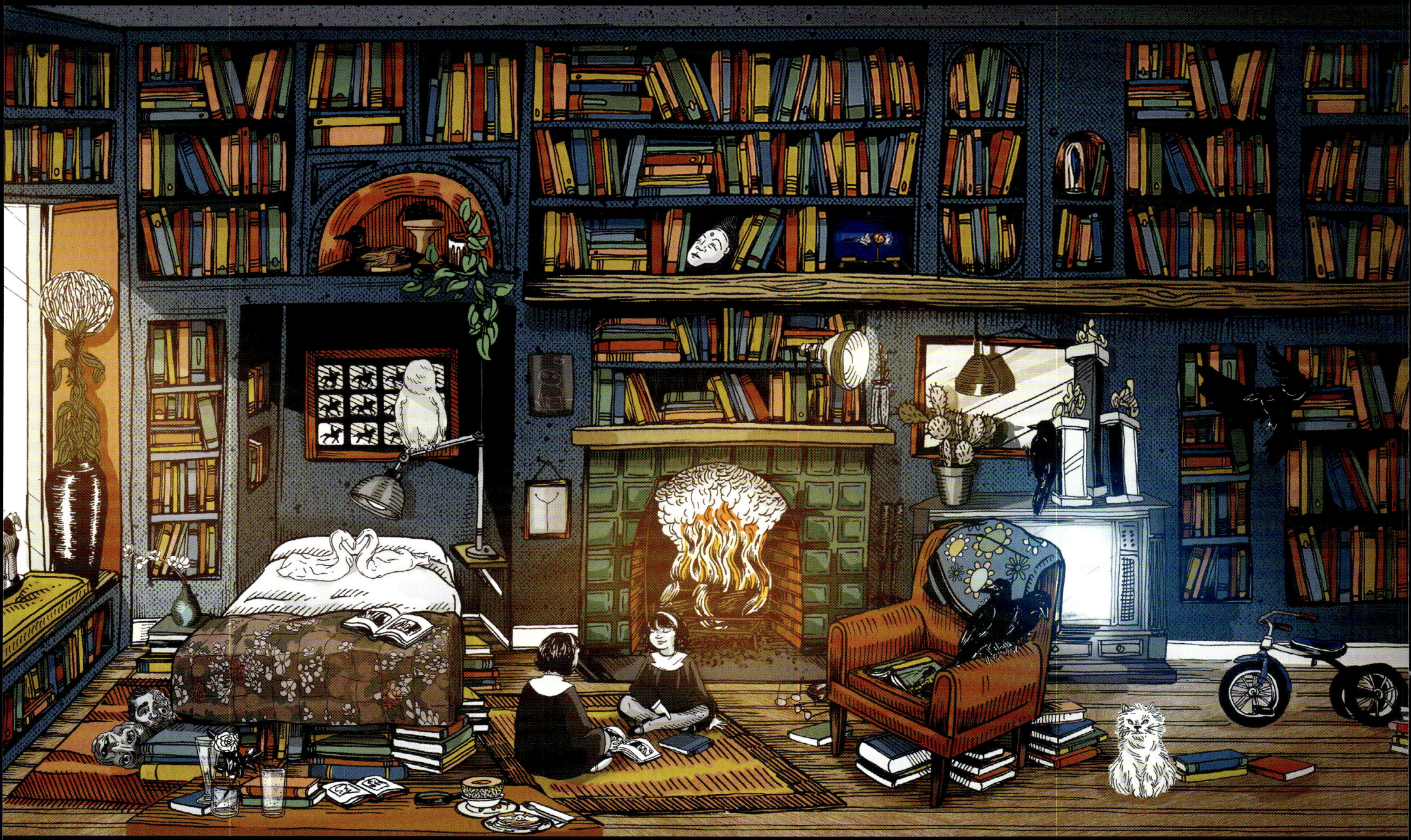

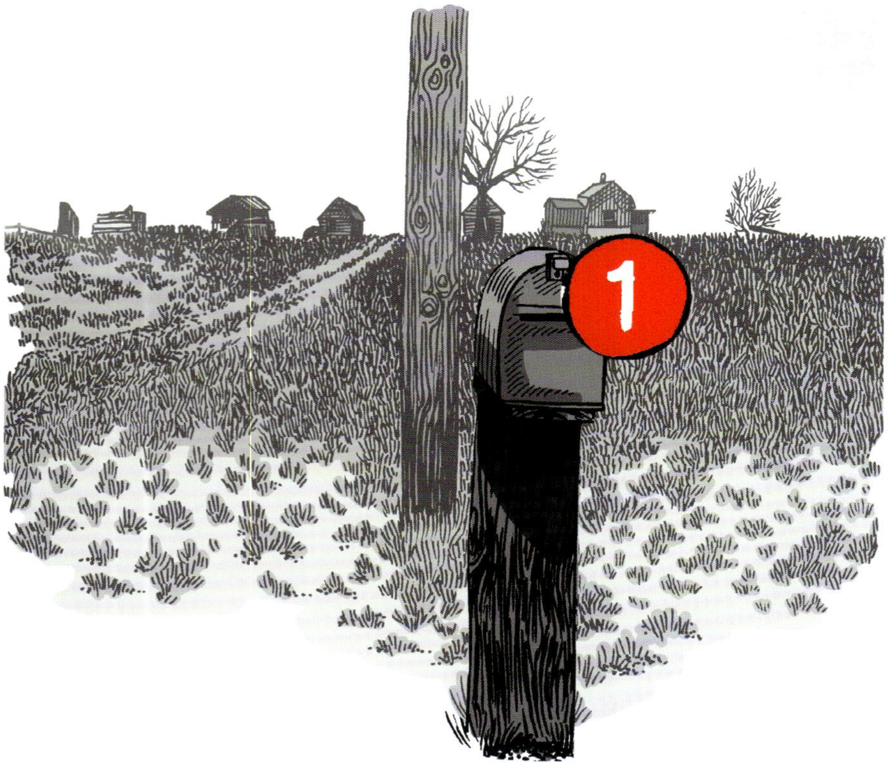

Robert Adams

For Robert Adams, the American West, with its broad landscapes and temporal stillness, exists as a statement of America, a definitive measure of a nation. His photographs, now collected in *American Silence*, an expansive exhibition at the National Gallery of Art, distill the vast region into recognizable black-and-white totems—a suburban home, an empty highway, a trodden beach. Before he became a photographer, Adams was an English professor. According to the curator Sarah Greenough, he recognizes "that a perfectly seen photograph, like a perfectly rendered poem, can reveal universal truths hidden in brief instants of time." Adams keeps his literary sentiments visible in his work, enlightening the mundane scenery of the everyday with lasting significance.

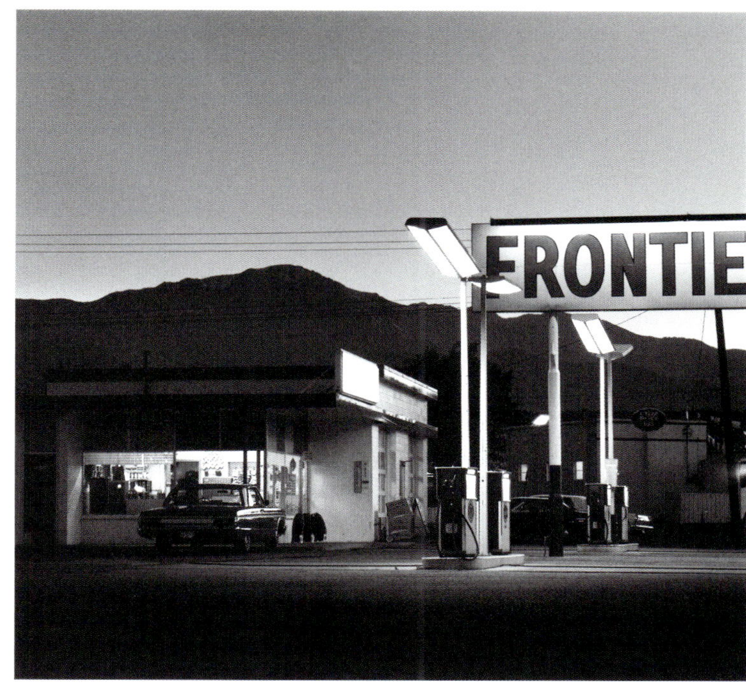

Robert Adams, *Pikes Peak, Colorado Springs*, 1969
© the artist and courtesy Fraenkel Gallery, San Francisco

American Silence: The Photographs of Robert Adams at the National Gallery of Art, Washington, D.C., May 29–October 2, 2022

Tracey Rose

"Reckoning, recompense, and repatriation"—these are the primary themes of Tracey Rose's work, says curator Tandazani Dhlakama, who has co-organized a solo exhibition of Rose's provocative photographs, films, sculpture, and installations at Zeitz Museum of Contemporary Art Africa (MOCAA) in Cape Town. A mixed-race South African woman, Rose fearlessly navigates a thicket of postcolonial narratives. "As you walk through the exhibition you are supposed to get a sense of anarchy," Dhlakama notes. *Tracey Rose: Shooting Down Babylon* covers more than two decades of Rose's practice, including iconic early images such as *The Kiss* (2001), which depicts a mixed-race couple sitting on a plinth like a classical sculpture, and *Lucie's Fur Version 1:1:1*, a 2003–4 series about Christianity and the origins of humankind, starring characters such as the Messenger, an angel in an Afro. As the title suggests, history is in the crosshairs.

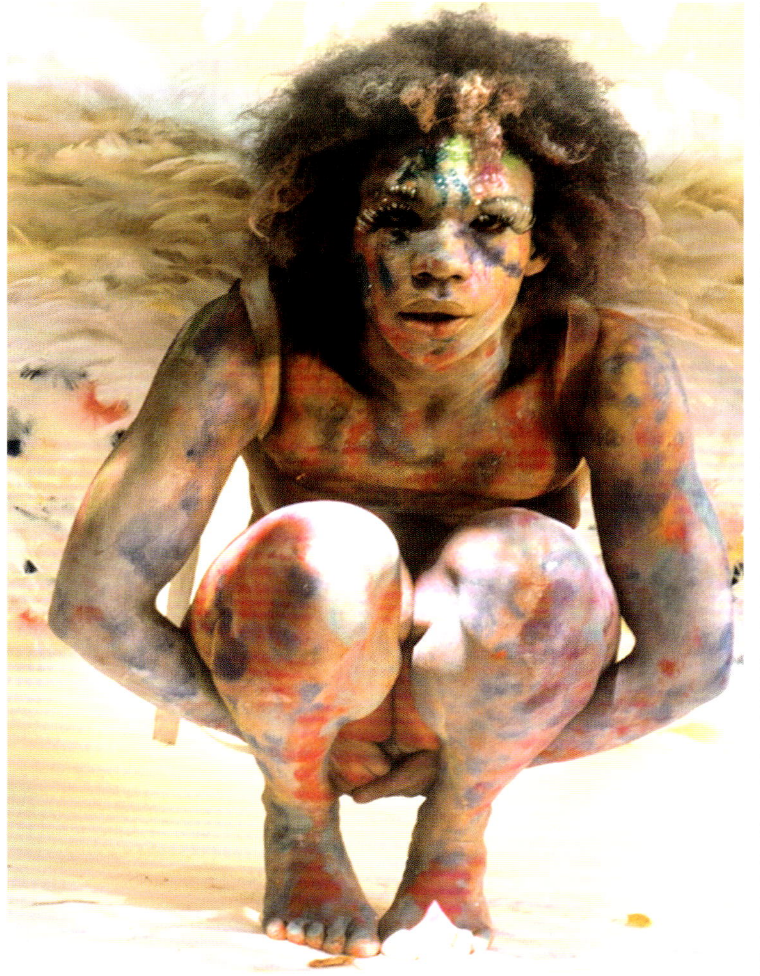

Tracey Rose, *Lucie's Fur Version 1:1:1–The Messenger*, 2003
Courtesy the artist

Tracey Rose: Shooting Down Babylon at Zeitz MOCAA, Cape Town, through August 28, 2022

Thomas Demand

Scenes eerily staged with cardboard paper cutouts come together to form the uncanny valley of Thomas Demand's work, on view in a career retrospective at the UCCA Center for Contemporary Art in Shanghai. *Thomas Demand: The Stutter of History* compiles several of Demand's exacting, large-scale artistic interventions, from a set of stop-motion films to the negotiations of historic flash points that at first glance might appear banal and lifeless. "We are looking not at a disaster but at an image of disaster," Demand has noted of his photograph concerning the control room during the Fukushima power plant meltdown, "although it's very hard to separate the two." Demand studied sculpture in the early 1990s, using photography as a mode of documentation, a format that would become his signature. By blurring the lines between the real and the constructed—and emphasizing the stutters or gaps in perception—Demand stages an uneasy encounter between experience, information, and memory.

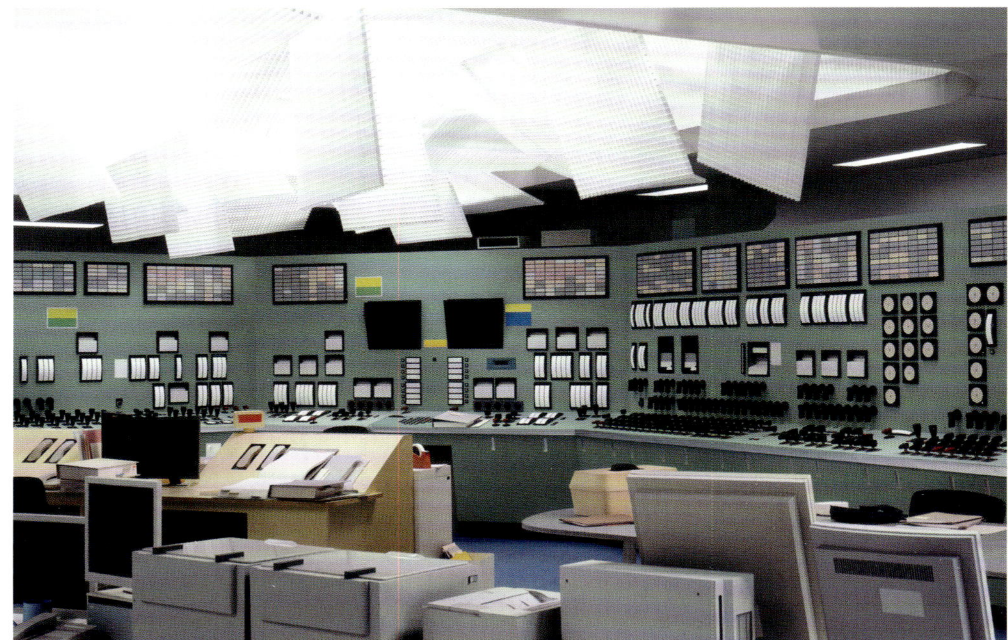

Thomas Demand, *Kontrollraum (Control Room)*, 2011
© the artist/VG Bild-Kunst, Bonn, and courtesy Matthew Marks Gallery and Sprüth Magers

Thomas Demand: The Stutter of History **at UCCA Center for Contemporary Art, Shanghai, April 2– June 19, 2022**

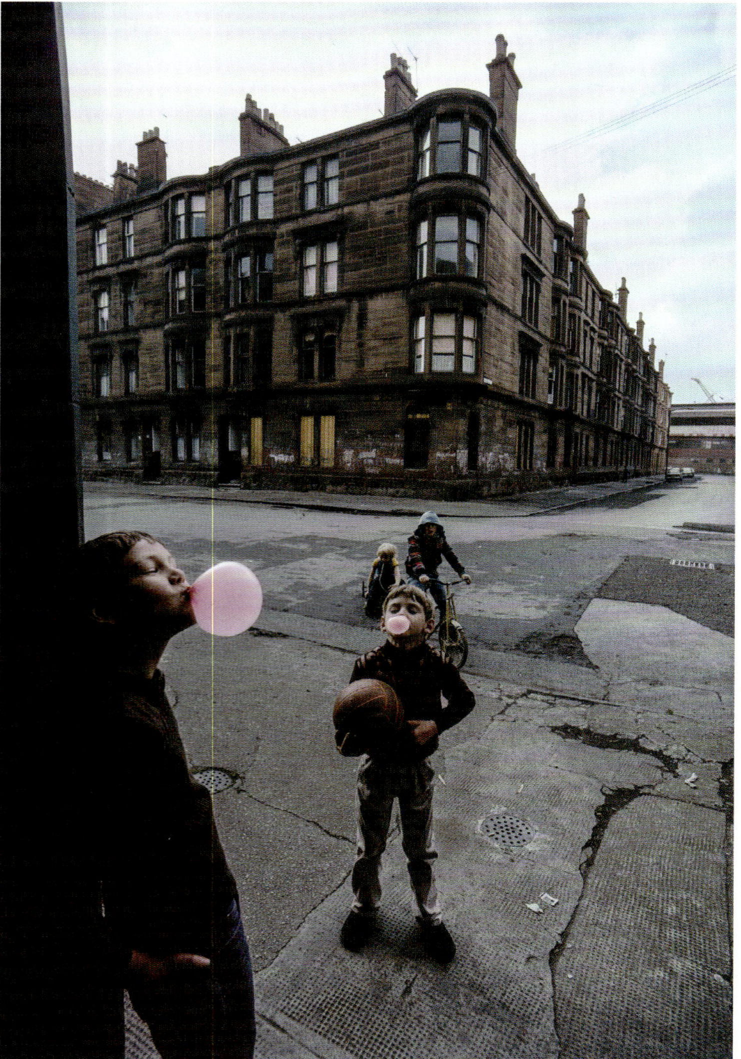

Raymond Depardon, Glasgow, Scotland, 1980
© the artist/Magnum Photos

Raymond Depardon

"I feel like I have something of the nineteenth century in me," Raymond Depardon said in a recent interview. "Maybe I held on to something from the last century . . . bringing the setting into my photos, with some close-ups, but relatively few." It is with a touch of irony, then, that the photographer's latest exhibition, presented by the Triennale Milano and Fondation Cartier pour l'art contemporain, is titled *La vita moderna*. The career-spanning display includes eight series of photographs, two films, and the photographer's complete catalog of published books. On the streets of Glasgow and on farms in rural France, his social conscience becomes clear through decades of engaged photography. A Magnum photographer since 1978, Depardon falls into a lineage of iconic French image makers—though, unlike Henri Cartier-Bresson, his photographs rely less on decisive moments and more on the patient ethnography of a bygone generation.

Raymond Depardon: La vita moderna **at Triennale Milano, Italy, through April 10, 2022**

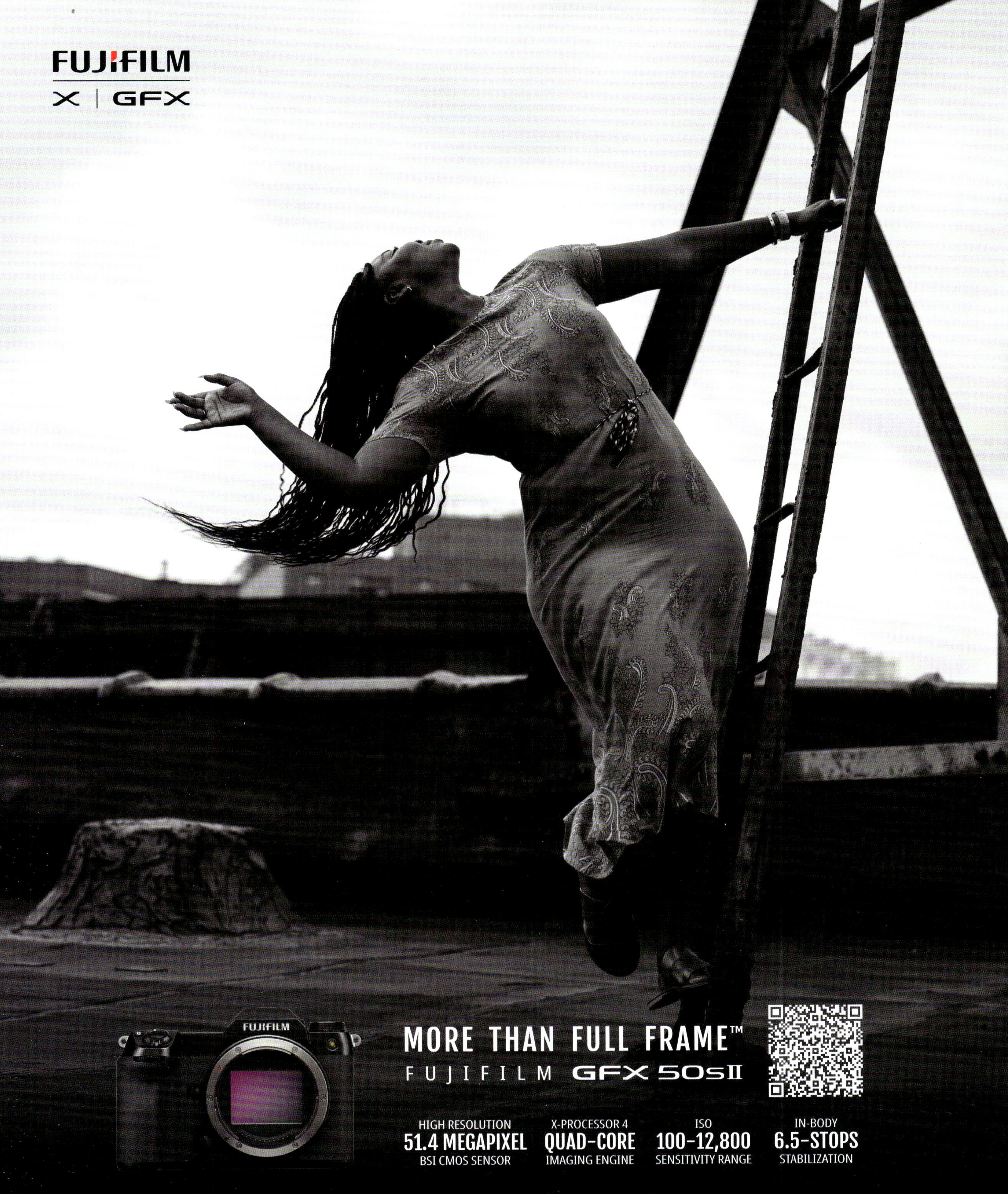
FUJIFILM
X | GFX
MORE THAN FULL FRAME™
FUJIFILM GFX 50sII
HIGH RESOLUTION
51.4 MEGAPIXEL
BSI CMOS SENSOR
X-PROCESSOR 4
QUAD-CORE
IMAGING ENGINE
ISO
100–12,800
SENSITIVITY RANGE
IN-BODY
6.5-STOPS
STABILIZATION
Photo © 2021 Shotti NYC | FUJIFILM GFX50S II Mirrorless Digital Camera with FUJINON GF80mmF1.7 R WR at 1/200sec at f/4, ISO 640. Shotti NYC is a FUJIFILM compensated professional photographer.

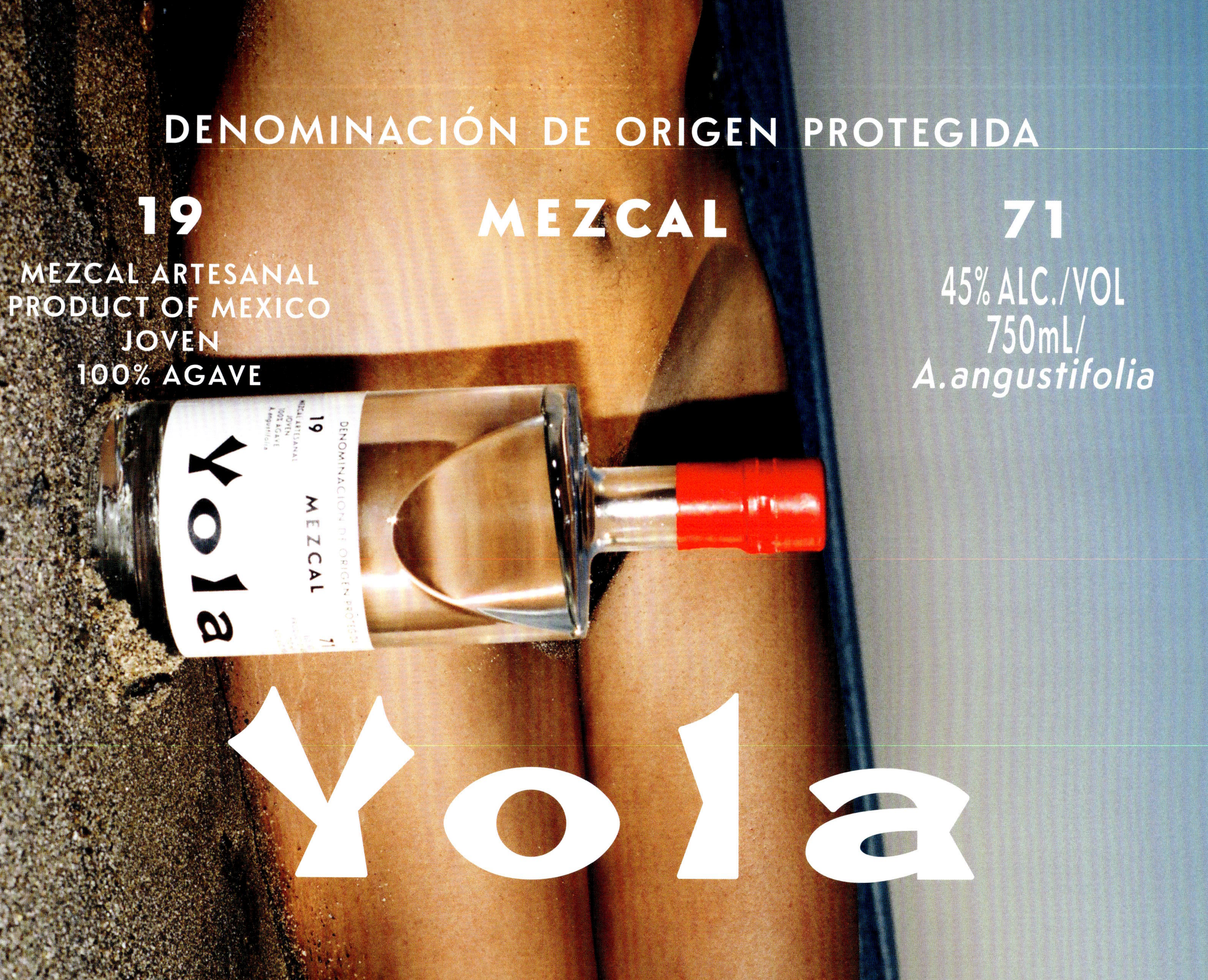
DENOMINACIÓN DE ORIGEN PROTEGIDA
19
MEZCAL
71
MEZCAL ARTESANAL
PRODUCT OF MEXICO
JOVEN
100% AGAVE
45% ALC./VOL
750mL/
A. angustifolia
Yola

Collecting

How will a recent acquisition of photographs by women expand ideas about gender and nation?

Britt Salvesen

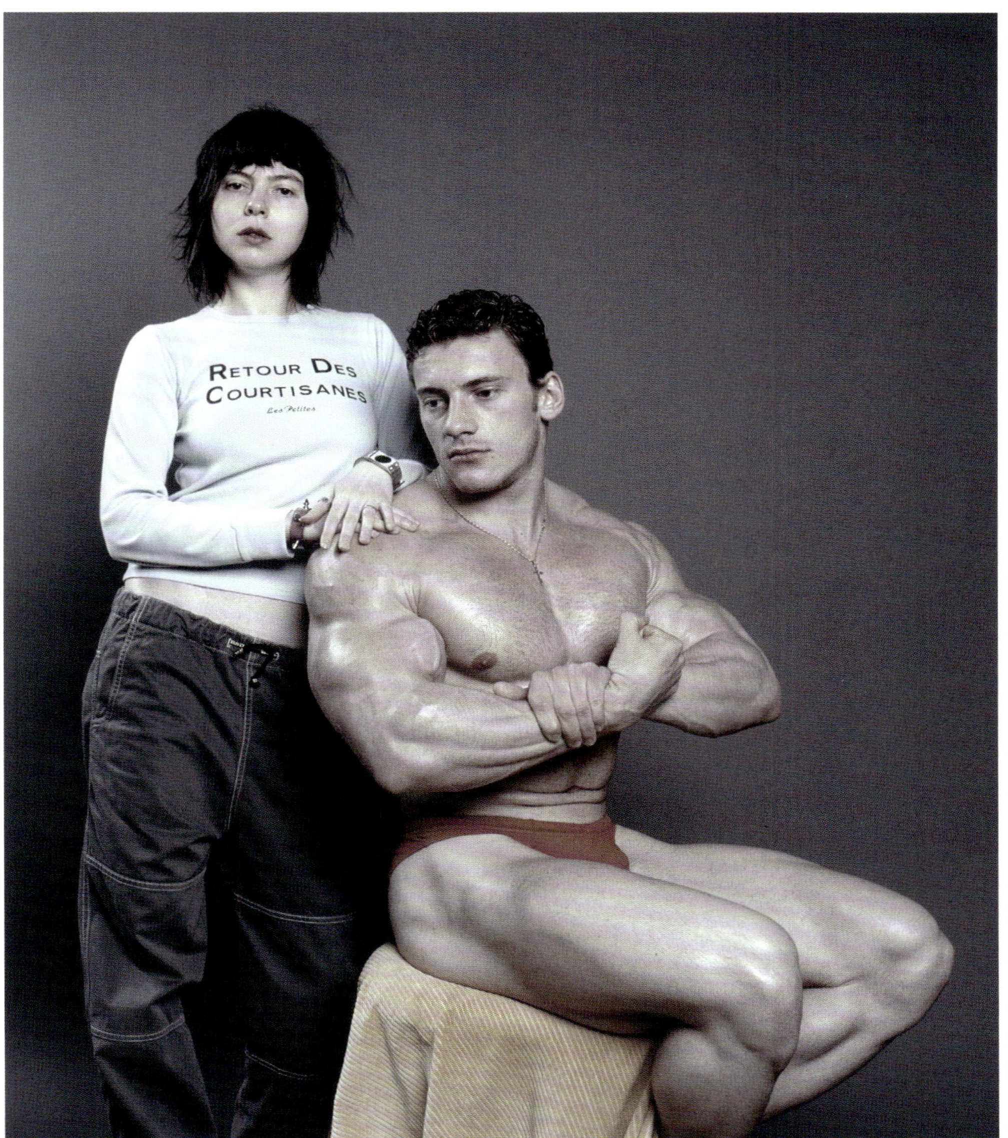

Alexandra Croitoru,
Untitled (Bodybuilder I),
2003
© the artist and courtesy the Los Angeles County Museum of Art and the Brooklyn Museum

Untitled (Bodybuilder I) is part of a portrait series made in 2003 and 2004 in which the Romanian photographer Alexandra Croitoru paired herself with a stereotypically masculine companion. In each example, the man is seated and looks away from the camera while Croitoru stands behind him, touching his shoulder and staring into the lens. In this image, she appears with a bodybuilder who trained at her local gym; in another, she is pictured with Adrian Năstase, who served as prime minister of Romania between 2000 and 2004. (Năstase was later tried and imprisoned for corruption.)

Croitoru is based in Bucharest, where she studied and now teaches at the National Academy of Arts. In contrast to this kind of overtly staged, performative work, her recent series are more documentary in nature. But a common thread is always an examination of the machinations of gender and power in Romania. As Croitoru explains, "I am quite a cynical person, and I usually question everything around me. So my art practice mirrors this way of relating to the world—asking uncomfortable questions, and not offering answers."

Croitoru's images recently came to the Los Angeles County Museum of Art (LACMA) through a joint acquisition, with the Brooklyn Museum, of Sir Mark Fehrs Haukohl's collection of two hundred objects by eighty-one artists working in eighteen countries. Haukohl, a Milwaukee native and Houston resident, is an art collector and philanthropist with wide-ranging interests. Already well-known for his holdings of Italian paintings from the sixteenth to the eighteenth century, he began around the year 2000 to acquire photographs by European women artists, presciently endeavoring to form a kind of time capsule of the twenty-first century. Haukohl's engagement in this area has been energetic and insightful.

LACMA's photography department held about 120 contemporary works by European women when Haukohl approached us. There was an overlap of only eleven artists between Haukohl's and LACMA's collections with no duplication of individual images among this group. As a curator, I believe the opportunity to consider how the women represented in the Haukohl collection are redefining the categories of gender, nation, and photography is essential. We will also be augmenting the acquisition year by year, focusing especially on artists who have immigrated to Europe from other parts of the world. While many photographers will doubtless continue to reflect critically on the legacies of the past, others will envision futures in which creative expression can expand—or transcend—any given notions of the medium.

Britt Salvesen is the curator and head of the Wallis Annenberg Photography Department and the Prints and Drawings Department at the Los Angeles County Museum of Art.

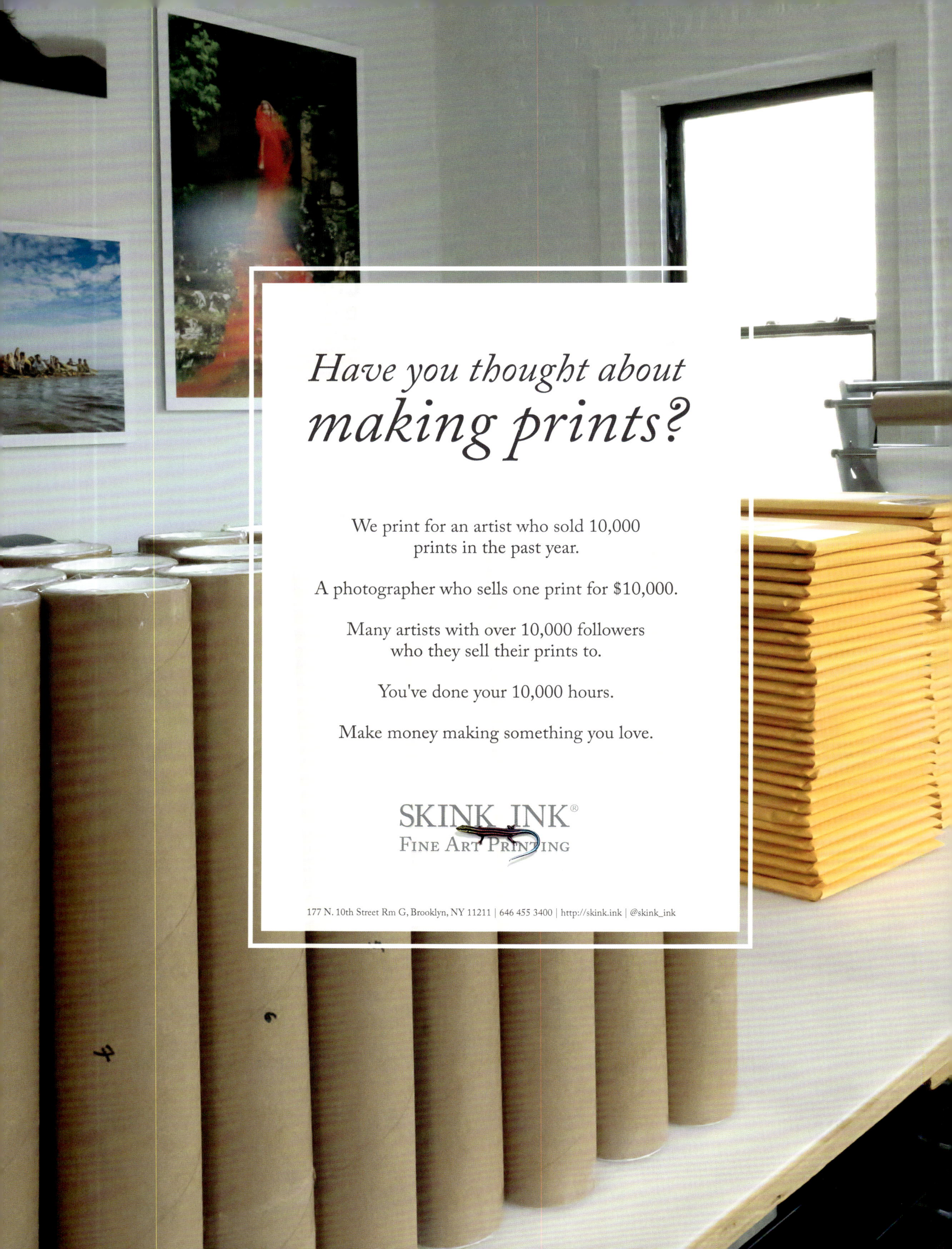

Have you thought about
making prints?

We print for an artist who sold 10,000
prints in the past year.

A photographer who sells one print for $10,000.

Many artists with over 10,000 followers
who they sell their prints to.

You've done your 10,000 hours.

Make money making something you love.

SKINK INK®
FINE ART PRINTING

177 N. 10th Street Rm G, Brooklyn, NY 11211 | 646 455 3400 | http://skink.ink | @skink_ink

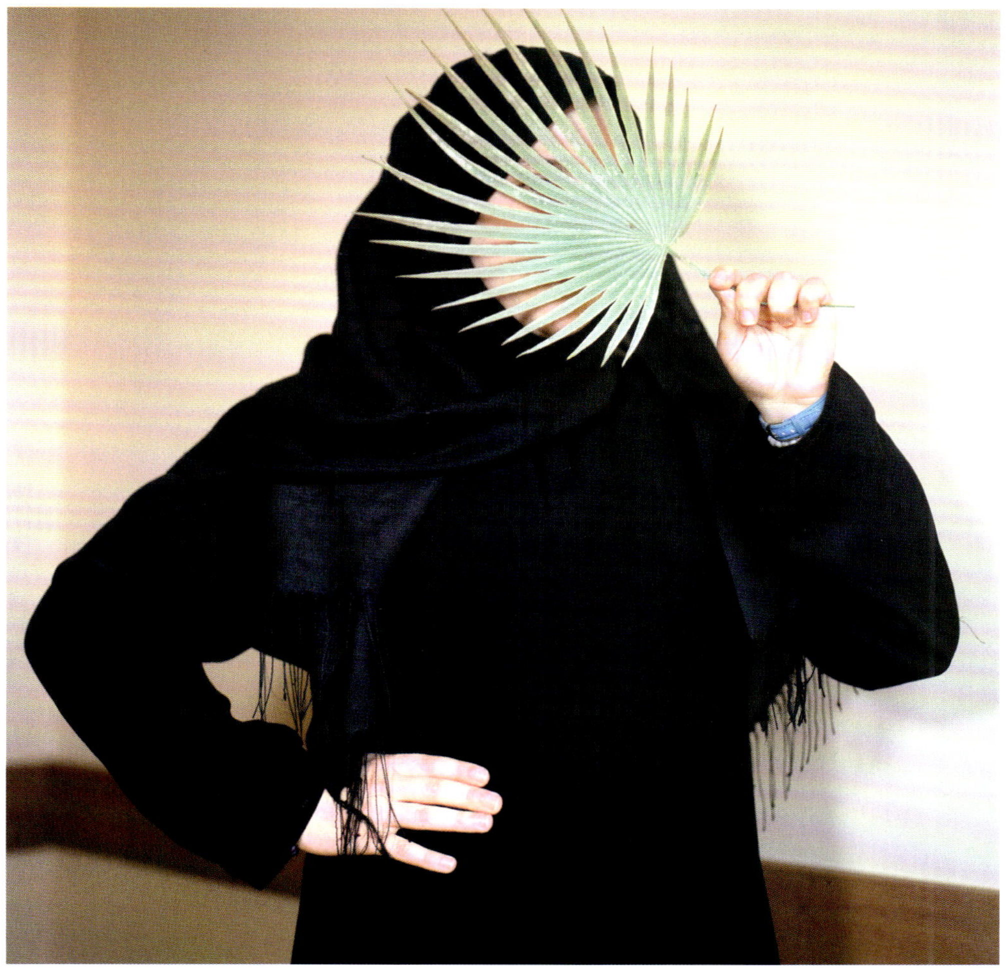

Recalling her childhood in Turkish Koran schools, Sabiha Çimen finds collaborators in the girls she photographs.

Kaya Genç

Sabiha Çimen was twelve when, in 1998, she enrolled at a *hafiz okulu* (guardian school) in Istanbul. Since 1970 more than 160,000 girls in Turkey, aged eight to nineteen, have studied in these single-sex schools, memorizing the Koran's 6,236 verses, which takes around three years, and becoming protectors of Islam's sacred book. Çimen's upbringing made such a deep impression on her that, a quarter of a century later, these schools became the subject of *Hafiz* (2021), her first photobook. Intensely intimate, Çimen's portraits, made between 2017 and 2021, surveil the double lives religious students lead in contemporary Turkey, where it is legal for parents to send children even as young as two years old to study at Koran courses.

Çimen belongs to an ethnically Kurdish Persian family. Her older sisters had gone through the same education, which was a rigid and traumatizing process; Çimen attended the Koran course with her twin sister. "I used to imagine these schools like prisons as a kid, but once inside, I saw I was mistaken," Çimen, who was named a Magnum nominee in 2020 and has published her photography in *The New York Times Magazine*, *Le Monde*, and *Vogue*, told me last fall in an Istanbul coffee shop. "It was a vibrant environment. You couldn't find such wise and bold women together anywhere else in the world."

Studying there alongside six hundred other girls for three years formed a large part of Çimen's DNA. But on graduation in 2001, Turkey's headscarf ban postponed her plans to attend college. In those listless years, she became infatuated with photography. During an *umrah* pilgrimage in 2002 to Mecca, Islam's holiest city, Çimen saw a Canon camera in a Saudi Arabian shop window. Over the next two years, she used it to keep a diary, making portraits of her mother and one of her sisters, and finessing her craft as a self-taught photographer. At college Çimen studied international trade and business, a field she had no interest in. She pursued a master's in cultural studies, savoring Homi K. Bhabha and Giorgio Agamben's texts, and wondering whether she should be a scholar. For her graduate thesis, she worked in Fatih, the Istanbul neighborhood

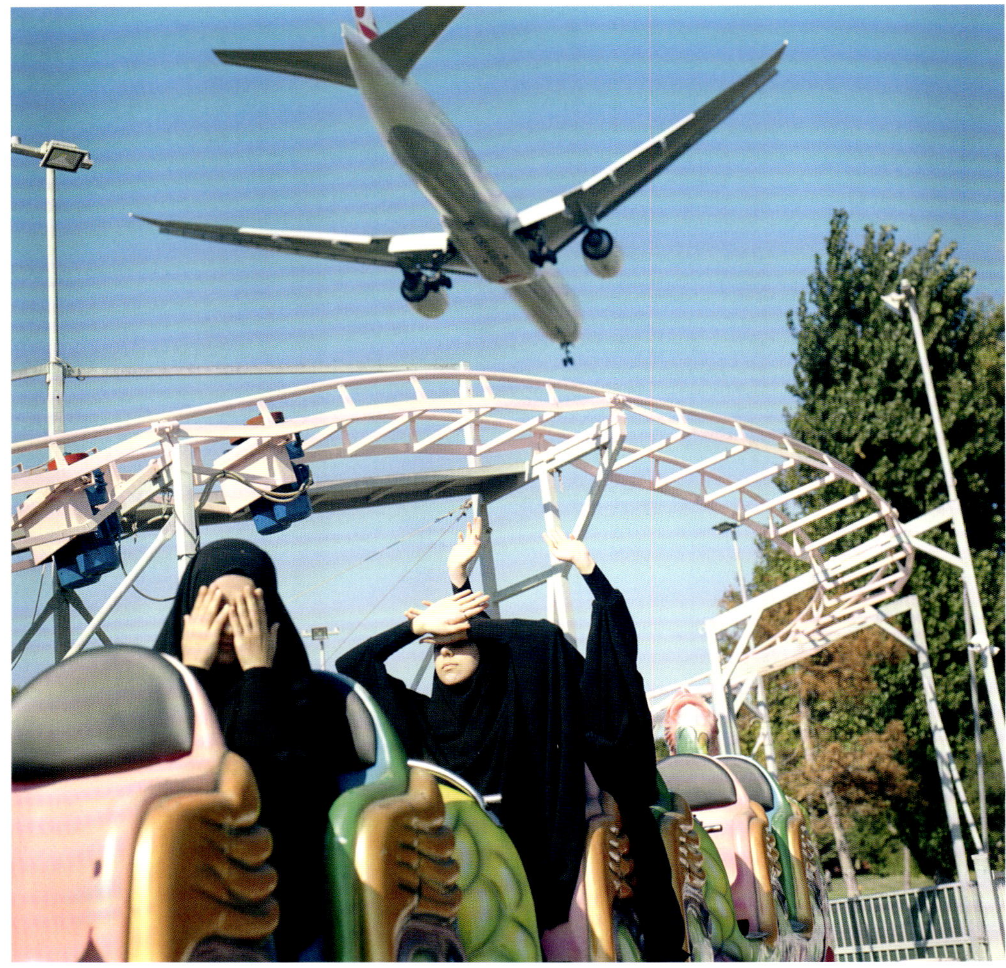

where she resided, photographing Syrians who had once been dermatologists, engineers, and architects, but who now worked at kebab and barber shops.

In 2015, Çimen bought a secondhand, medium-format Hasselblad. Once assured of her technical competency, she searched to find a subject for an extensive project. "These memories from my religious-education days haunted me," she recalls. One day, Çimen summoned up her courage, visited the school she had attended, and gave a presentation to the current group of girls proclaiming: "Like you, I was a student here, in 1998. Now, I have this project about which I don't know precisely what to do. We'll discover it together! Would you like to spend time with me?"

Girls reluctantly agreed. On the first day, Çimen placed her camera on a desk to acquaint the students with its features. She

Çimen seems fated to be a guardian for the young students whose experiences she shared and captured.

spent a fortnight with them, living in their quarters, eating lunch, hearing their stories, and mostly avoiding the teachers. She went on to photograph Koran schools across Turkey: in Kars, Hatay, Malatya, and Rize. "Those girls are bashful, and I struggled to earn their trust," she says. "Those I photographed in Istanbul were more outward looking but harder to work with."

Hanging out with the girls, Çimen witnessed their strict discipline. Reading novels was banned. Smartphones were out of the question. Girls went to sleep at nine at night and woke up at five with the morning call to prayer. "They were like recording devices, memorizing the Koran around the clock," she says. Getting permits to portray their world proved a challenge. One mufti (religious administrator) bluntly murmured: "You can't photograph Muslim women.

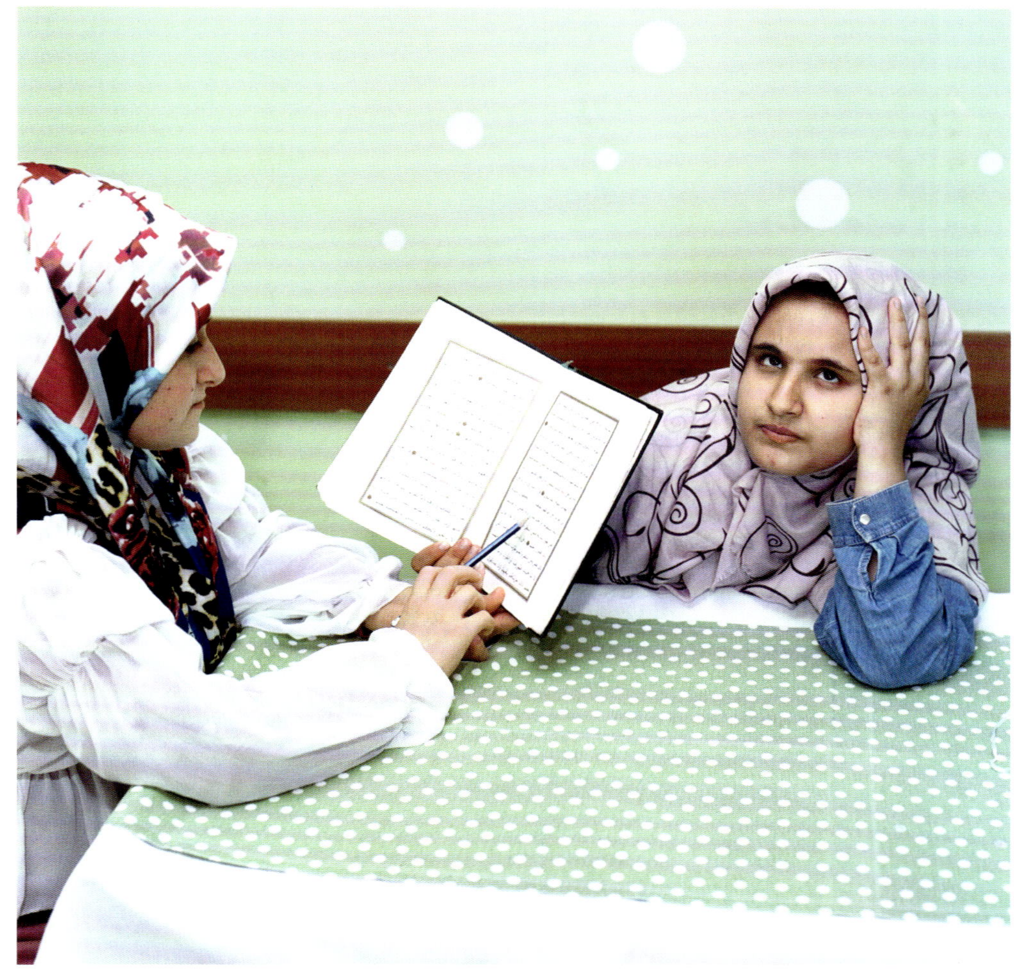

It's forbidden in Islam." Undeterred, Çimen realized her dream.

Hafiz's world is Dickensian, with gangs of girls abounding in its corridors. There are fragile girls, tough girls, playful and traumatized girls. They hide behind a locker, a curtain, or a palm leaf. They Rollerblade, tend roses, play hopscotch, hold dead fish, look at caged birds, pore over a loaf of bread, eat ice cream, perform at a religious play. They're primarily daydreaming—something Çimen did often in her student years. She explains that Koran-school graduates retain "organic ties" to each other throughout their lives. When some of these girls showed an interest in photography, Çimen mentored them, giving tips on which cameras to buy and how to look for interesting subjects. "Incredible talents will emerge among them. It was fate that placed me here, and the same can happen to them," she says. During the photoshoots, Çimen resisted lifting her camera and remained on the same level as her subjects. She gave girls the time and space to slowly open themselves up to her. While Çimen was photographing a wall at a Koran school one day, a girl asked: "Why don't you photograph me instead?" This question became a turning point in what Çimen calls their "invisible agreement." Afterward, on an outing, students spotted an exploded watermelon on the pavement— "I said: 'Stop, girls! I want to photograph you around this watermelon.' Having internalized my style, they soon began to gravitate toward things I like to put in my compositions."

I wonder who the audience will be for *Hafiz*, a poetic book that took Çimen three years to compile from three hundred images. Turkish photographers? Pious young girls? What will her book tell foreigners about their lives of religious devotion? "I wish that these kids and their families would be my audience," muses Çimen, "but sadly, it won't be them." Out of *Hafiz*'s print run of two thousand, only one hundred books are in Turkish. "As for those Islamist men who have always been against me, never looked at my art and instead tried to ban it—they won't be my audience either." Yet Çimen seems fated to be a guardian for the young students whose experiences she shared and captured, serving as their *hafiza*—the Turkish word for memory.

Kaya Genç is a writer based in Istanbul and the author of *The Lion and the Nightingale: A Journey Through Modern Turkey* (2019).

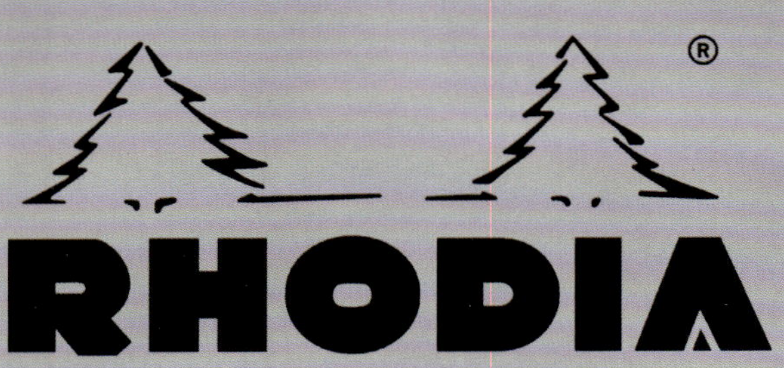

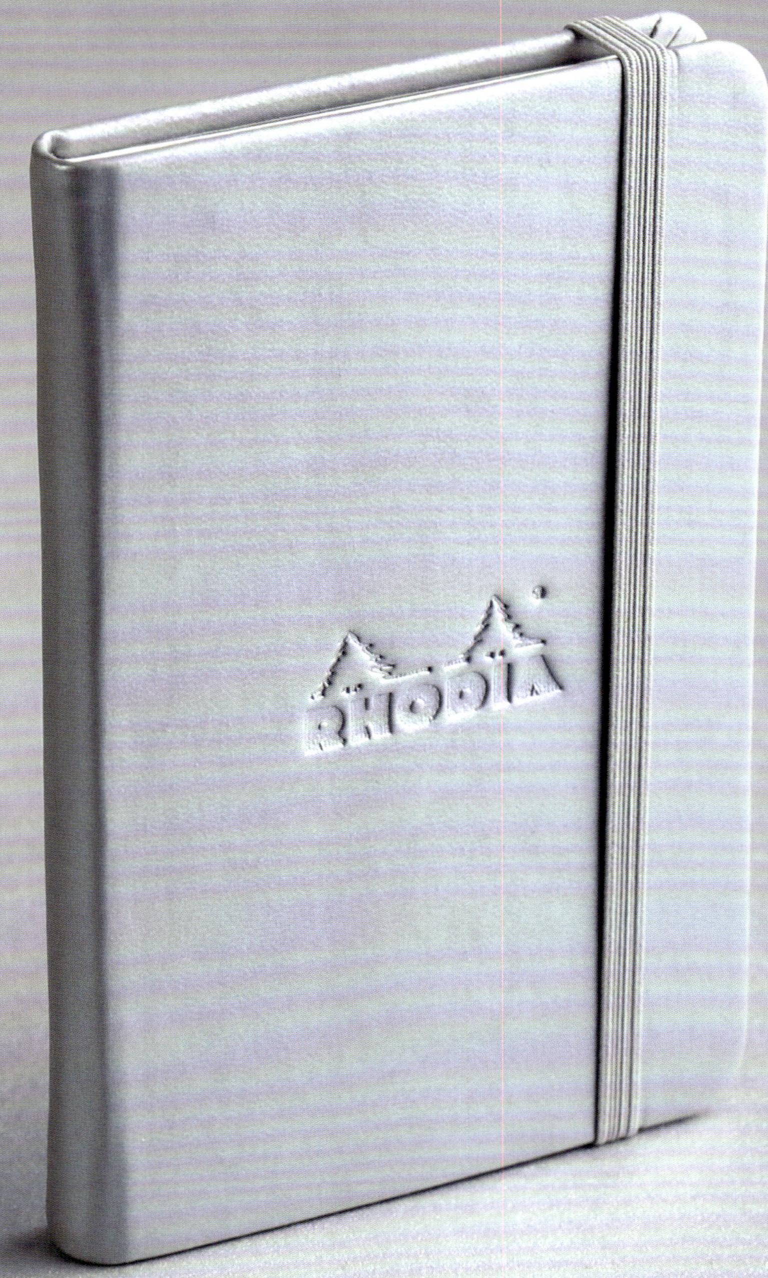

A modern notebook since 1934

Made in France

Distributed by Exaclair, Inc.
sales@exaclair.com ◆ www.exaclair.com

In her Chinatown loft, Kunié Sugiura presses conventional boundaries of photography and painting.
Randy Kennedy

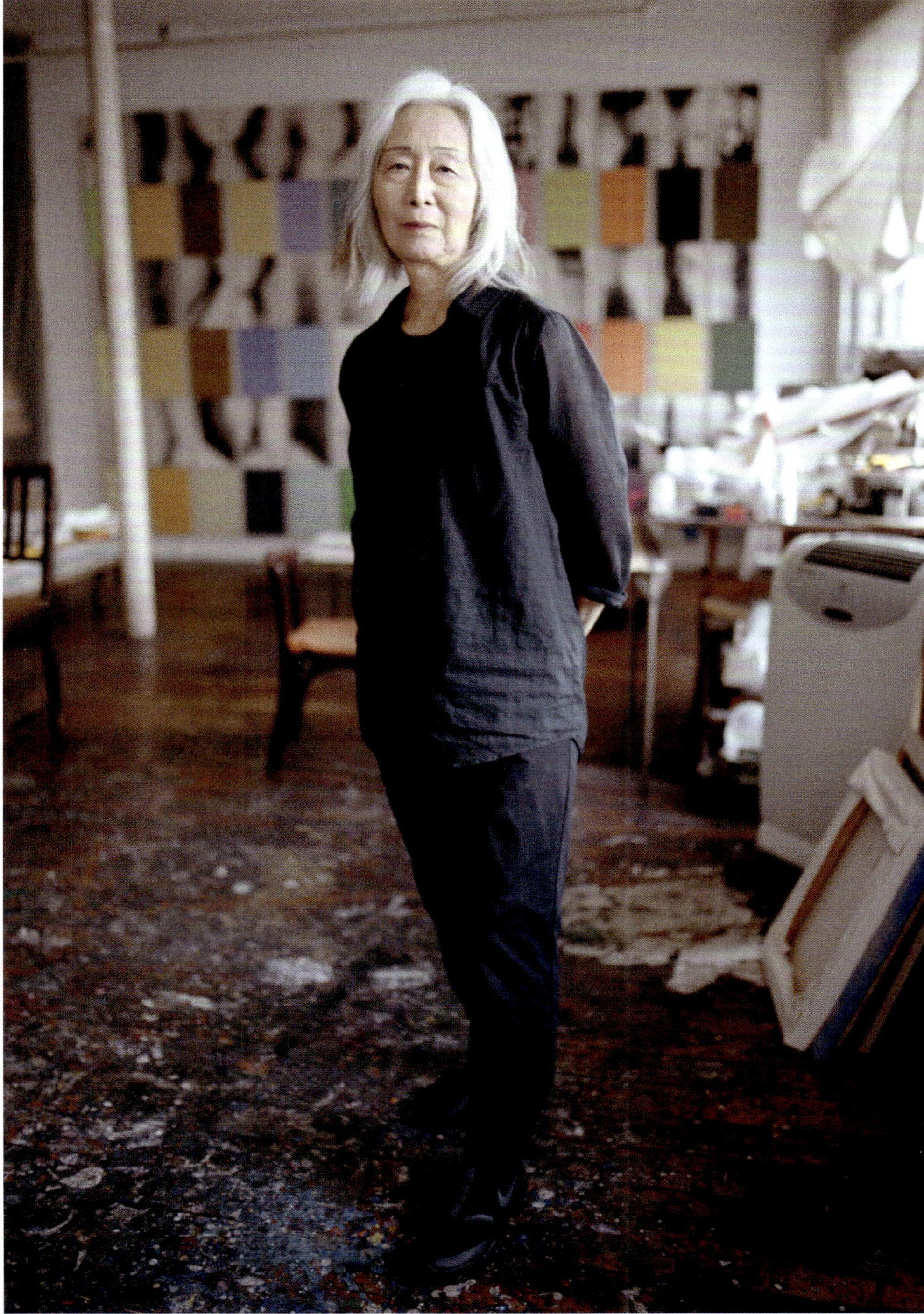

In 1811, when the Commissioners' Plan established the map that was to dictate Manhattan's development north of Houston Street, city fathers settled on the gridiron as the ideal form not for its Euclidean elegance but for the sake of rank commerce: "Right angled houses are the most cheap to build," they declared.

Meanwhile, in the city that already existed, streets slouched and coiled like vagabonds, their winding shapes defined by rivers, shorelines, swamps, and large rocks. Among these vintage arteries, Doyers Street, a narrow, two-hundred-foot dogleg angling between the Bowery and Pell Street, is unlike any other. The crime journalist Herbert Asbury, who covered downtown New York, once called it "a crazy street" and said "there has never been any excuse for it." Turning onto it feels like stumbling into Venice or Kowloon and makes me think of Walter Benjamin's sentiment in *One-Way Street* that as soon as we gain our bearings in a city, habit erodes our sense of wonder about it. Somehow, visiting Doyers never stops feeling like the first time because it never stops feeling like being lost.

Recently, I went to the old gray brick building at number 7 and rang the buzzer of Kunié Sugiura, who has lived and worked there in a rough, roomy, fourth-floor loft since 1974, making art that combines photography and painting in ways that confound conventions of both (often involving cameraless photographs and paintings that function more as sculptural objects than as canvases).

Sugiura, seventy-nine, born in Nagoya and raised in Tokyo, moved to the United States in 1963 to study at the School of the Art Institute of Chicago, where she fell under the sway of one of her professors, Kenneth Josephson, who was at work establishing the terms of what would come to be known as Conceptual photography.

Sitting at a long worktable in the front of her loft, framed by tall windows overlooking Doyers, Sugiura told me: "I liked photography because photography was not really what it looked like. It's such a subconscious thing, and you can experiment. Of course, all the other art students at that time completely looked down on us." She moved to New York in 1967, partly because she sensed it was on the verge of generational upheaval. "And I knew that great social change is when culture happens," she says. "But mostly, I just thought New York City was a lot of fun. Even going to a deli here was entertainment."

In the early 1970s, Sugiura began layering photographic emulsion, exposed with her Minimalist images of the city—a storefront, high-rise windows, approaching headlights, the hull of the Staten Island Ferry—on surfaces such as aluminum, wood, and ceramics, until

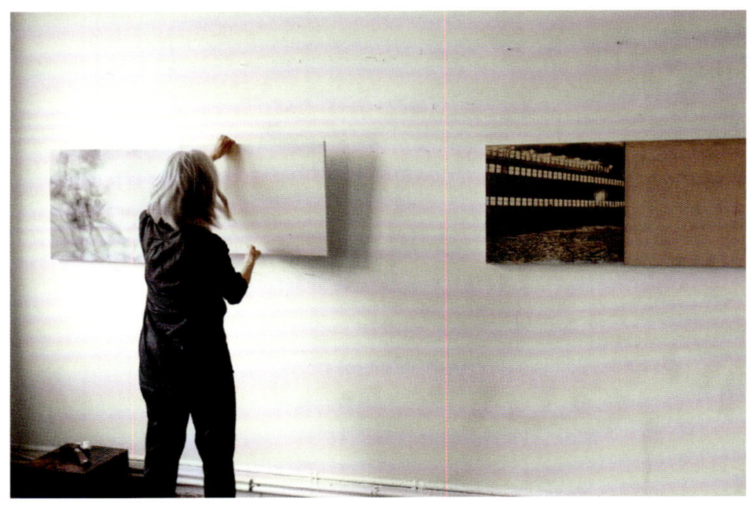

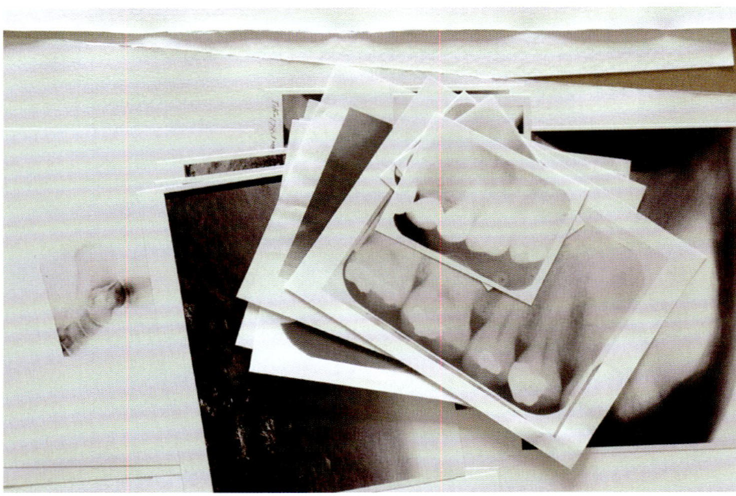

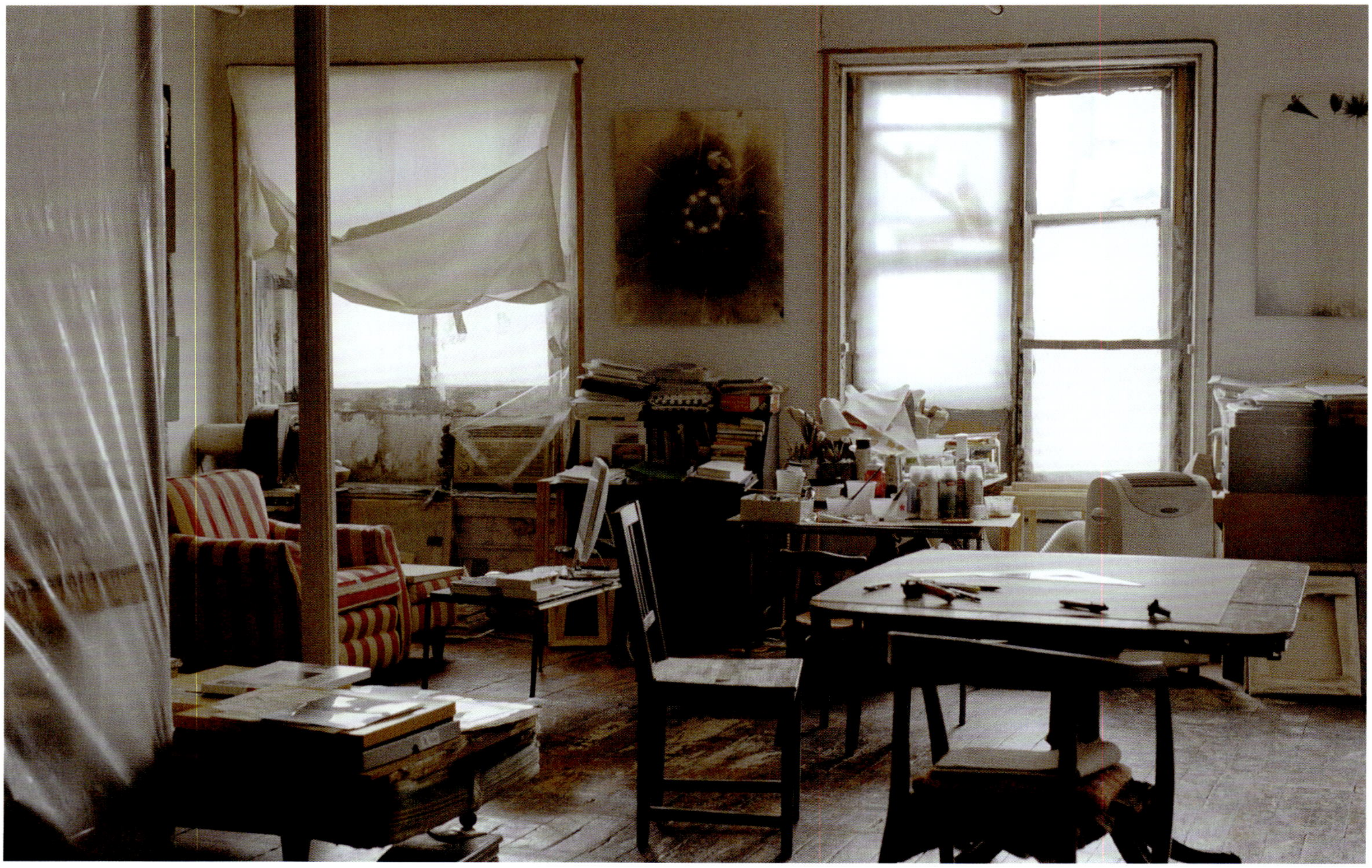

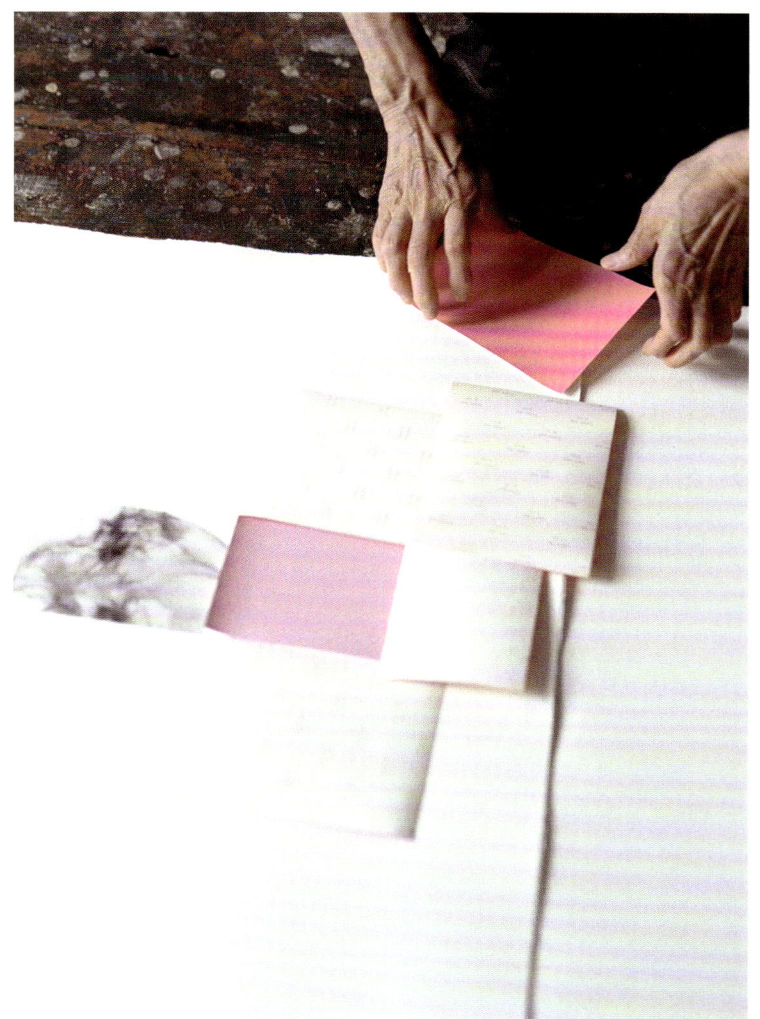

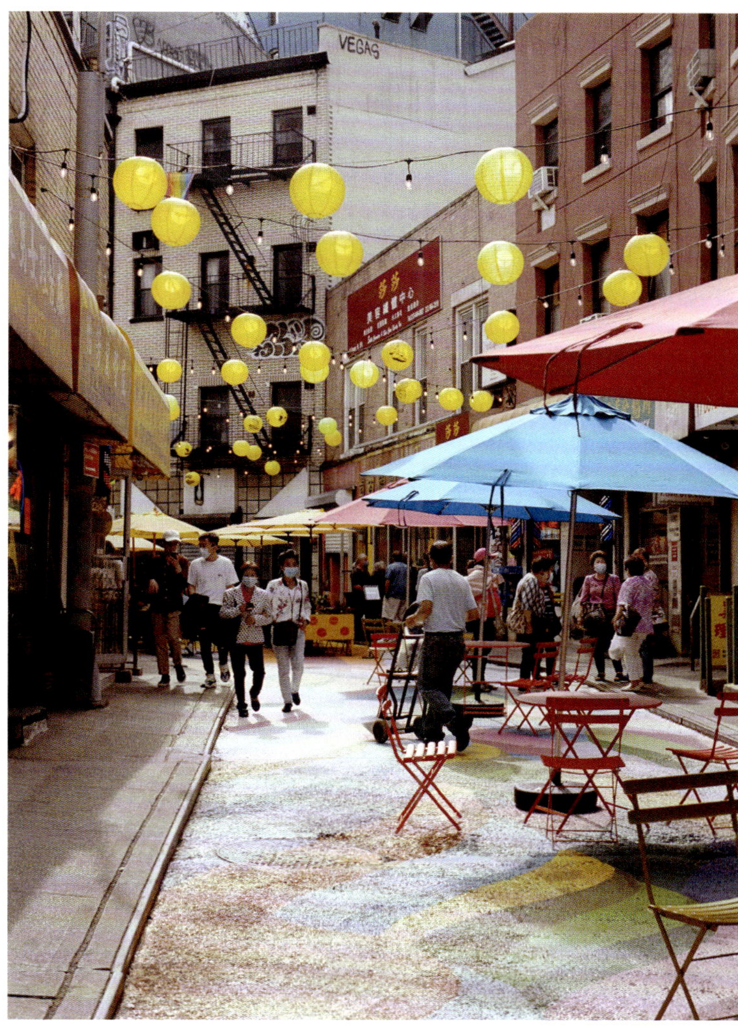

In the early 1970s, Sugiura began layering photographic emulsion, exposed with her Minimalist images of the city.

settling on canvas, a nod to the influences of Robert Rauschenberg and Andy Warhol, though her work had a quiet poise that resembled neither. As the process developed, she incorporated monochrome or striped painted canvases along with the emulsions, sometimes grouped in wooden armatures that suggested frames but seemed more like elegantly deconstructed Shaker furniture. (The critic Karen Rosenberg once said that Sugiura's early pieces appeared as if "Walker Evans had teamed up with Anne Truitt.") Over subsequent decades, she has continued to press restlessly at photography's boundaries, experimenting with collage, painterly photogram techniques, and landscape-like pigment prints.

Sugiura was featured early on in the Whitney Museum of American Art's 1972 Annual Exhibition, curated by James Monte, and her work has appeared in exhibitions over the years at OK Harris, White Columns, the Museum of Modern Art, New York, the Museum of Fine Arts, Houston, and the Museum of Fine Arts, Boston, among many others.

In the early 1970s, after the breakup of a marriage, she met the pioneering dealer Richard Bellamy "who told me he would be my agent—whatever that meant—but he really began to help my career and introduced me to other downtown artists like Neil Jenney." She began hunting downtown for a space to live and work and chanced on the Doyers Street building, which had once housed the city's first Chinese-language theater and later became a flophouse before being virtually abandoned in the 1960s. In 1971, the sculptor John Duff claimed the building for artists, making a loft on the top floor, where he remains today, and Sugiura moved in with two artist friends three years later, sharing the building with a Buddhist temple and, for a while, a loft of rowdy Cajuns with connections to Philip Glass's musical circle and the artist-run restaurant Food, founded by Gordon Matta-Clark.

"This was where I really was first able to have the life of an artist," she says. "It has sometimes been crazy or hard, but Doyers still feels like a sort of hidden place in the city, even in Chinatown, and the light that comes in my windows is northeast light, which is always beautiful. It's my home."

Randy Kennedy is the editor in chief of *Ursula* magazine, published by Hauser & Wirth.

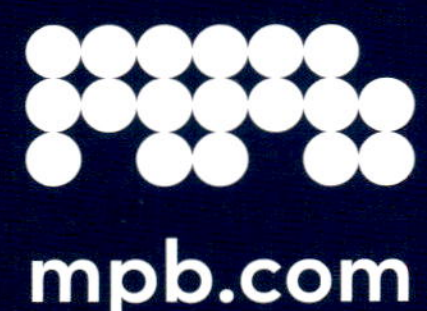

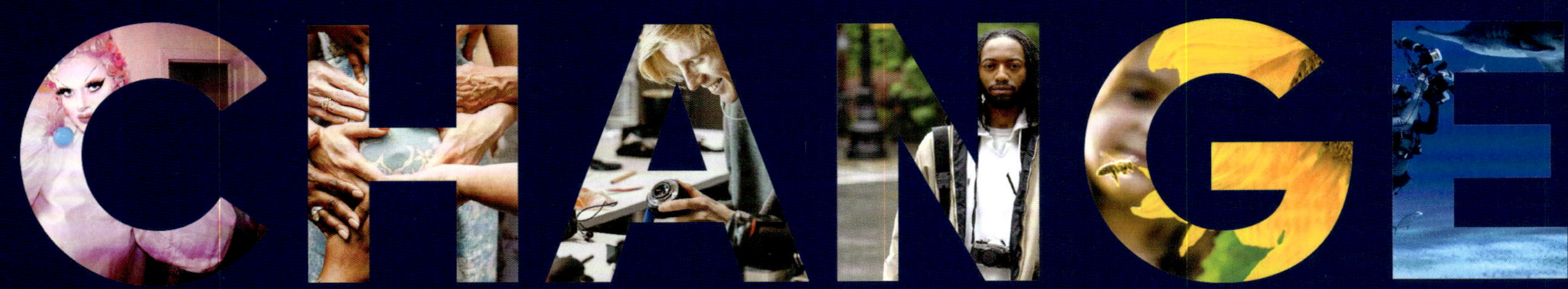

Photography and videography can change us.
They change the way we feel.
Our understanding.

They change our hearts and minds.
They change the rules.

Testing the limits of our comfort zones.
Changing the way others see the world.
See themselves.

Together let's change the way we do things.
Change the narrative.
Change the bigger picture.
Open up opportunity.
Give more people a voice.
Put camera kit in more hands.
Create a more sustainable future.
A future with more people included in it.
Here's to the stories to come.

MPB

Change gear.
Buy. Sell. Trade. Create.

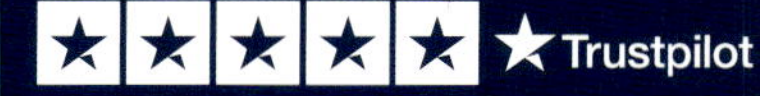

Rated 'Excellent' 4.9/5 based on 14,000+ reviews

Backstory

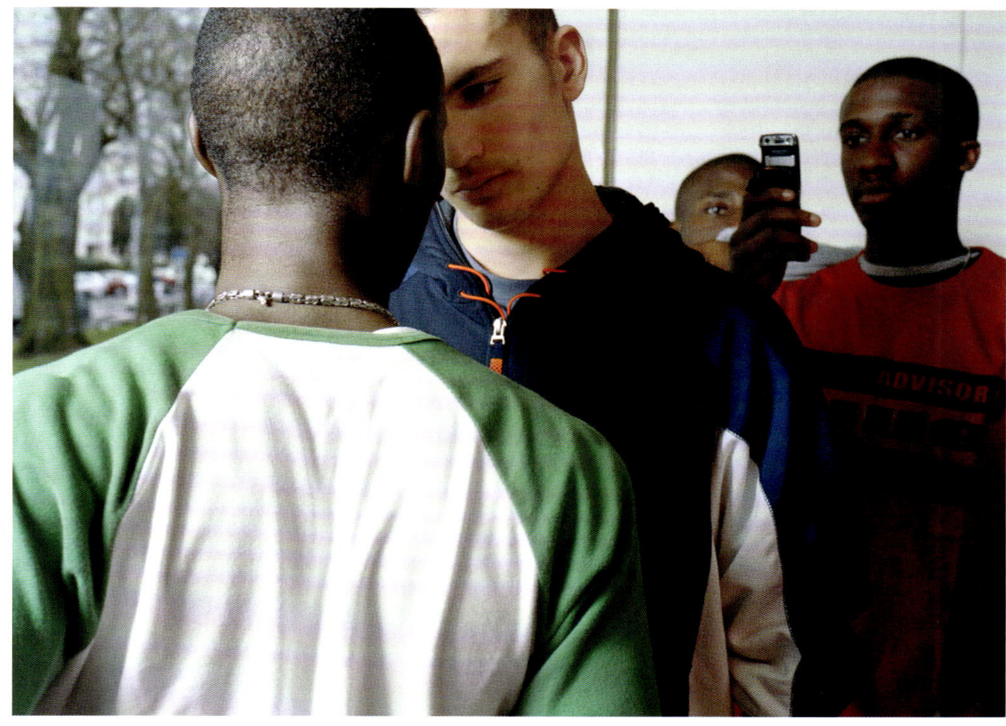

A new photobook revisits Mohamed Bourouissa's incisive images of young people on the peripheries of Paris.
Elisabeth Zerofsky

Mohamed Bourouissa was still an art student in 2004 when he took his first photographs of young people, mostly his male friends from the banlieues, or suburbs, of Paris. He had wanted to represent their particular sartorial aesthetic. At the time, the Parisian transportation system was laid out such that the easiest way for kids living in different banlieues to meet was to take the direct train to Châtelet–Les Halles in the center of the city. On arrival, their dynamic style—a lot of brightly colored athletic wear—stood out among the drab but formal uniform of most Parisian kids, clearly marking them as residents of the peripheries. They were obviously *issus de l'immigration*—second- or third-generation French youth whose families were from the former colonies—though no one really articulated these distinct identities at the time.

Not long afterward, in the fall of 2005, widespread demonstrations broke out in the banlieues following the deaths of two young men from one of the neighborhoods who were running to escape police. Bourouissa realized he'd been on to something and spent the next three years working on a modified concept of the project. He relocated it out to the banlieues, to the spaces of the *périphérique*, as the series, made from 2005 to 2008, came to be called, these urban areas that border the city but are clearly not of it. And, pivoting from what had begun as a documentary project, Bourouissa decided to stage the photographs. Bourouissa's background was in painting, and he wanted to incorporate the formal compositions and attributes he had come to love from

Bourouissa considers the fact that *Périphérique* is being published now an indicator that it has stood the test of time.

classical French painters—the tensions expressed through the gestures of the hands, the suggestiveness of the gaze.

"All these things that are really part of European culture," Bourouissa told me recently, "I wanted to reinterpret with this new French youth, with its own history, its own codes." For example, in *La main* (2006), from *Périphérique*, a young woman reclines on a bed like a figure of erotic romanticism, gazing at a man who is leaning over her with a hand placed on her abdomen, which is illuminated by a strip of light from a window. A third figure, another man, looks on ambivalently from a darkened corner behind them. Another from the series, *La république* (2006), shows a scene of collectivity; whether the group is engaged in some kind of combat, or rebellion, or something else, we don't know. A French flag is planted provocatively in the upper corner as the men signal to each other in a kind of sacral drama. Still, the staging is subtle, not necessarily immediately obvious enough to draw a stark distinction from documentary photography.

Périphérique, which in fall 2021 was collected in a monograph published by Loose Joints, is heavily male: its subjects are mostly young men, and masculinity itself is a clear topic of study. Some of these men were Bourouissa's friends, the people he saw most often and knew best. But the choice was also, in part, pragmatic—the public spaces of the banlieues were then, and still are, male spaces, where young men hang out together and where complicated notions of masculinity are worked out. "How do you affirm yourself when your parents are devalued by society?" Bourouissa asks. Social standards, he observed, demand that everyone be powerful, strong, and rich. How does one construct a sense of one's own power in relation to others if it cannot be inherited? Amid the poverty that surrounded him and his friends, the answer was through the body. "It's almost like a reproduction of the mechanisms of power in the body," Bourouissa says. "There is a physical experience of what we live through. And we incorporate that experience into our bodies as a kind of memory."

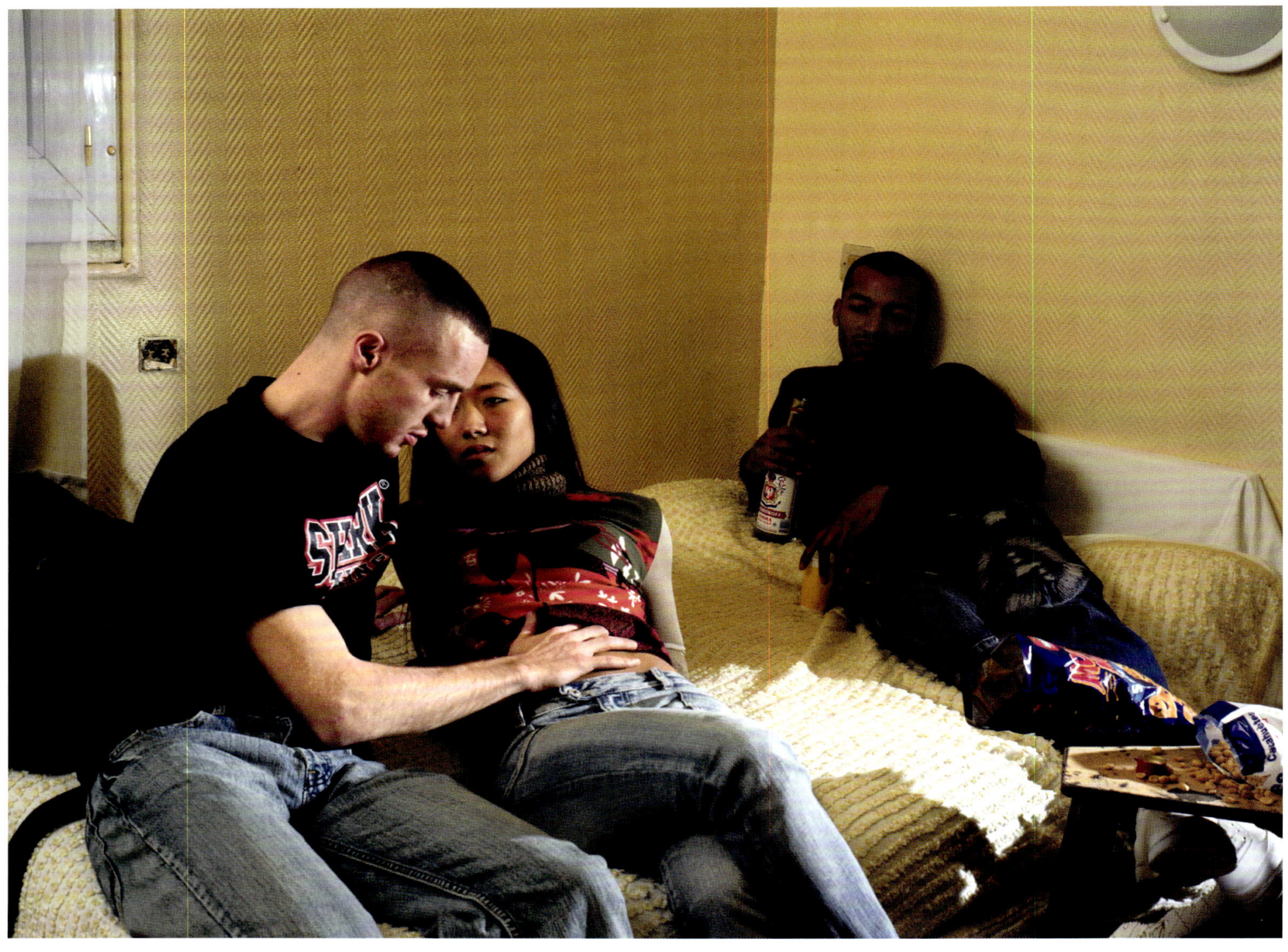

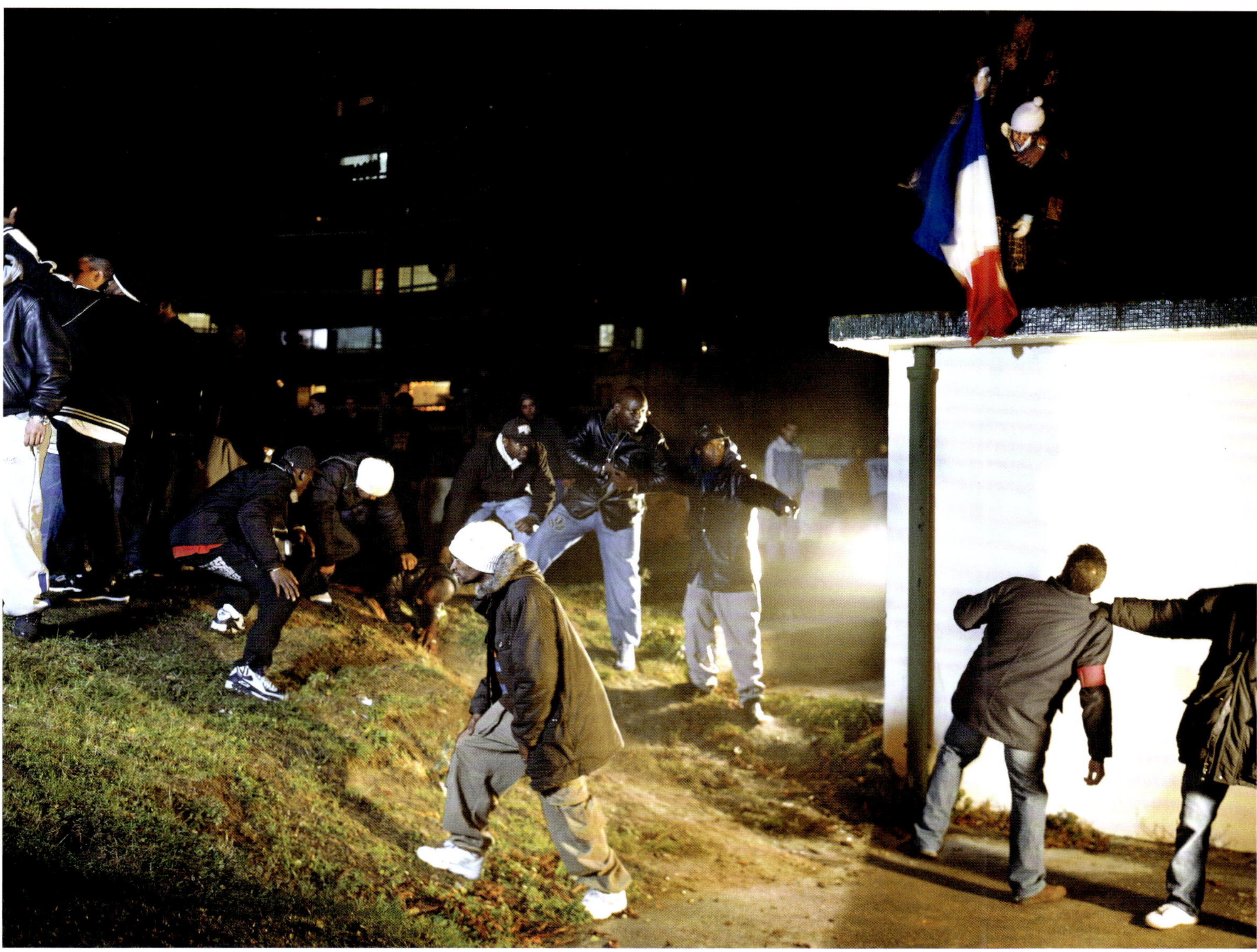

Périphérique brought Bourouissa widespread recognition before the age of thirty. Photographs from the series were included in New York at the New Museum's inaugural Triennial, in 2009, an international exhibition of young artists titled *Younger Than Jesus*; are in the permanent collection of the Musée national de l'histoire de l'immigration, in Paris; and were recently displayed at a solo exhibition in Copenhagen, at the Kunsthal Charlottenborg. Many of Bourouissa's admirers suggested that he continue focusing on the topic, but he decided to diversify and moved on to other projects, including *Shoplifters* (2014), for which he repurposed a collection of disarming Polaroids of shoplifters in New York, and *Brutal Family Roots* (2020), an immersive installation that used acacia trees to reflect on migration and dispersion. Still, he considers the fact that *Périphérique* is being published in book form now, for the first time, more than a decade after the work was created, an indicator that it has stood the test of time.

It is tempting to look at *Périphérique*, from the mid-aughts, and ask what, if anything, has changed. Clearly, with regard to poverty, stigmatization, and the myriad issues affecting identity and history in the banlieues, with France's ongoing cultural battles playing out in the background, one might take a pessimistic view. But Bourouissa insists that when he looks at those photographs now, he sees certain, very clear, differences: *Race* was a word that no one spoke at the time. "No one dared to name it," he says, but that has changed. Now, people, especially young people, talk about matters of race, and the French are starting to "untie" what that word means, its implications in historical understanding, and the afterlife of history in France today.

Elisabeth Zerofsky is a writer based in Berlin and a contributor to *The New York Times Magazine*.

Curriculum
Sohrab Hura

"Incoherence is important to me," Sohrab Hura observed in a 2019 interview. "It is a reflection of the violent deluge of imagery that I feel I am living with every day." Hura's evocative work is animated by a deeply personal way of parsing the world, through projects that have focused on cities along the Ganges River, the geography of the lower Mississippi River, and more recently in Kashmir. Relying on a complex narrative structure, his award-winning book *The Coast* (2019) comprises a carefully sequenced collection of repetitive and immersive images. A member of Magnum Photos and an editor and curator in his own right, Hura, who is based in New Delhi, projects his vision while also advocating for other image makers in his orbit.

Bruce Lee and Being Like Water
Be formless, shapeless, like water. Now, you put water into a cup, it becomes the cup. You put water into a bottle, it becomes the bottle. You put it in a teapot, it becomes the teapot. Now, water can flow, or it can crash. Be water, my friend. —Bruce Lee

Bruce Lee's imperative reminds me of how photography often gets treated as fixed, perhaps because everything needs to be identifiable and familiar. When younger, I was constantly told that I should be doing one kind of photography in order to find authorship. But sticking to that approach felt forced. I was able to learn that photography could be like a conversation with a friend, a lover, a parent, or even a stranger—malleable.

Short Stories by Ismat Chughtai and Saadat Hasan Manto
Whether it's "Lihaaf" ("The Quilt," 1941) by Ismat Chughtai or "Toba Tek Singh" (1955) by Saadat Hasan Manto, both writers engaged with their times using brutal honesty. When I first discovered these writings as a young photographer in India, photography was meant to be documentary in an evidentiary way. Reading their short stories made me recognize that one could search for a photographic vocabulary that opened up thoughts rather than closed them off.

Apichatpong Weerasethakul, *Uncle Boonmee Who Can Recall His Past Lives*, 2010
In this film, everyday ordinariness seems like magic, and the past merges with the present and the future. But that's how life usually is. The film gets conveniently described as magic realism, a label often attributed to what one finds unfamiliar. In my series *Snow* (2015–ongoing), what I, as an outsider, had at first thought of as being magical metaphors were, in fact, lived realities for many in Kashmir.

Kathmandu
If one could point to the heart of the photography ecosystem in South Asia, it would surely lie in Kathmandu. Over the last fifteen years, image-based practices in Kathmandu have thrived, and the city has become a meeting point, of sorts, for people from all over, including India and Pakistan, with flows and exchanges across political and geographical borders. Photo Kathmandu, Photo Circle, Nepal Picture Library, and other arts institutions have made the hegemonic position of New Delhi in the region's photography scene quite redundant.

The Secret Life of Dayanita Singh
Over a decade ago, my photo lab called asking if they could show my work to a "client." After an hour, they called again telling me there was a package to come pick up. In this package, I found one hundred rolls of Kodak Tri-X with an anonymous note asking me to keep working and not think about anything else. I was taken aback. Over the years, from time to time, a new package would appear with that same note. I started to have an inkling of who that person might be after hearing stories that this person had been leaving film for young photographers at different processing labs way before I received mine. Many of the photographs in my first book, *Life Is Elsewhere* (2015), were made on those rolls of film.

December 6, 1992
This was the day that Hindu supremacists demolished the Babri Masjid, a sixteenth-century mosque, claiming that it was the birthplace of the Hindu deity Rama, the protagonist of the Ramayana, and set into motion acts of communal violence that unfolded over the next thirty years. The date remains a cornerstone for many artists who have thoughtfully and rigorously engaged with the myth of Ramayana. Both Rummana Hussain, with her performance works in the 1990s, and Anand Patwardhan, with the 1992 film *Ram Ke Naam* (*In the Name of God*), foresaw the violent, dystopian future that we are living in today. *Sita's Ramayana* (2011), by Samhita Arni, shines light on the feminist perspective of Ramayana. The 2018 film *Kaala* (Black) by Pa. Ranjith punctures the fallacy of the binary notion of good versus evil, which, based on skin color and caste, perpetuates social hierarchies and fundamentalism.

Anjali House
In 2008, I started to work with children at Anjali House, in Cambodia, and was charmed by the way they moved with the camera: carefree, raw, unaware of the baggage of being a photographer. I realized the stiffness in the formality—or, more precisely, the consciousness—of my own process. I had to unlearn everything I knew. The children's photographs are a constant reminder of this magical way of looking at the world, no matter how cynical one might sometimes feel as an artist.

Adyar Banyan Tree
This banyan tree at the Theosophical Society in Chennai is believed to be almost 450 years old and one of the largest in the world. When I started photography, I imagined my practice similar to the way a tree grows. Then, two friends took me to the Theosophical Society and led me into a dense forest where overlapped banyan branches create a canopy so thick that on a hot summer day they formed a patch of shade. Only the forest's barren center remained lit with sunlight. The forest had once been a single tree and, over time, its aerial roots reached the ground and grew into individual trees while the main tree trunk died. I now see my own tree more clearly. It is an incomplete aerial-root tree surrounded by other aerial-root trees— younger, stronger, far more generous and expansive than mine. Each finds its own way to the light. It was never about the tree itself but about the larger forest.

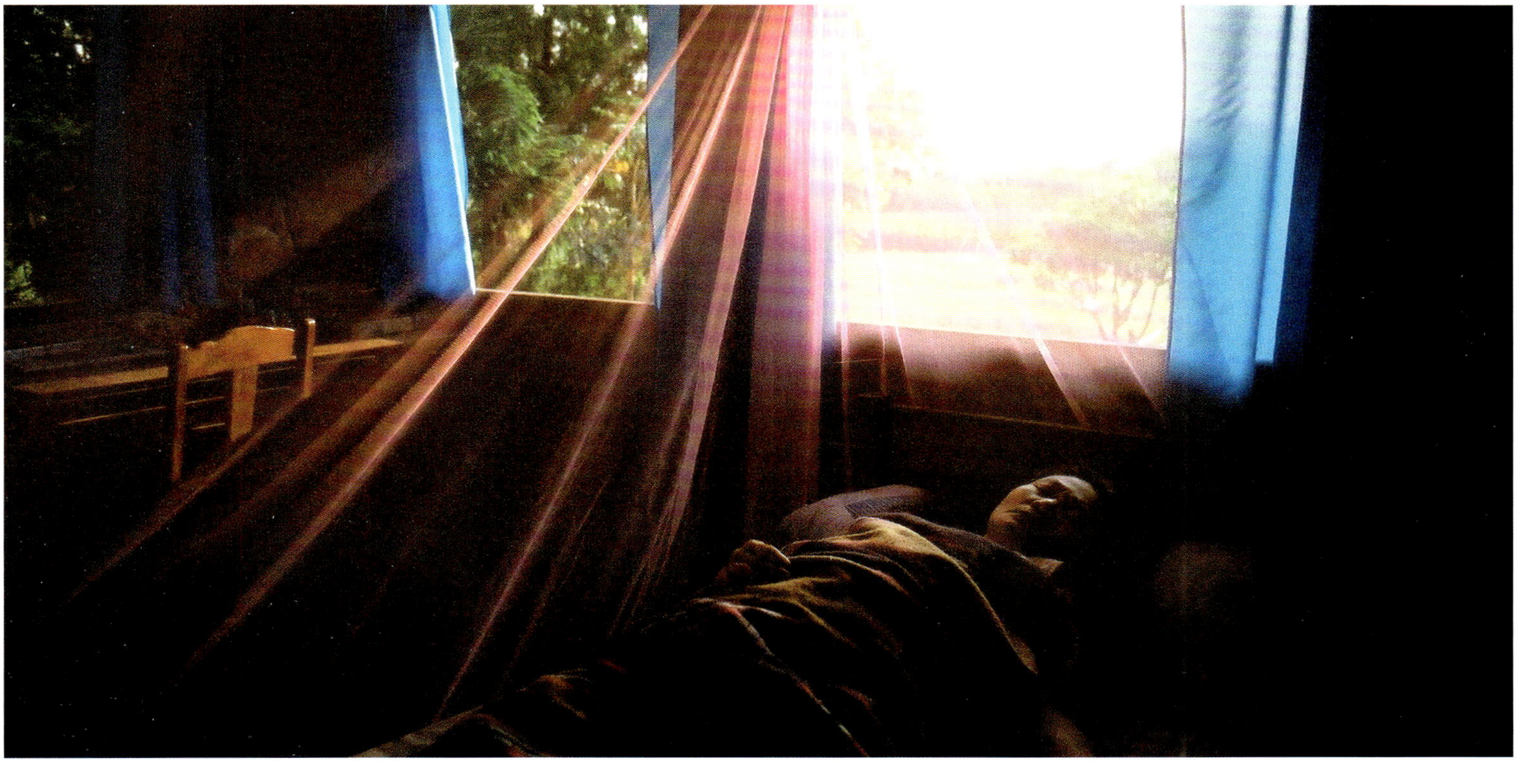

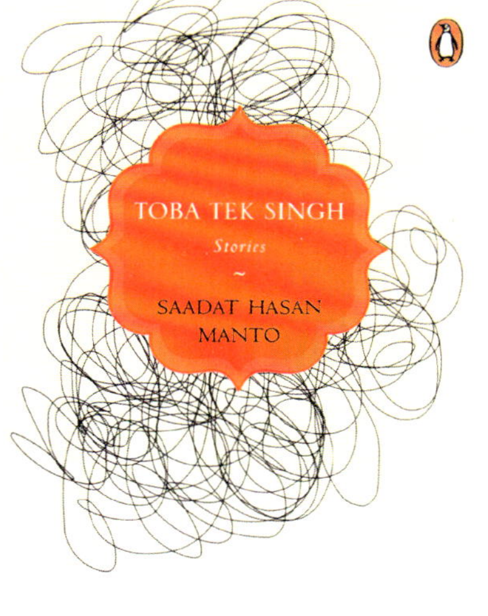

TOBA TEK SINGH
Stories
~
SAADAT HASAN
MANTO

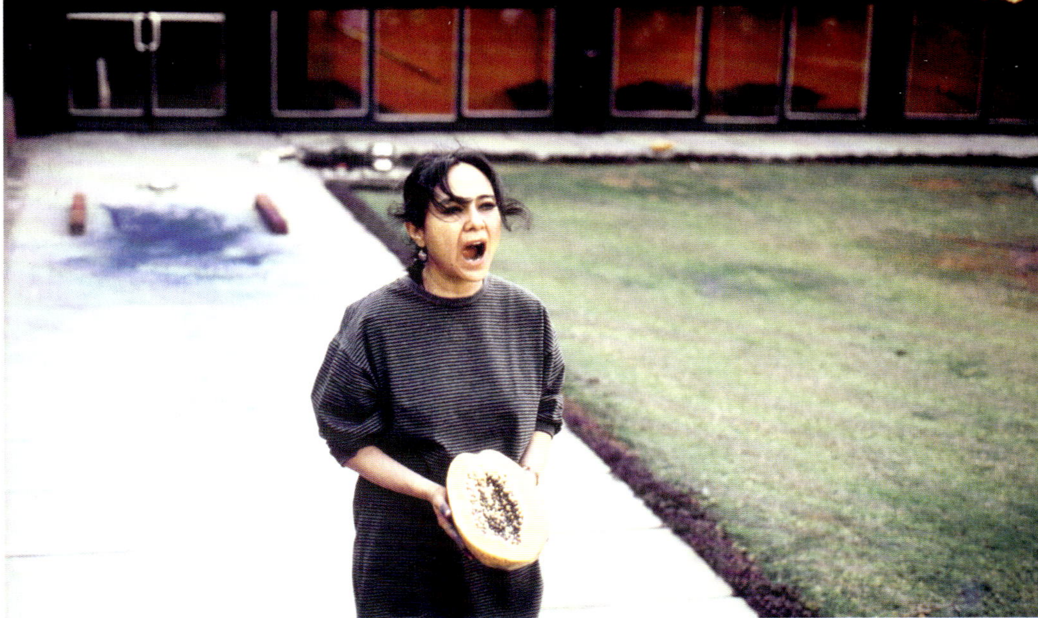

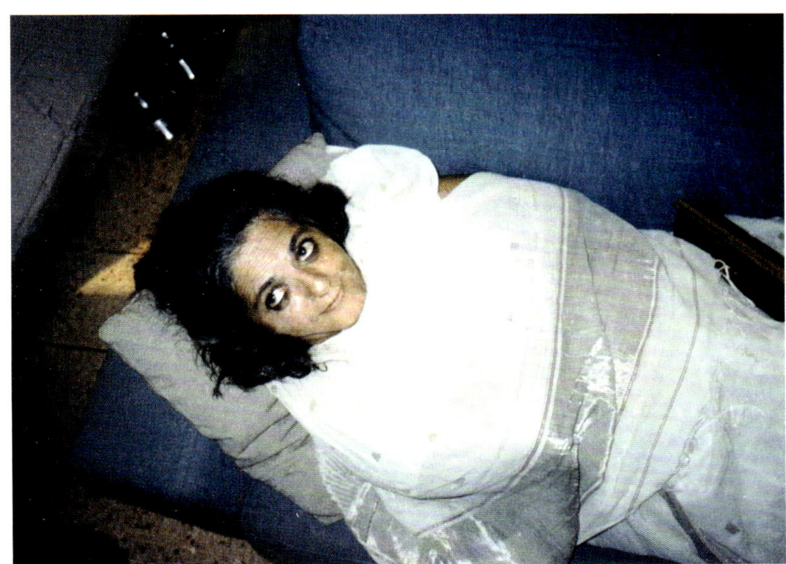

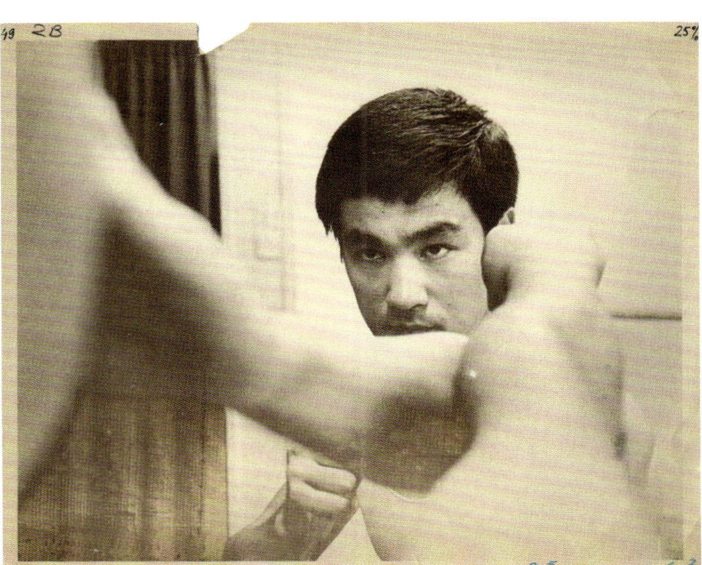

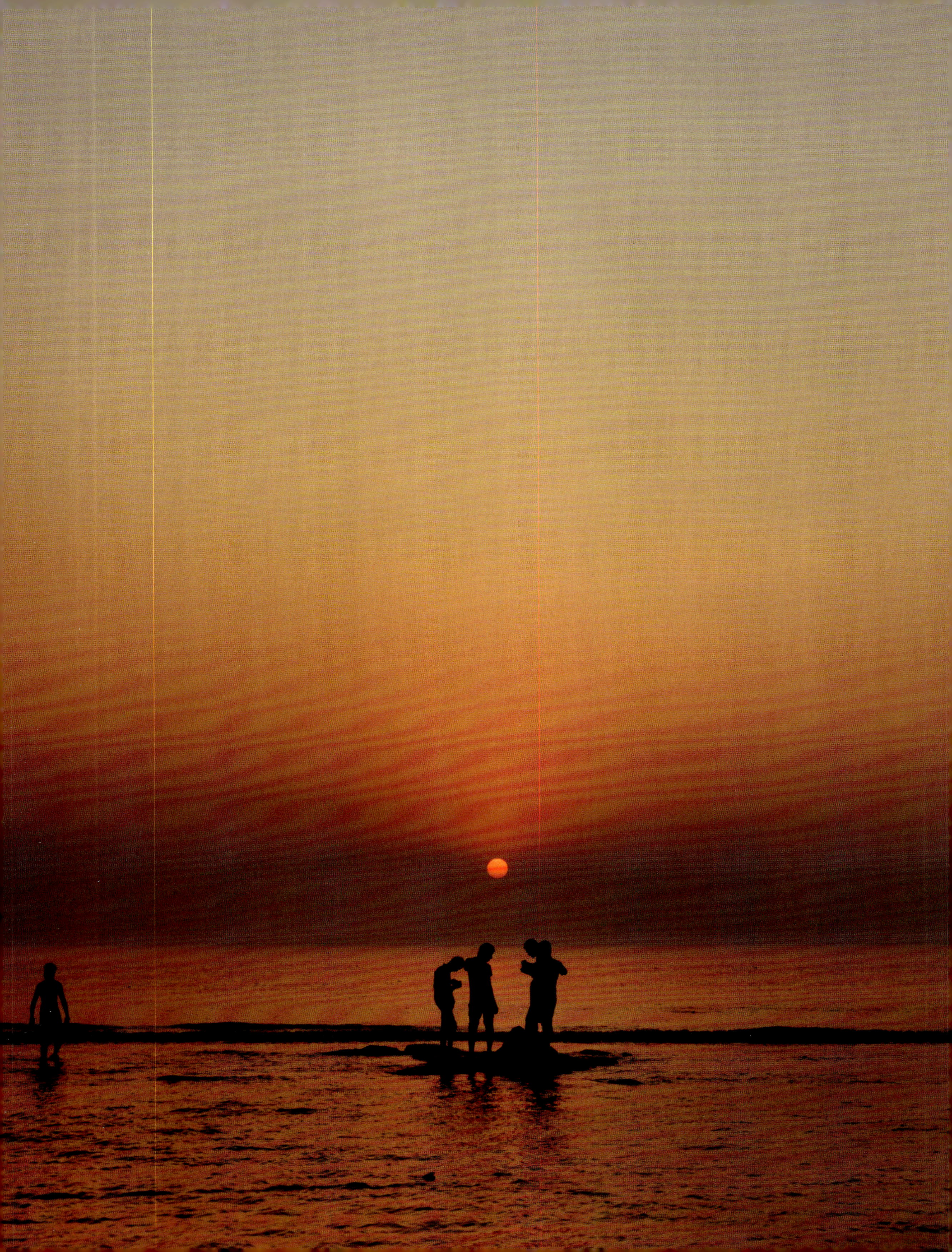

Celebrations

This year, *Aperture*, founded in 1952, turns seventy. That the magazine has managed to consistently publish for seven decades is a milestone, a minor miracle, a testament to the indefatigable spirit and stubborn will of its staff over those decades. Given this anniversary, it seemed fitting to delve into our archive—a resource of inspiration and instruction—to revisit some earlier themes of the magazine.

In doing so, one stood out—admittedly, an idiosyncratic issue from 1974 titled "Celebrations." "Today, there is a great need for emphasizing the climactic affirmations of life's events and feelings," the preface states, arguing for photography, a medium that inherently embodies a close read of the world, to do just that. "A photograph that celebrates is an affirmation of existence," the editors proclaim, and this affirmation of life might take many forms—be it through visual equivalents, documentation of literal celebrations, or invocations of the spiritual and the sublime.

In this 2022 "Celebrations" issue, we build on their ideas through depictions of holidays, ceremonies, and festivities—as well as by considering the ritual of careful observation as a means of grieving or marking time. We see visceral exuberance against a backdrop of political strife in Beirut, the thrill of wanderlust, excavations of family histories, and the powerful, constant urge to gather, whether in Kinshasa's vibrant nightlife of the 1950s and '60s or London's sweaty dance floors of our era, where jubilation carries on, despite an ongoing, and unpredictable, pandemic. Now might be a complicated moment for celebration—even if tempered by caution—but the photographs presented here remind us that pausing to look can be its own form of revelry.　　**—The Editors**

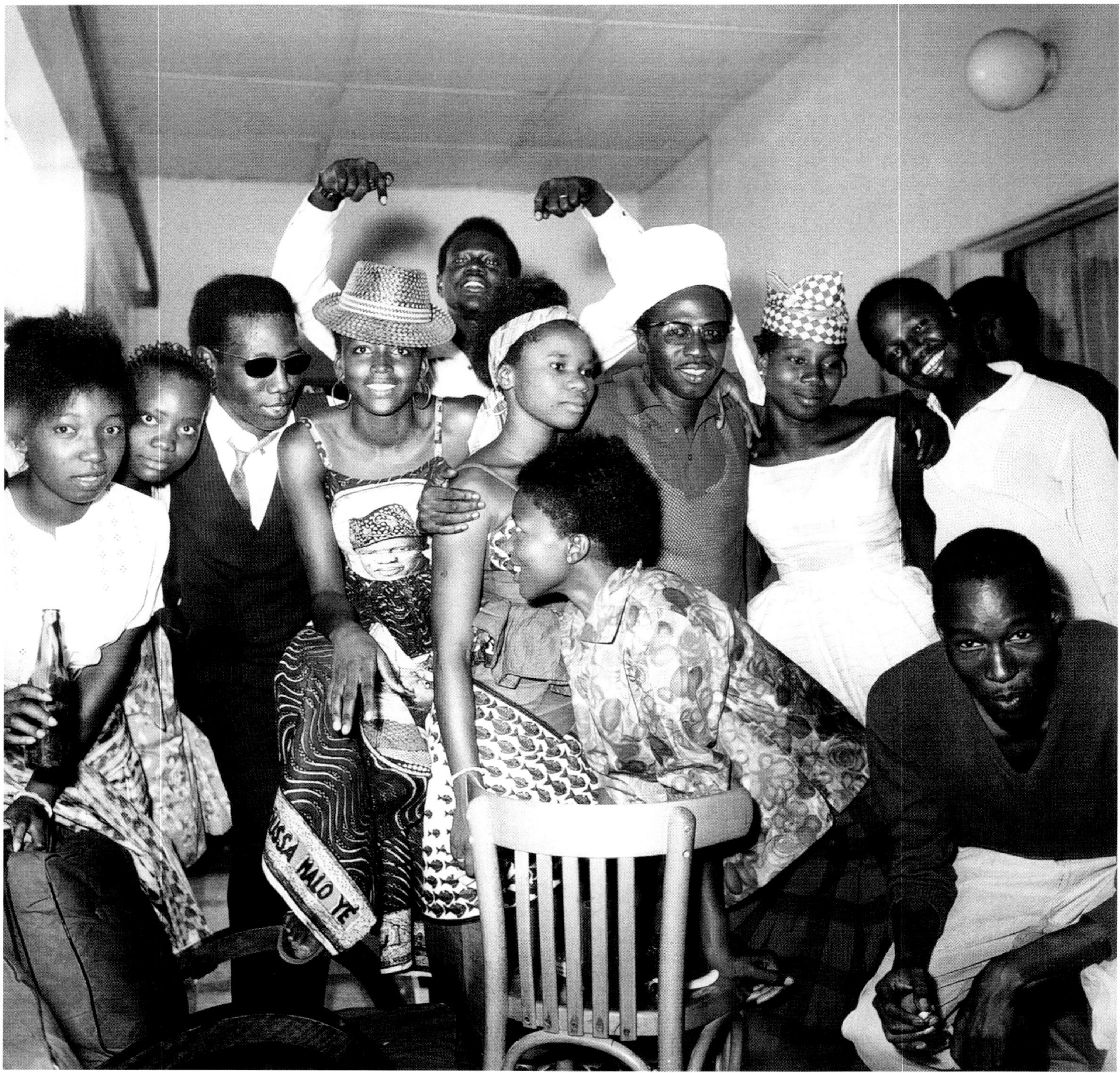

This page:
Malick Sidibé, *Soirée familiale*, 1966–2008
© the artist and courtesy
Jack Shainman Gallery,
New York

Opposite:
Frances F. Denny,
Cake (Cambridge, MA),
2013
Courtesy the artist

What Makes a Celebration?

Lynne Tillman

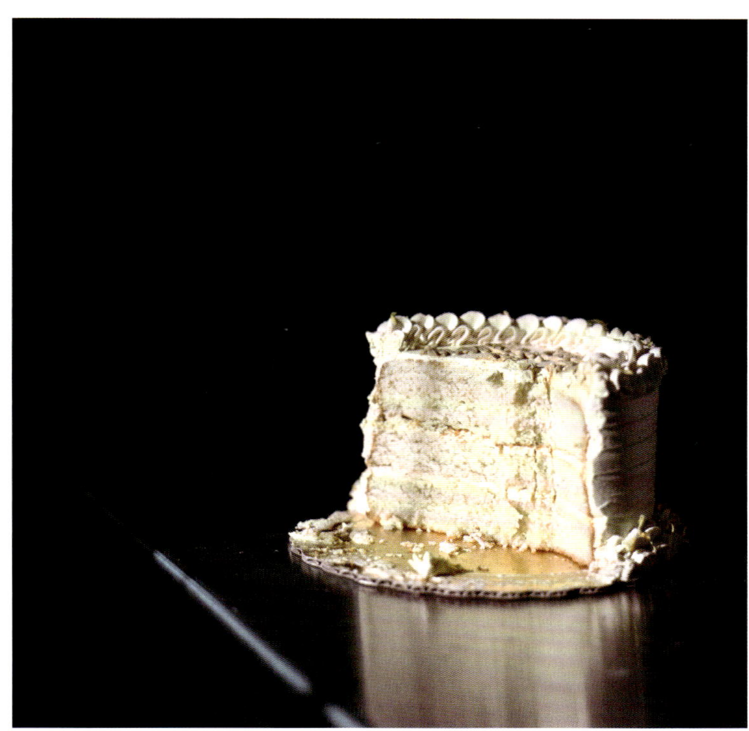

A pack of wolves gathers to celebrate the birth of a pup. They look up at the sky, eagerness in their eyes, and howl in unison. All of them welcome births with joy, and must have from their beginning, I think; and wonder what the first humans celebrated. Newly standing up, likely some covering on their naked, hairy bodies—did they celebrate their difference from other animals? Probably not. At the birth of a tiny, bloody one emerging from another's body, did they howl like wolves? To celebrate is a behavior that the human species took time to develop, though cave drawings might be a version of celebration.

From long-ago, unpictured days, humans have found ways for communally expressing grief and showing joy. Affection, attachment, love, fellowship, feelings toward others must have been transmitted with grimaces, hugs, shrugs, headshakes, gestures for all occasions. Then, events must have sprung up: a huge bonfire at harvest time, a totem pole to honor gods, sun worship at dawn, a merging of clans in something like marriage. Feelings for and about oneself and others—pride, shame, rage, jealousy—ancient texts attest to them.

There are the spontaneous or the planned or the obligatory celebrations, analogous to Claude Lévi-Strauss's idea of "the raw and the cooked," the dialectics of culture, "categorical opposites drawn from everyday experience." Of the cooked: U.S. civil society has Thanksgiving, an ignorant and disturbing holiday, mostly enjoyed or suffered for overeating, decidedly not enjoyed by First Americans whose ancestors were massacred by white Europeans. Halloween, nonobligatory and semi-raw, is fun, most especially for children, when disguise offers them a chance to be superheroes and scare adults, while adults can regress to childhood. About which the comic Richard Lewis quipped: "At Halloween, my family dresses up as obstacles."

Few people celebrate failure, but the British commemorate a failed revolution with Guy Fawkes Day. On the street, children ask, "Penny for the guy?" A resilient irony rescues the British from maudlin sentimentality, except at Christmas.

Weddings, Christmas, birthdays, the planning for these occasions sows happiness, worry, and agitation; then come their festive, or not, results. Ask a friend: "Did you get gifts for Christmas when you were a child?" or, "Did you have birthday parties?" The response will be immediate and specific, details often vivid and surprising, or so vague and bland as to indicate trauma. Holidays can be the most ambivalent days of your life.

"I'm going home for Christmas" might begin a stand-up comic's routine, while many movies depend on family fractiousness for plot points. Getting home may be difficult, flights bumped, but being at home can be bumpier. Philip-Lorca diCorcia's 1978 scene of an overdecorated living room in Hartford is Christmas gone wild. Without people, it's an expectant, perfectly idealized Christmas. The reality of adults arguing near the tree imposes itself on the picture, while a lament can be heard: Why did we ever come home?

Sociologists claim celebrations foster social cohesion by honoring key community figures, denoting public accomplishments and private ones, such as success in love with marriage ceremonies and medals awarded for daring and courage in war. Celebrations proclaim significant moments and events, and also shape the appropriate responses—a gold watch for retirement after fifty years. They teach people when to applaud or weep, and sometimes people do both at weddings and funerals.

President Barack Obama's 2008 election night was tense, exciting, dramatic. A Black man had been nominated for president in a nation whose written Constitution recognized slavery, embedding racism within it. Black communities were buoyed by possibility, and enthusiasm for Obama crossed races. Many non-Black Americans didn't feel it, not at all. And his win most likely aroused their already active and latent racism.

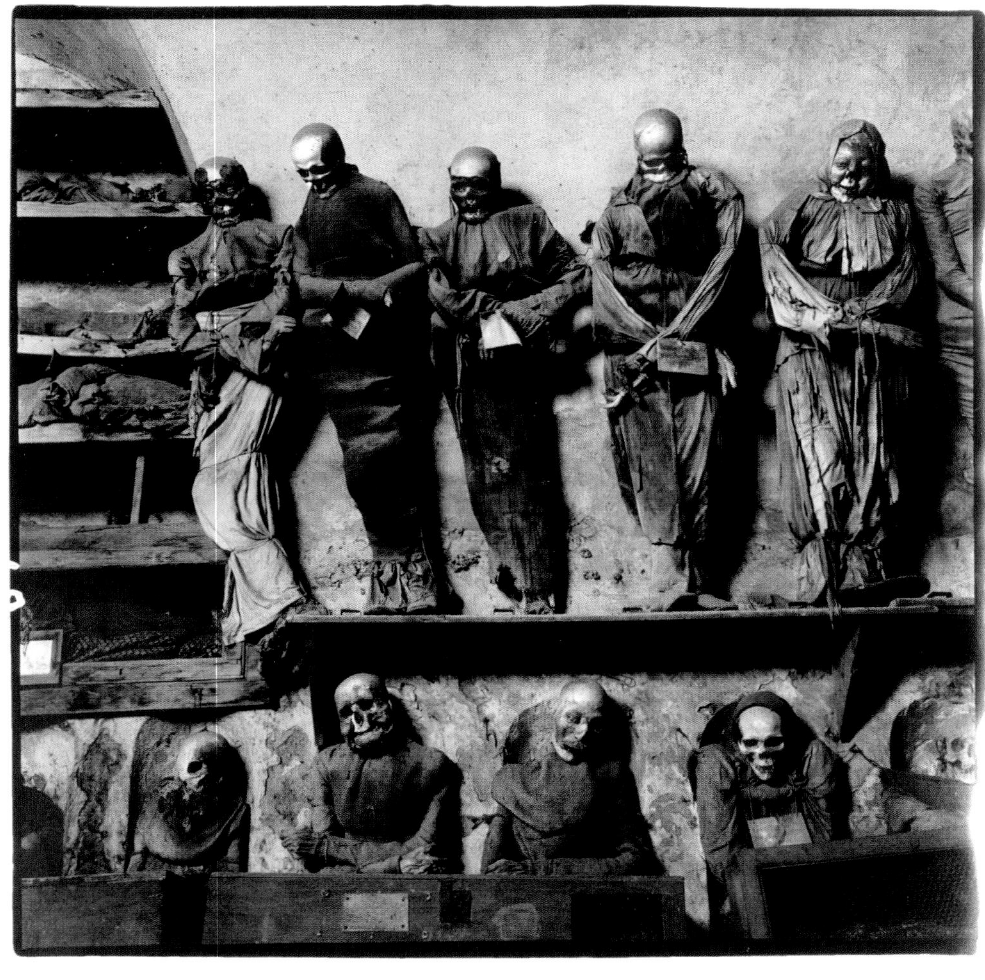

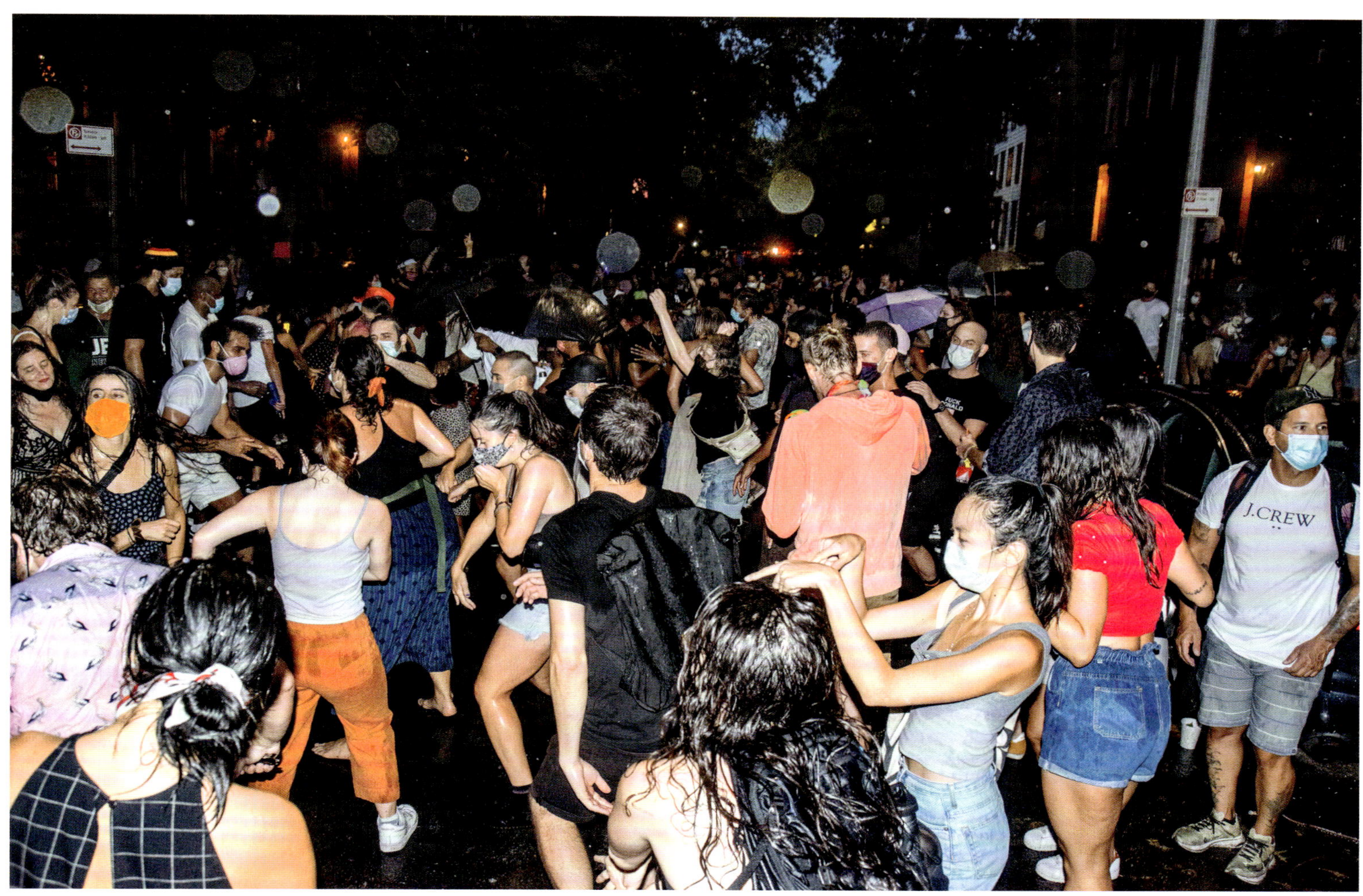

Ruvan Wijesooriya, *Rain and Shine at St. James Joy*, Brooklyn, 2020
Courtesy the artist

In Chicago, where Obama lived and was a U.S. senator, Michal Czerwonka documented the ecstasy at his 2008 victory gathering in Grant Park. Two American flags and Obama's image on a placard wave behind a crowd of beaming supporters; in the foreground, an exultant young Black man has raised his fist in the Black Power salute. The gesture also foregrounds the civil rights movement, without which a Barack Obama wouldn't have had a chance in hell. He had run on hope, and hope animates Czerwonka's photograph. Now, it is an image of unfulfilled wishes.

Covid lockdown, masking, and being housebound, everyone felt like a prisoner. In the summer of 2020, about two months into the pandemic, whatever fears these Brooklyn neighbors felt, they ran into the streets, masks on, to escape their boredom, for a block party known as St. James Joy. "There was dancing in the street," to quote Martha and the Vandellas. Pictures of the event burst with human energy and the beauty of spontaneity, exemplifying what well-planned events can't ever do—let the moment happen, when sudden pleasure roars, when nothing else matters, it's just full on partying.

Now, with vaccinations, apartment doors have opened. People meet and greet. There's still need for caution—the threat of new variants—but there's reason enough to celebrate the advent of almost ordinary life. The first season of *Succession* launched with an episode titled "Celebration." The eightieth-birthday luncheon for the patriarch, Logan Roy (*le roi*), was attended by his entire nuclear, or unclear, family. No one enjoyed it, especially the birthday boy. The ironic festivity united the series' disunited characters, inviting *Succession*'s viewers into the family's vicious infighting. Some birthdays are like that.

Malick Sidibé's photograph of a jolly family gathering in *Soirée familiale* (1966) sings with ebullience. The family's liveliness

Celebrations proclaim significant moments and events, and also shape the appropriate responses. They teach people when to applaud or weep.

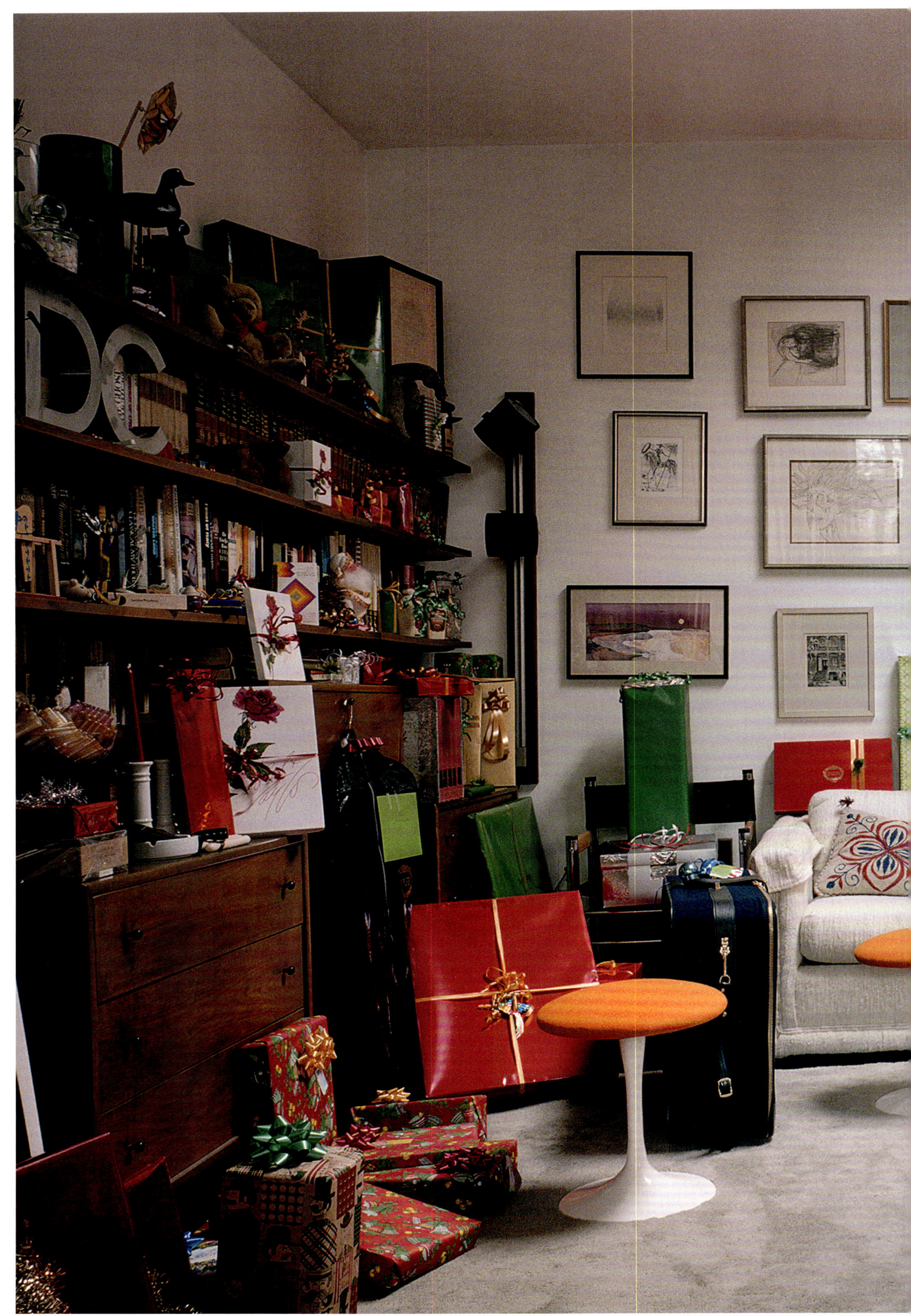

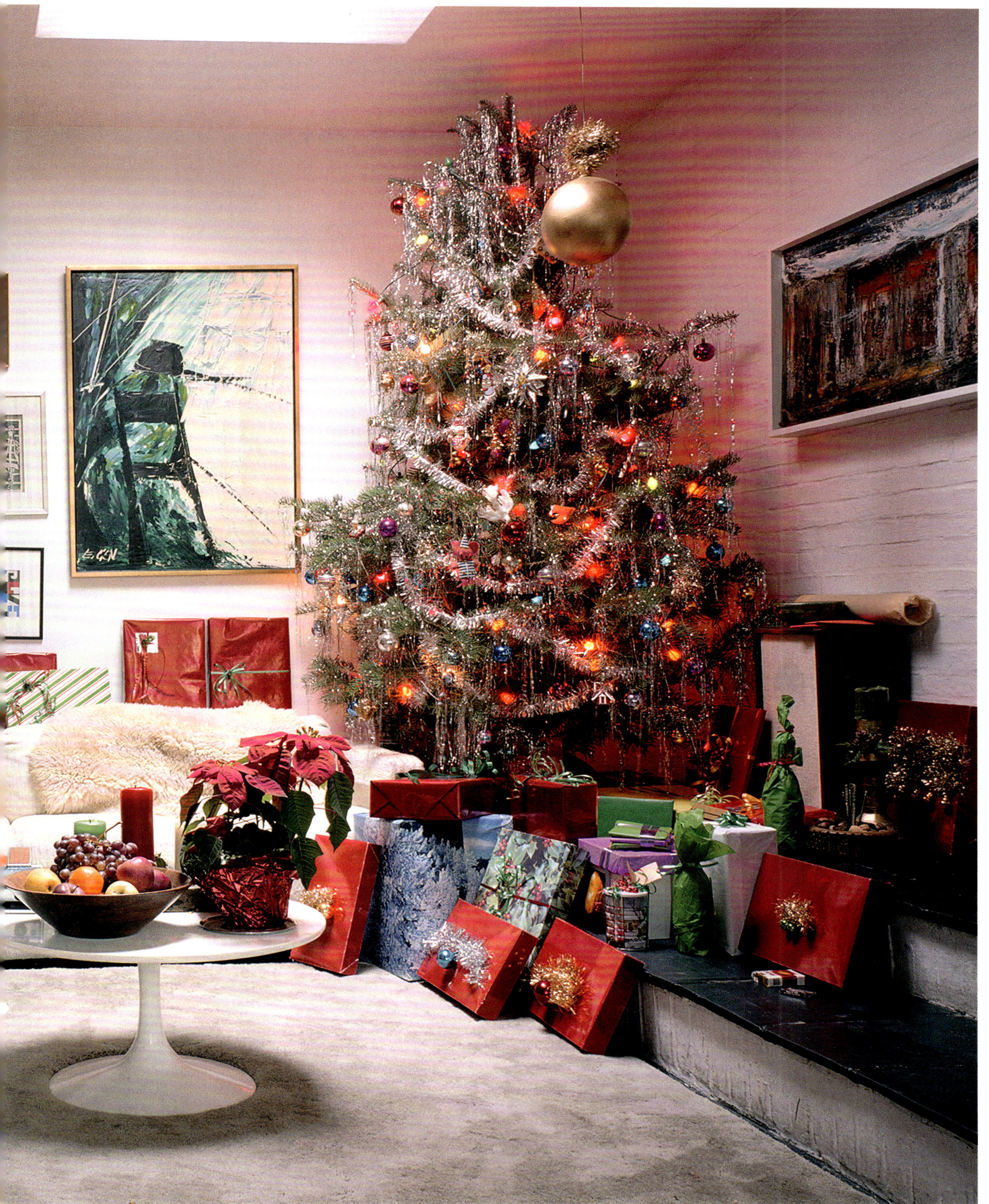

Obama's 2008 election night was tense, exciting, dramatic. Black communities were buoyed by possibility, and enthusiasm for Obama crossed races.

overflows the frame. Most of the group looks at his camera, but not everyone. Those not looking, otherwise engaged, register individuals as related to each other and unique from each other. Sidibé didn't insist, Look at me, the camera, smile, the standard gimmicks to organize group portraits. He let this family act as it wanted. Maybe they're being themselves, though one can't know. The family composition thrives with personality, a portrait of resemblances and differences.

In Frances F. Denny's *Cake, Cambridge, MA* (2013), a round, high, heavily frosted white cake is metonymic, either for a birthday or small wedding. *Cake* might even be a tiny monument to the uniformity of celebrations. Sitting on a black table that disappears under it, Denny's cake is spotlighted like a movie star. But half of it is gone, likely eaten, so the cake is undone. The assumption is that it was once whole, which comments on the ways viewers narrate pictures, imagining a before them and an after them. The exposed interior might be, curiously, about interiority, what lies beneath or inside a luscious surface. Nobody's waiting for a slice, and Denny's solitary half cake says, It's over. On reflection, the party might not have been as sweet as the cake, now just a leftover.

Photography's genesis must have been influenced by people's fascination with themselves; knowing death awaits is a perpetual insult to their narcissism. Might a picture subvert eternal disappearance? "Life is a movie. Death is a photograph," Susan Sontag famously wrote. She saw a still object, necessarily of the past, the subject absent—death. But a photograph is seen by the living who enliven it with meaning. It is, instead, a fitting subject for a photograph, this stasis.

The dead are also celebrated, honored, and photographers' concepts range as widely as burial customs. Peter Hujar's elegant style in *Palermo Catacombs #11* (1963) articulates the texture and architecture of the tombs. In the sixteenth century, the Capuchin friars used these crypts when their cemetery became

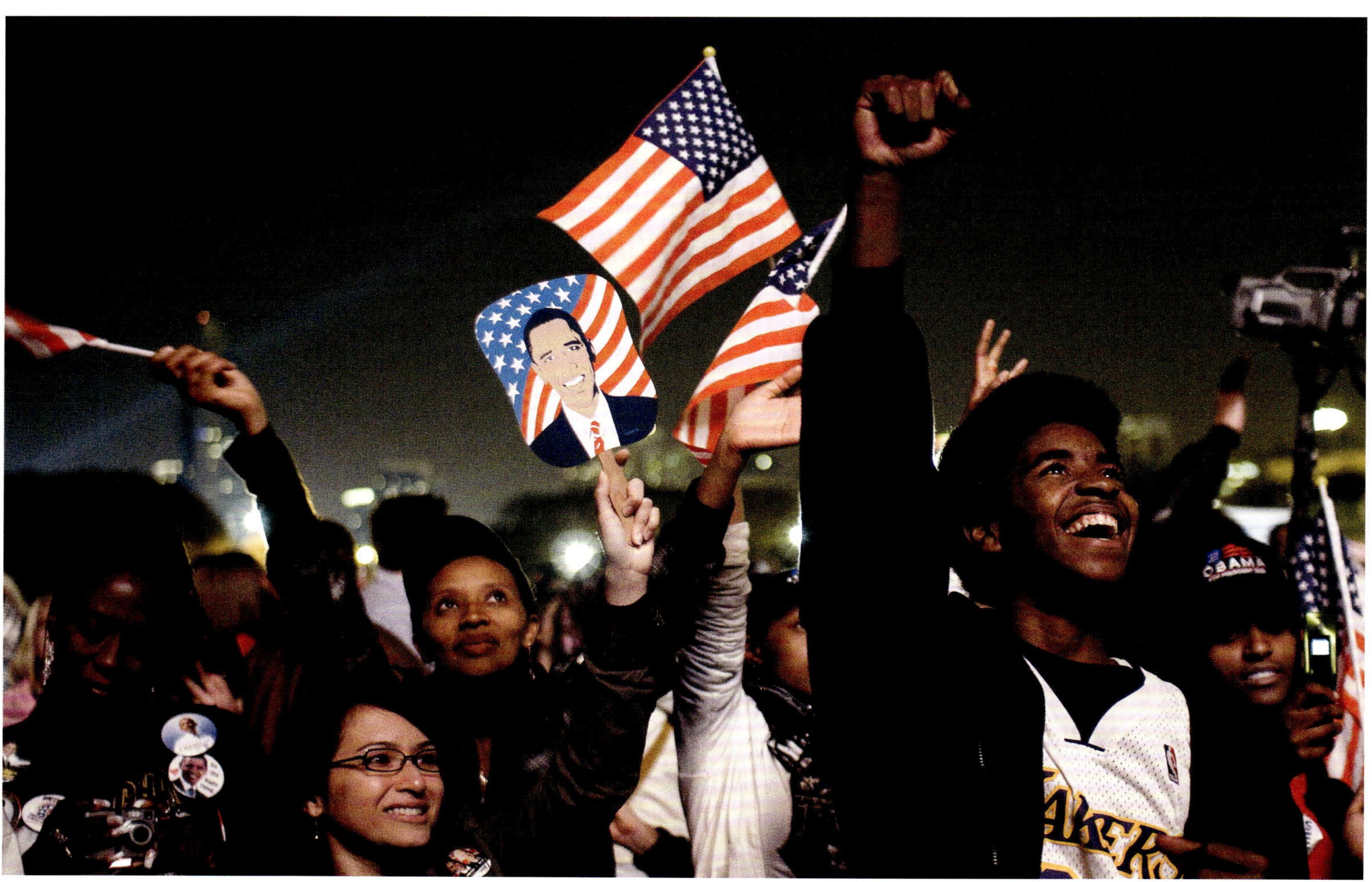

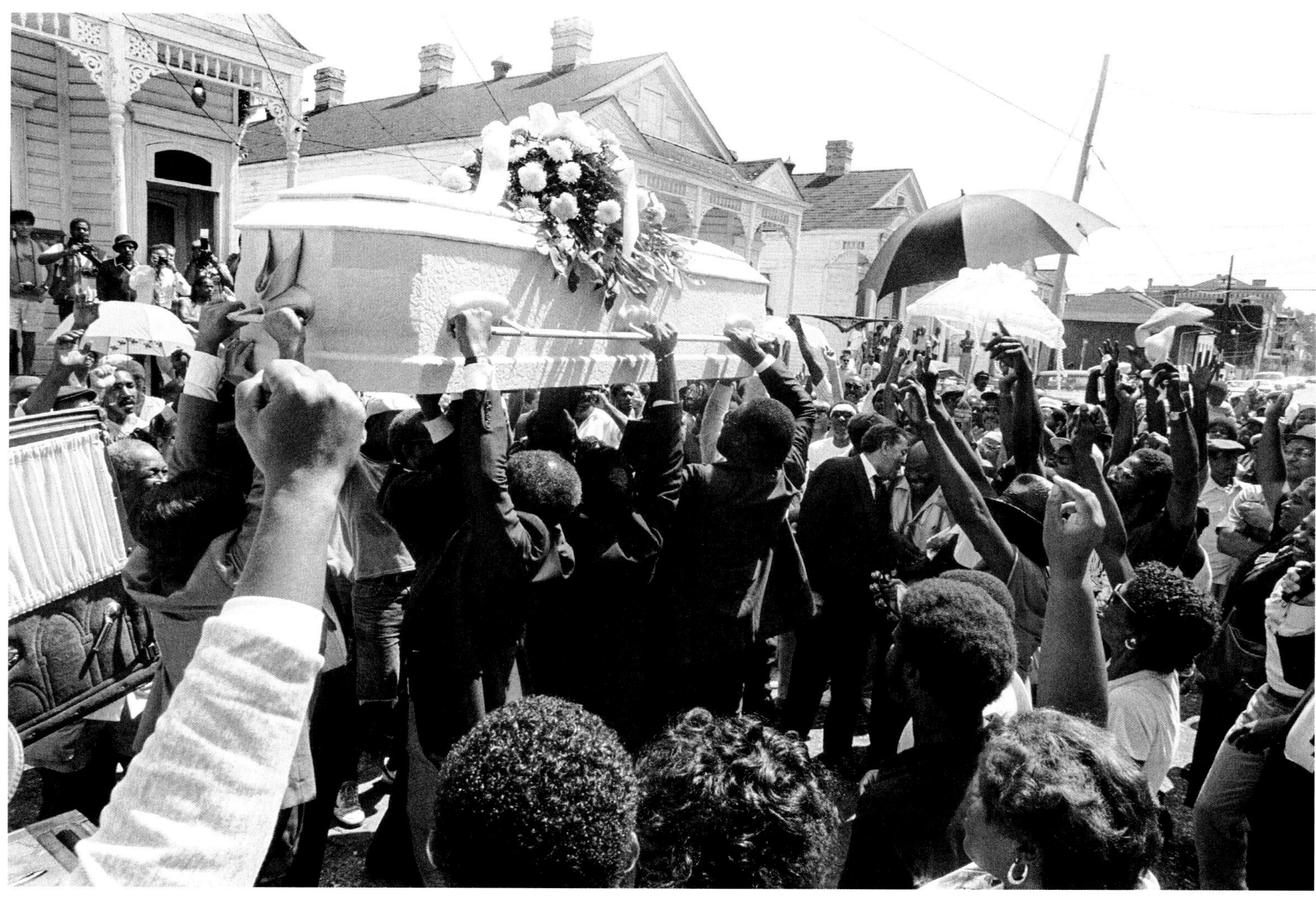

Chandra McCormick, *Jazz Funeral of American Jazz Drummer James Black,* Treme, New Orleans, 1988
Courtesy the artist

full. Initially, they dried the corpses, dousing them with vinegar to preserve them.

Hujar's photograph is shocking, the way death is. Hujar wants to see death, get close, focus on details. God is in the details, and maybe death is also. Their robes drape around their mummified bodies. Those faces, their icy expressions, what do they tell us? Standing up, the dead might just walk away. The liminal passage between life and death—she passed, he passed— is heightened by Hujar's inclusion of a staircase, signifying ascension and descent. The friars will walk up and down it, until, one day, they can't.

Far from Palermo, the death of a drummer, James Black, merits a traditional New Orleans jazz funeral in 1988. It's a joyous celebration. Chandra McCormick places the stark white, flower-bedecked casket, raised high by pallbearers, in the center, motoring the dynamic procession and the photograph. Some of the Black and non-Black mourners have raised their fists. So many people surround it, fan out from it, walking in front of and behind it, the coffin might be floating in the air, even though three pronounced arms do the work. James Black's life of making music has ended, and the tunes he played and loved will see him out. Exultant faces proclaim their fervent belief: James is going to a better place.

In the here and now, celebrating feels right. The vaccine— and the promise of helpful new pills—is freeing people to roam the streets, meet in bars, go shopping, see friends, dine out— even the usual seems a celebration. Nothing feels ordinary, though, while it is also very ordinary, except for the threat of the vexing unvaxxed and new variants. Still, it's a dangerous world where much more than viruses are killing people. Many would still prefer to stay home.

Lynne Tillman is a novelist, short-story writer, and cultural critic based in New York.

"Reach out and touch faith," Depeche Mode implored in "Personal Jesus." In Myriam Boulos's photographs, I could've sworn I heard her subjects whisper, "Reach out and touch me."

Faith is touch; touch is sacred. And the body is its own god.

Against a purple sky, two naked men tenderly embrace; one is, indeed, whispering, not to us—the welcome voyeurs—but into the ear of his beloved. Juxtapose the delicacy of that moment—men stripped of the confines that patriarchy makes of masculinity—with the altogether more robust, and much more tightly cropped, image of two women kissing. Swallowing each other whole, more like. It is difficult to ascertain where one begins and the other ends. There is power in their desire.

And that is what the revolution renders: powerful women and tender men.

In a global pandemic that has starved us of touch, who would not genuflect before the heady carnality captured by Boulos's gaze? In almost every photograph in her series *What's Ours* (2019–ongoing), hands knead into flesh, skin lies on top of skin, body hair on disjointed limbs serves like rivers on a map, luring us closer toward sustenance, enticing us with intimacy, destination freedom.

Boulos was born in 1992, in Lebanon, two years after the official end of the seventeen-year civil war. Her fluency for turning her country inside out with her gaze has landed her work in *Vanity Fair*, *Vogue*, and *Time*. She is based in Beirut, but she was in Paris on a two-month fellowship when we spoke last year.

Reflecting on *What's Ours*, Boulous has written that when the revolution began in Lebanon in October 2019, with protests against corruption and austerity measures, "It all felt as if we were coming out of an abusive relationship to finally say: No, this is not normal."

Those who truly want to be free know that is how the revolution succeeds. The revolution against the political tyrant alone is the minor one. Taking a leader down does little to topple the personal tyrants who live on street corners, in our bedrooms, in our minds. Their overthrow is the stuff of major revolution.

Who does the revolution belong to? What do we own if not our bodies? What is ours?

"My friends and I used to take pictures naked in the streets of Beirut," Boulos writes. "It was our own way of reclaiming our streets and our bodies. Everything that is supposed to be ours."

The inhabitants of Boulos's Beirut clearly trust her. Obsessed as she tells me she is with "the body and the present moment," it is as if she has stepped inside the embrace that she captures, presenting it to us with awe and reverence; as if she sliced through the thin veil that separates the "us" from the "them" and entered the embrace on another, ethereal level that does not disturb or distract the divine creatures she captures.

Her eyes, heart, and camera are the holy trinity.

"A revolution was happening in my country, a revolution was happening in me. It made me question everything," Boulos writes.

Revolutions—I know as an Egyptian marking ten years since my country's revolution—inspire you to say no to more, to everyone. One "no" leads to another like a stairway to liberation. When that staircase is yanked, you take a vulnerable punch to the gut. In Lebanon, a financial crisis, the pandemic, and the Beirut port explosion of August 2020 did not just yank at the staircase to liberation but seemed to fray it to bits.

"Since the explosion, I feel like a glass of water that overflows constantly," Boulos writes.

In a Zoom chat—she in Paris, I in Montreal—we talk about the leitmotif of compounded trauma and unresolved grief that connects our parts of the Middle East. And we talk about the body's need to fuck to mark its survival. She tells me of post-Beirut port explosion sex with an ex. I am reminded of how, soon after Egyptian riot police broke both my arms and sexually assaulted me in 2011, I began an on-again, off-again entanglement with a survivor of a postrevolution massacre in Egypt.

"An acute awareness of our mortality makes the physical especially important," I tell her. "This is your body saying to you, You are alive, and you have to do what you're meant to do, and that is fuck. Do it now!"

I am delighted that her new project is on women's sexual fantasies.

Faith is touch; touch is sacred. And the body is its own god.

We are each other's personal saviors because, as the poet and activist June Jordan wrote in her 1978 *Poem for South African Women*, "We are the ones we have been waiting for."

Myriam Boulos
What's Ours

Mona Eltahawy

Mona Eltahawy is the author of *Headscarves and Hymens: Why the Middle East Needs a Sexual Revolution* (2015) and founder of the newsletter Feminist Giant.

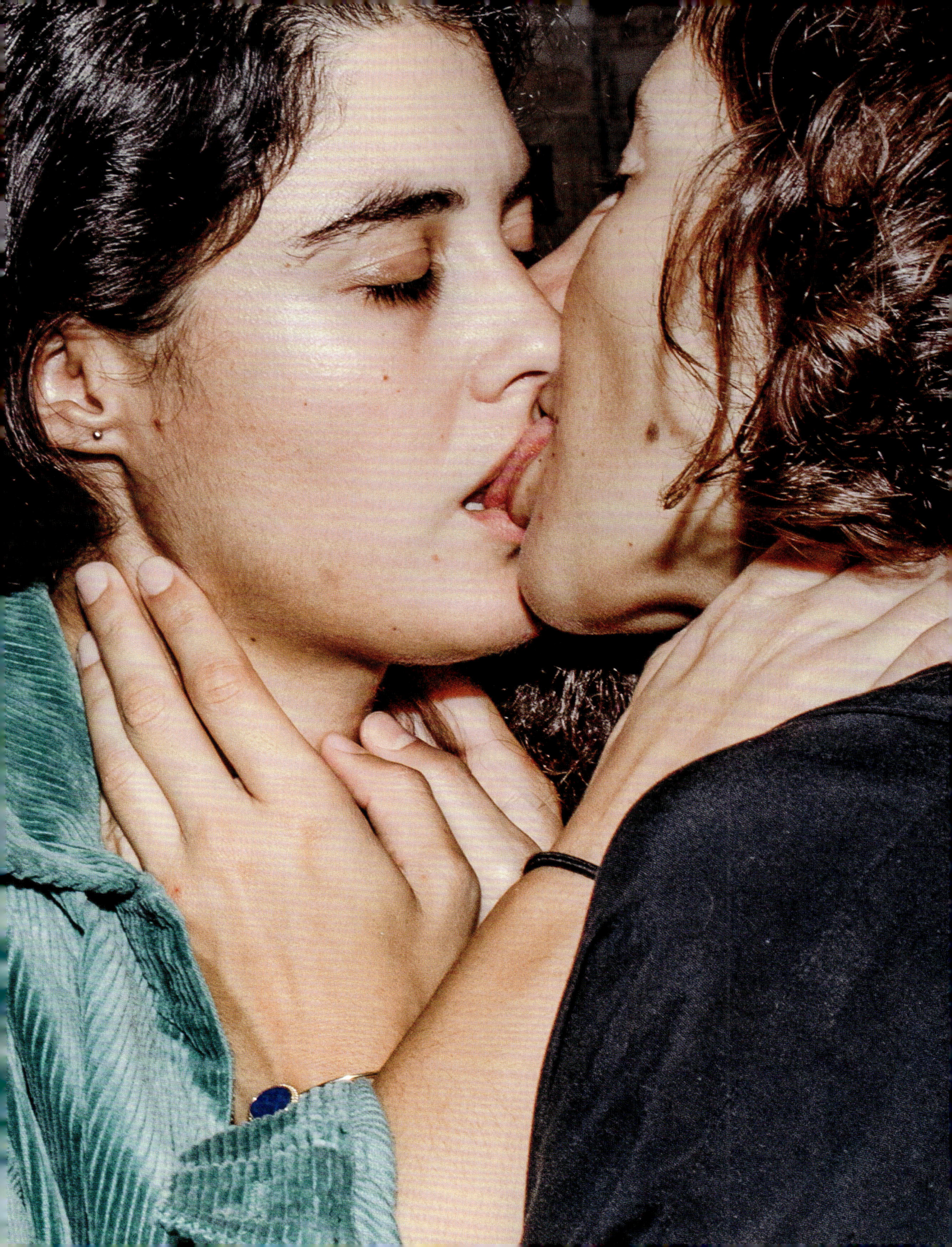

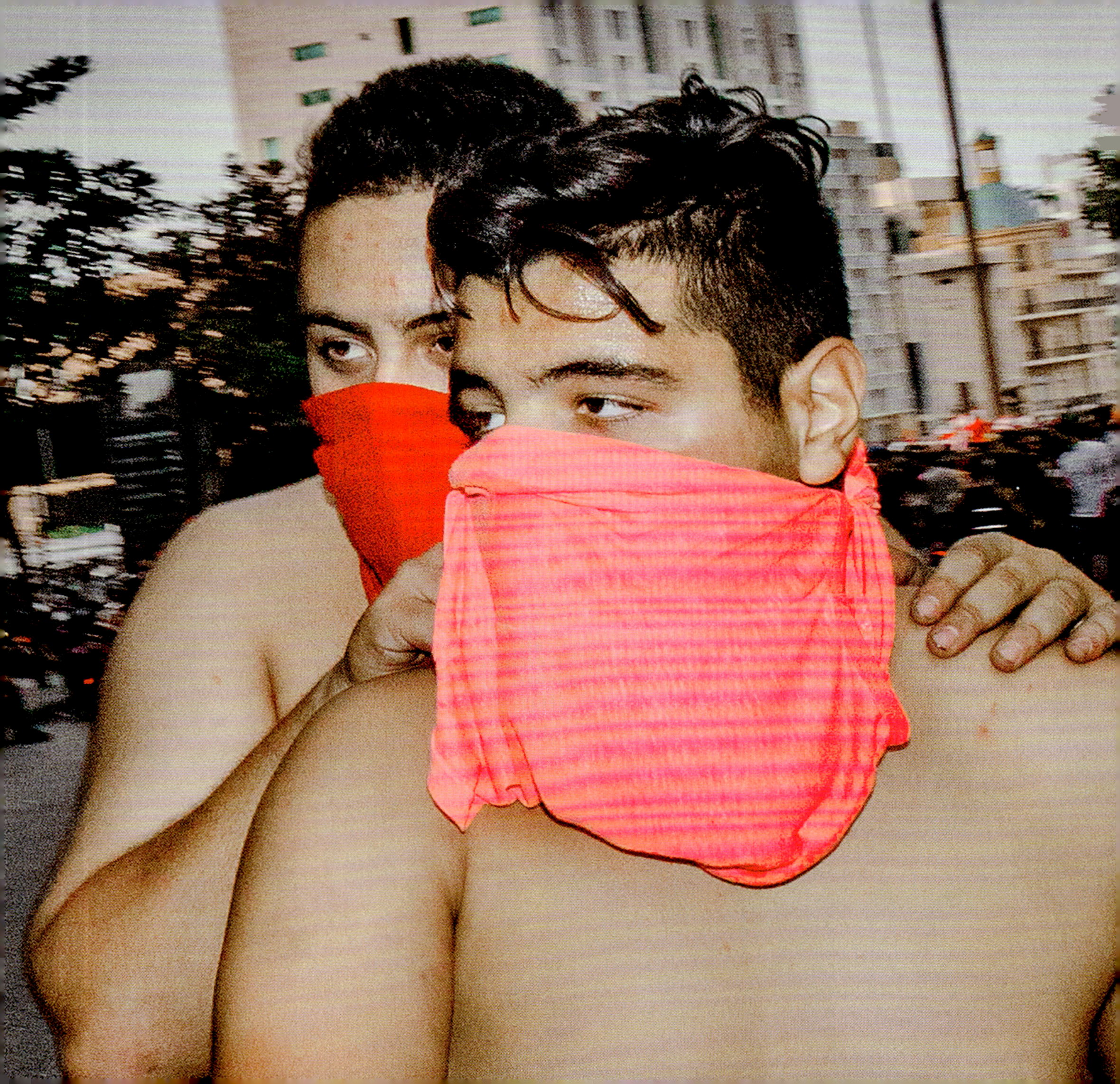

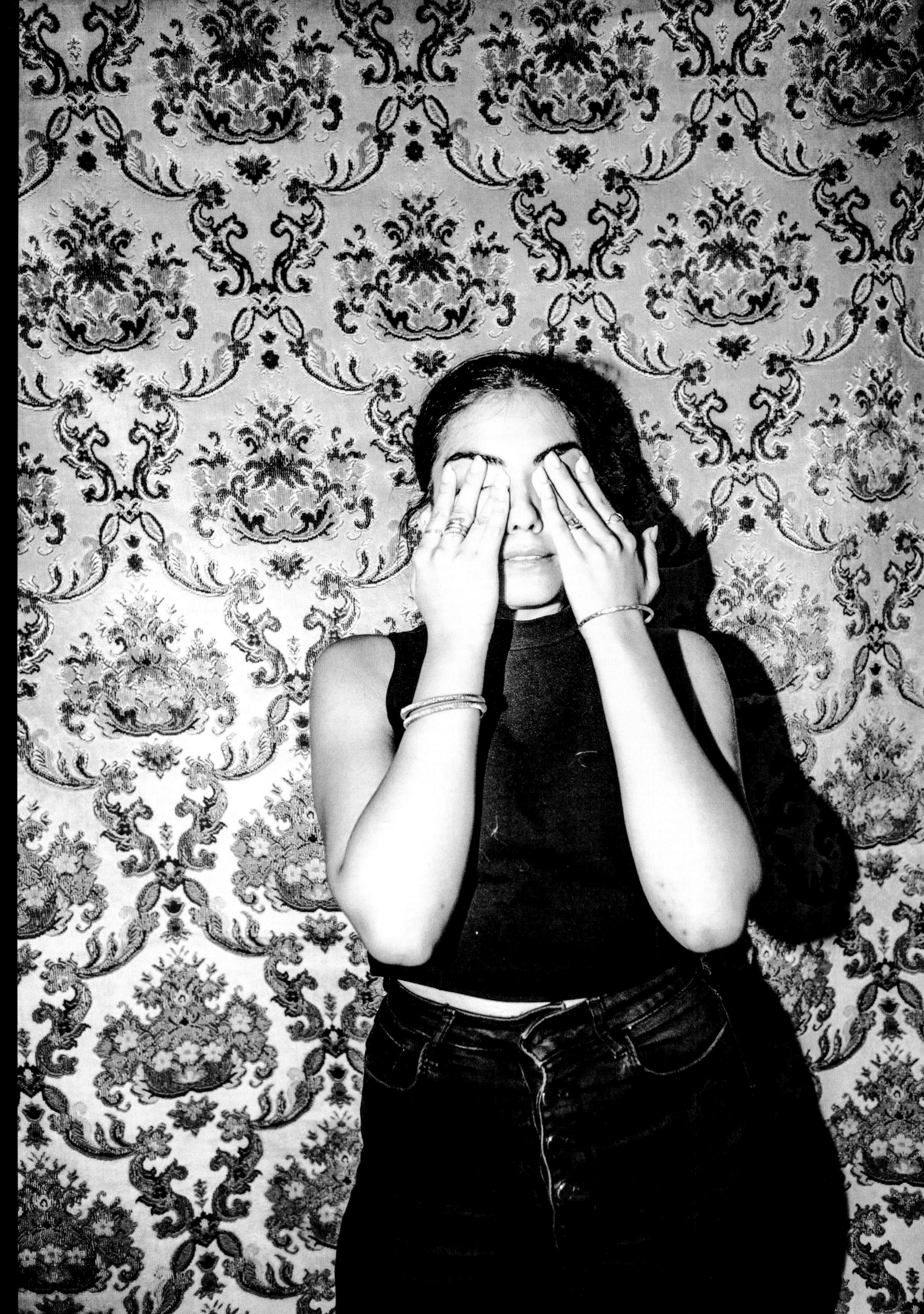

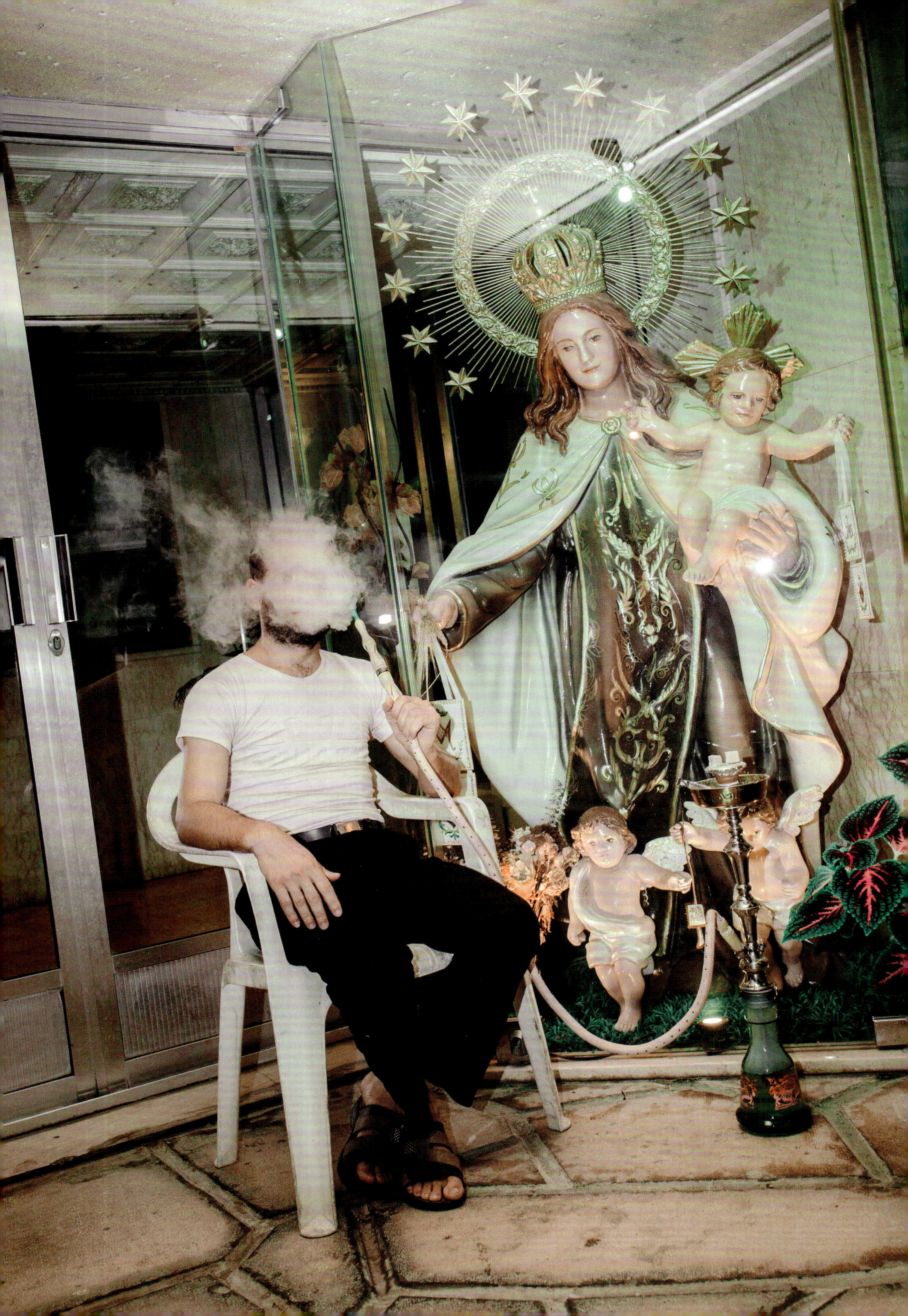

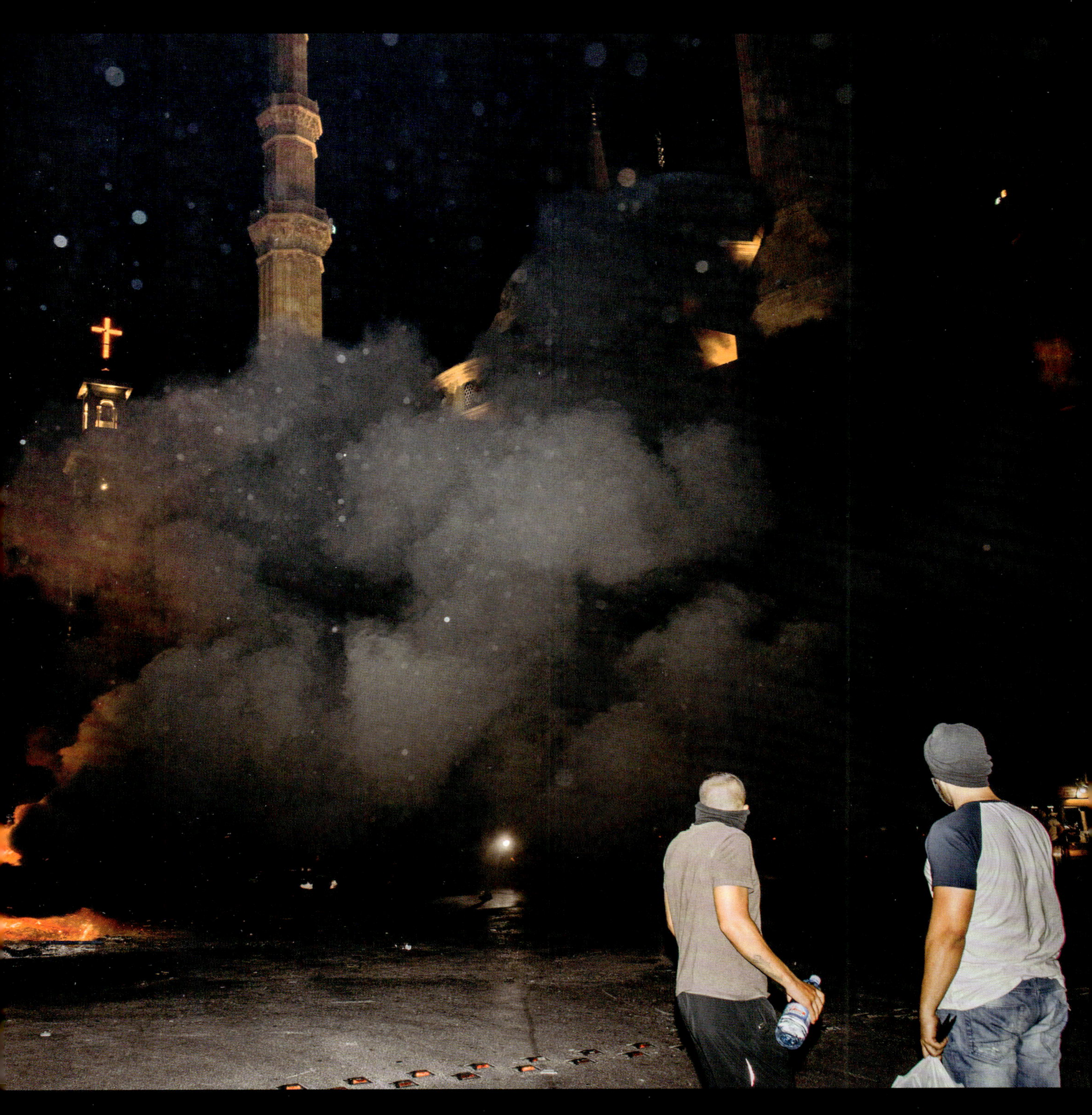

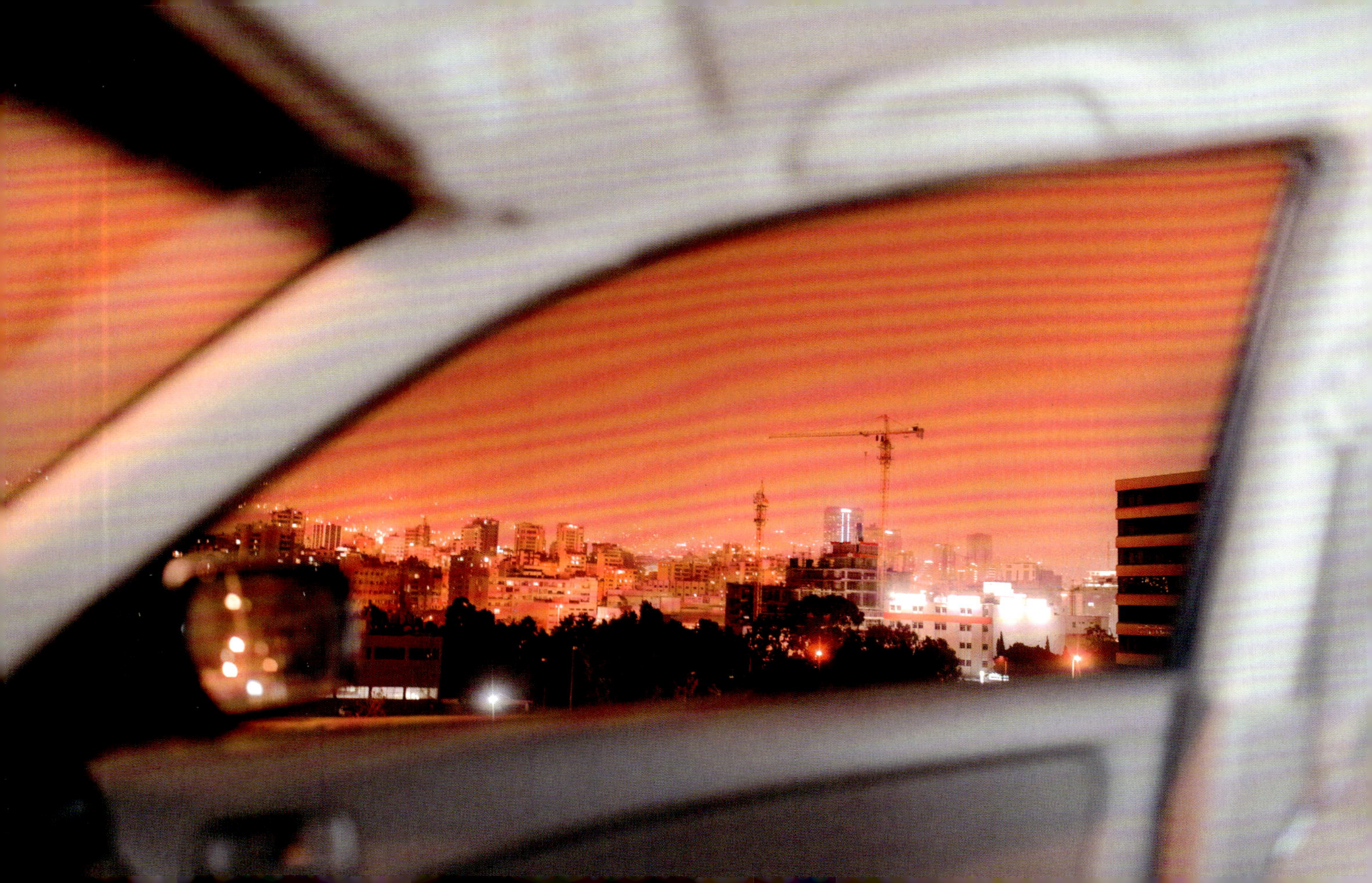

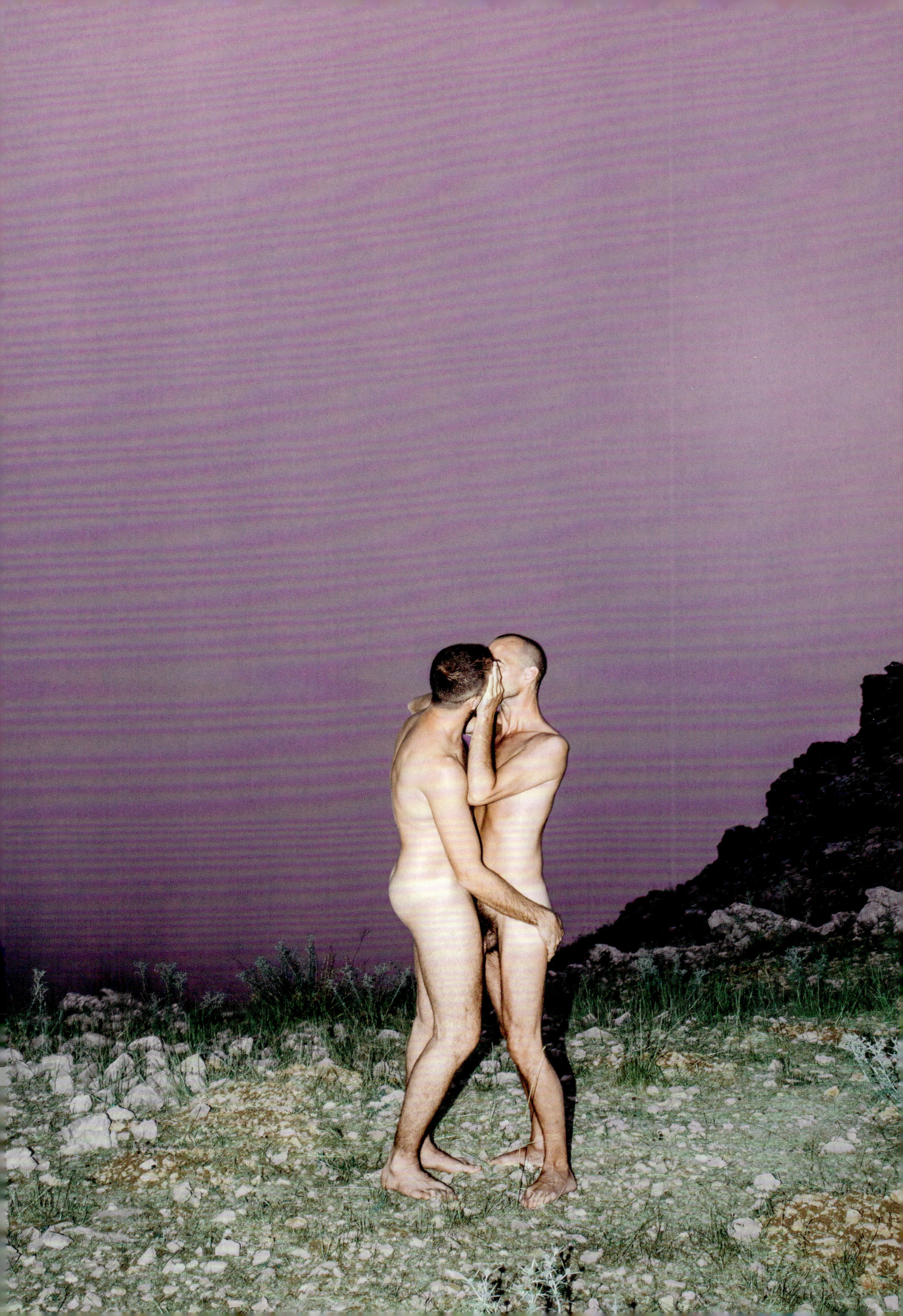

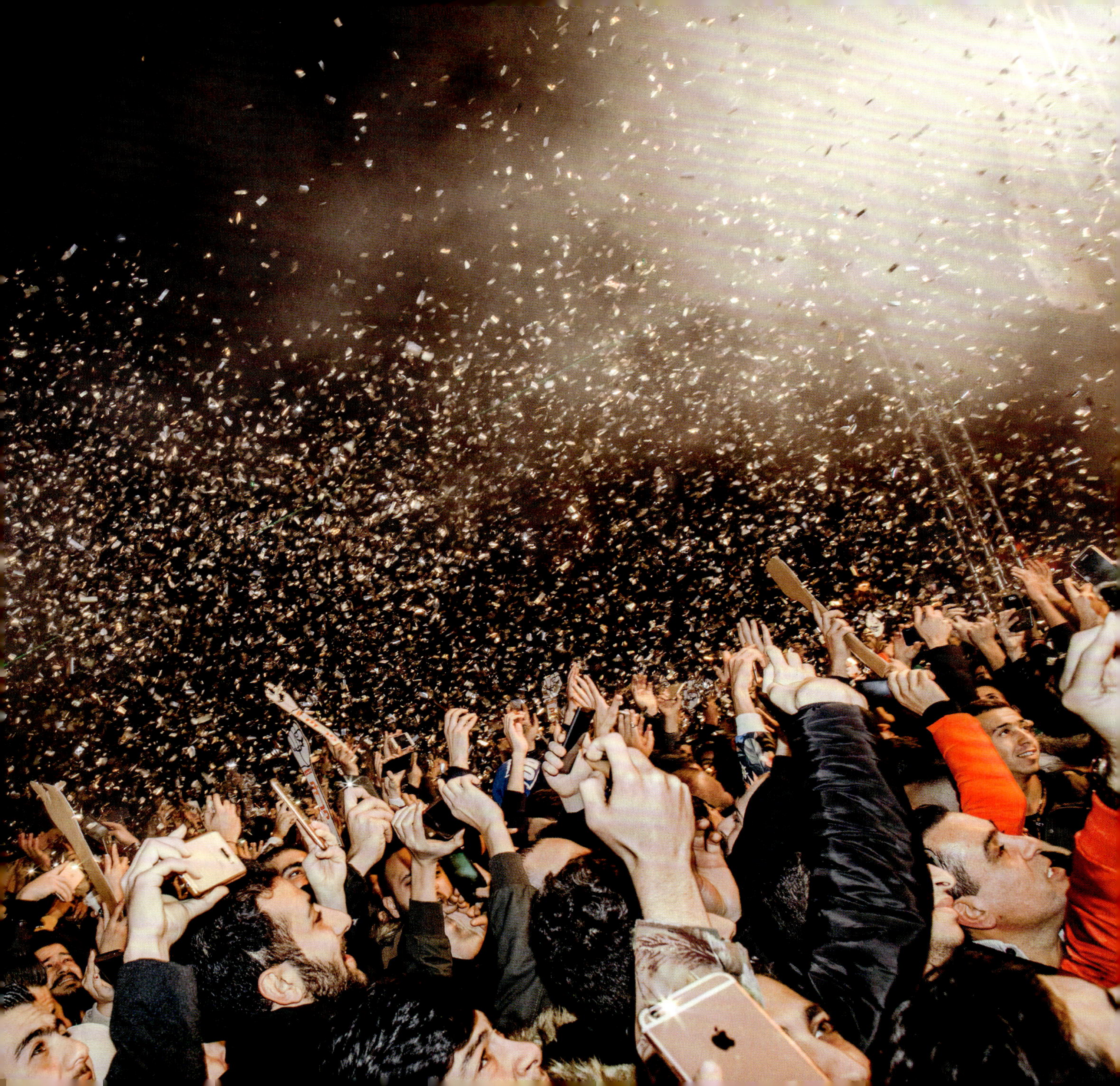

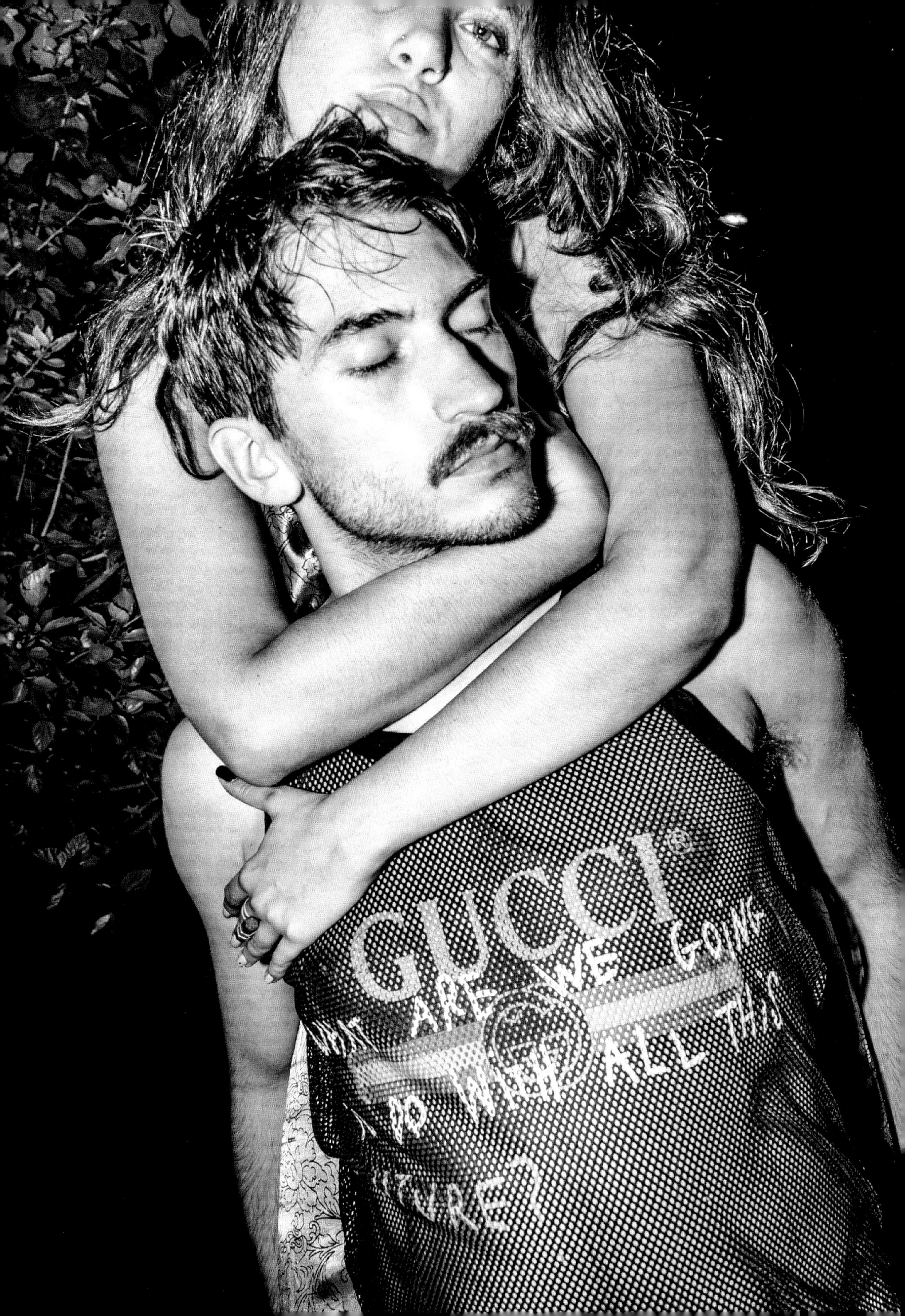

GUCCI®
WHAT ARE WE GOING
TO WITH ALL THIS
?

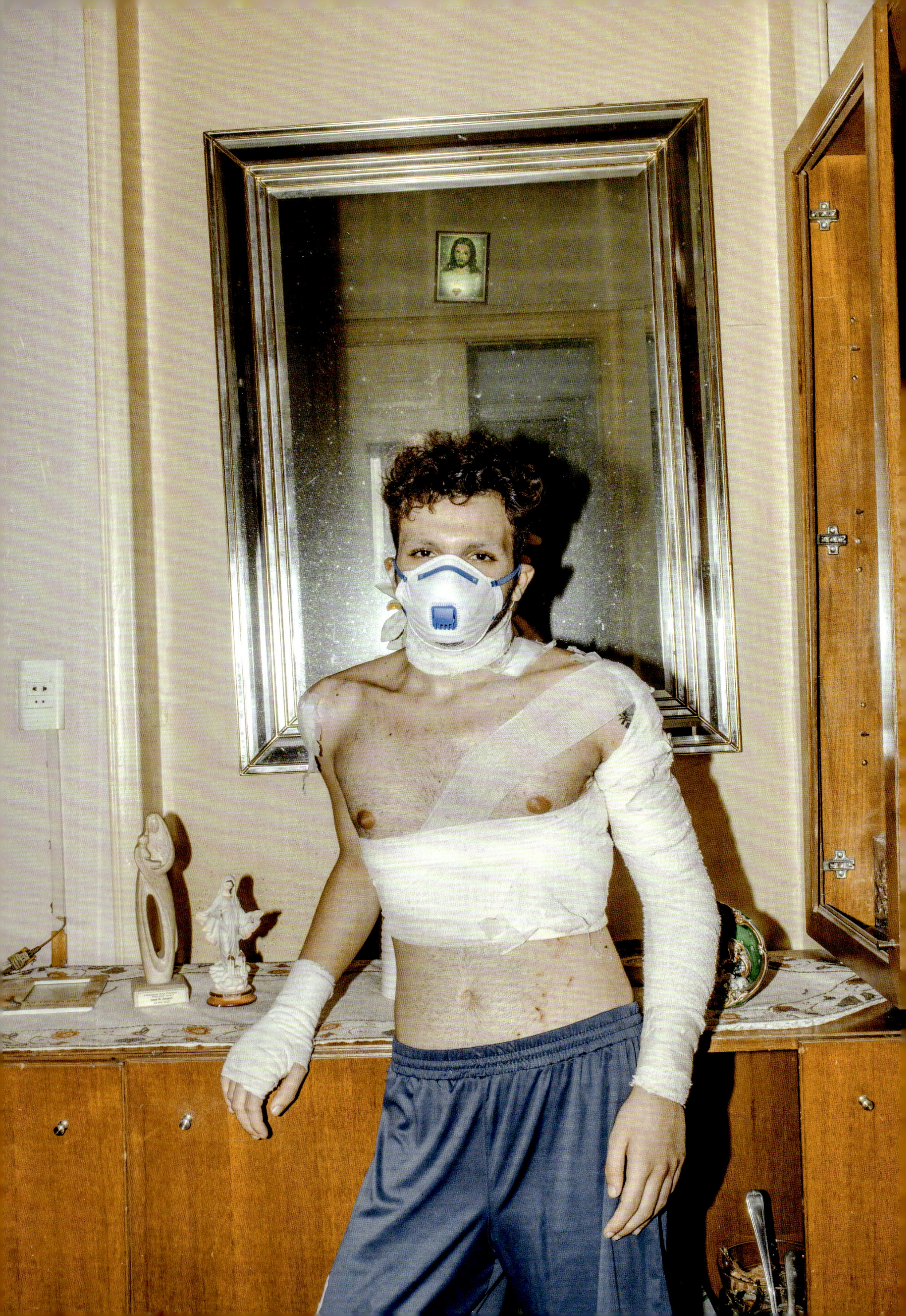

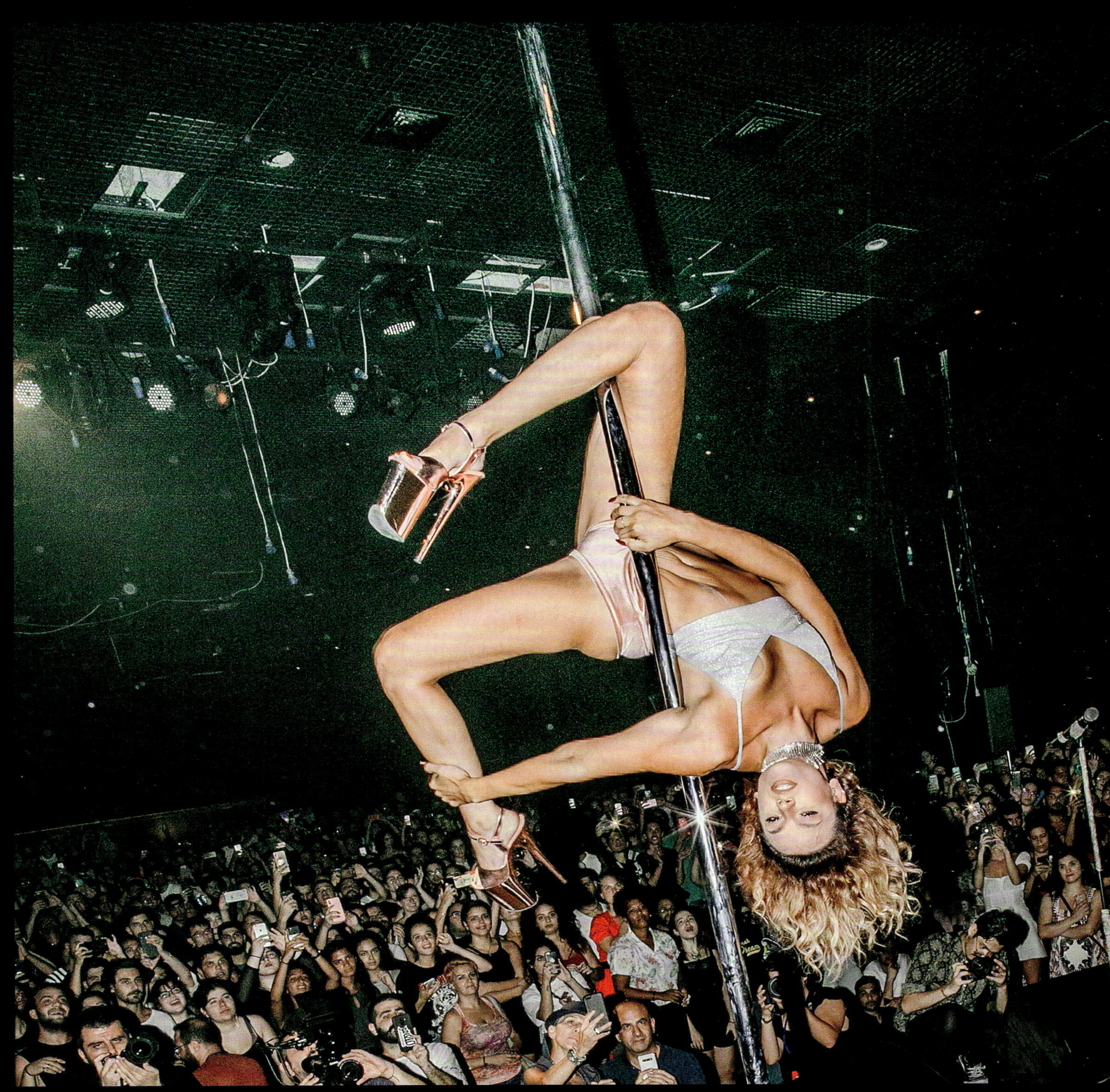

All photographs *Untitled*,
Beirut, Lebanon, November
2017–August 2020
Courtesy the artist

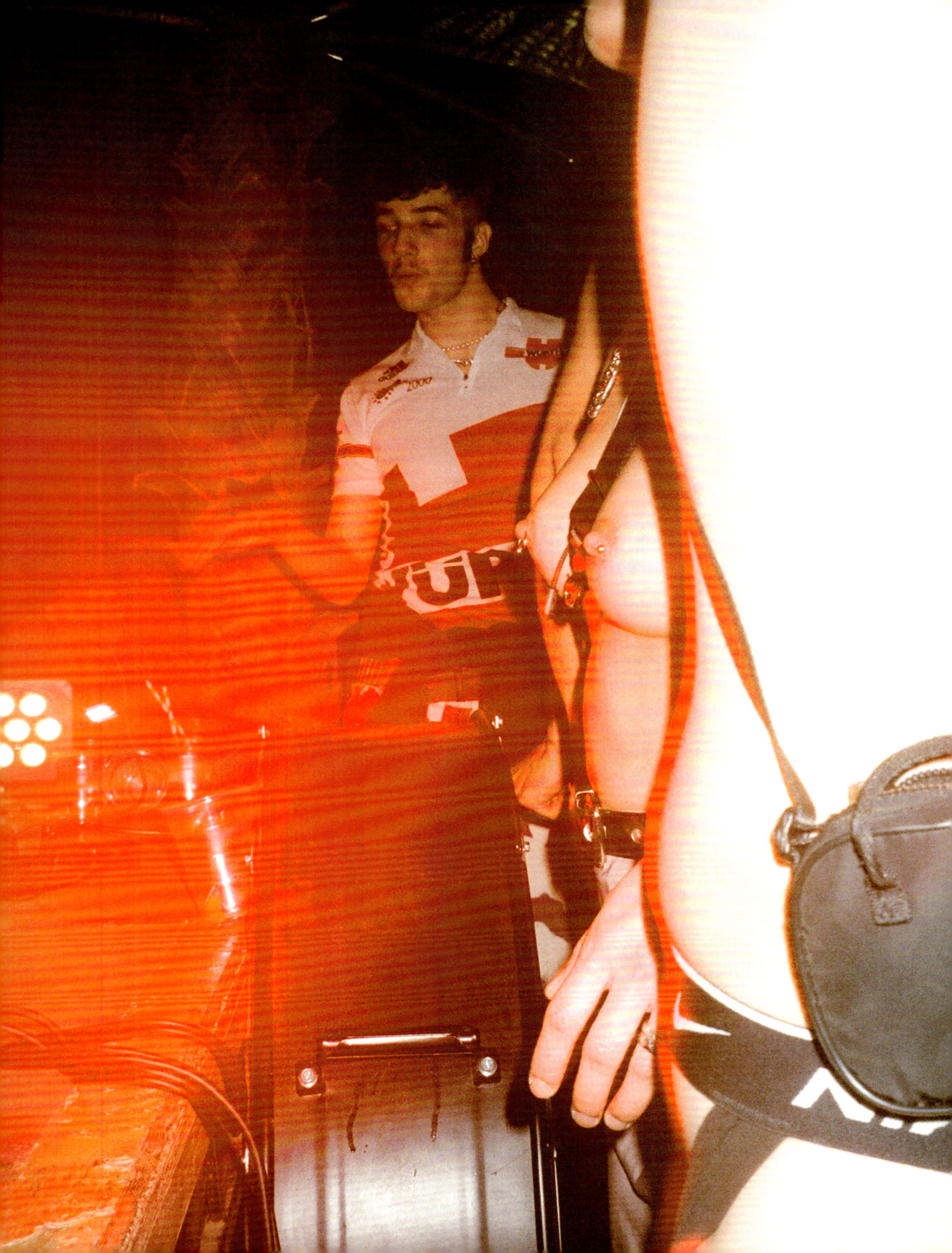

Because the Night

How can photographs convey the freedom and ecstasy of club culture?
Charlie Porter

In October last year, three days before I began writing this piece, I had my first proper dance in twenty months. I live in London where, after lockdown, clubs reopened in July 2021. I was forty-seven at the time, now forty-eight, and don't go out so much anymore. I also happen to co-run a queer rave with two friends, a party we've been organizing since 2013 called Chapter 10. In prepandemic times, we did seven or eight a year. A benefit of running a party: I can dance without the hang-ups that can come from entering someone else's space. I can think.

At Chapter 10, on Saturday night into Sunday morning, my thinking was all about openness and possibilities and creative energy. If I look back over the past thirty years, my adult life, clubs have been places of such generative thinking. During one critical period from about 2007 to 2008, when I was navigating out of a

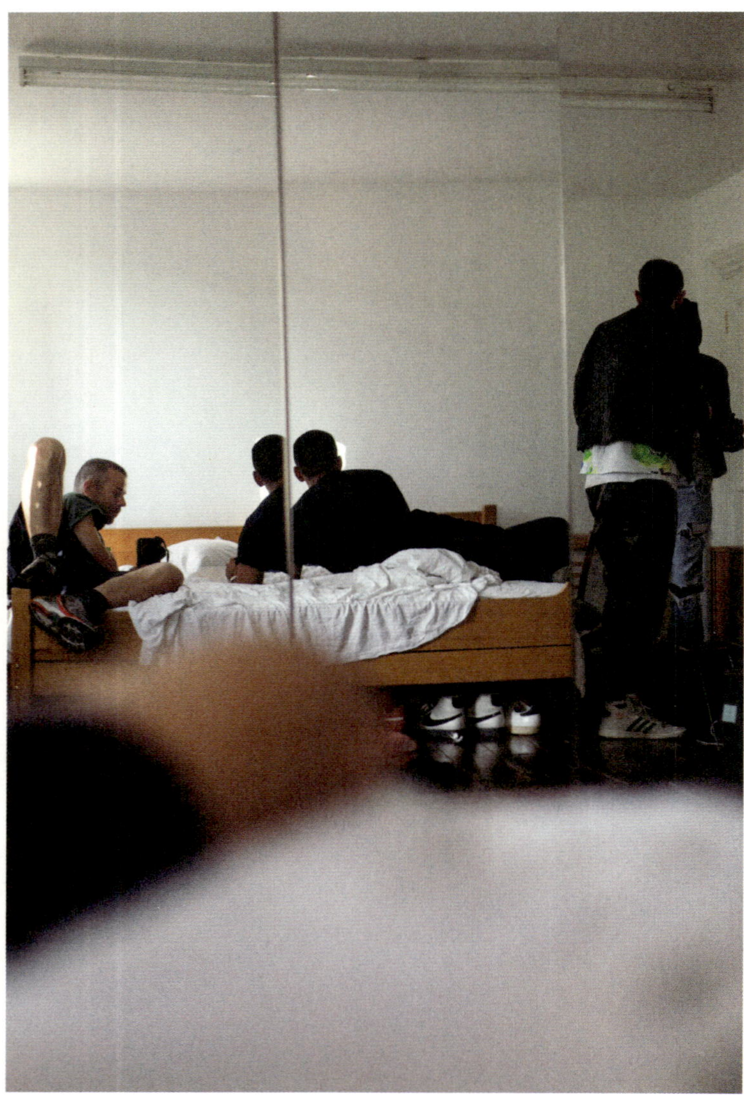

Wolfgang Tillmans,
London Olympics, **2012**
© the artist and courtesy
Maureen Paley, London

dead-end desk job in journalism, clubs pointed to a different way of existing in the world.

What does this way of being look like? Photography of nightlife can mythologize and can mislead. It can present a milieu that seems accessible only to elites, such as the 1970s images of Studio 54, the New York club housed in an old TV studio on West 54th Street. In the twenty-first century, footage on social media suggests that nightlife is a place of commerce and banality, of megaclubs with overpaid and undertalented DJs raised above the dance floor, dancers facing forward with their phones held high—consumers of leisure entertainment—rather than facing each other and being.

Critically, the most radical, creative, generative club of the twenty-first century bans photography entirely. At Berghain, in Berlin, those who make it past the door-humans are asked to hand over their phone so that a sticker can be placed over its lens. Anyone who peels it off and is caught attempting to take a photograph is thrown out. Berghain has an Instagram account, @berghain_ostgut, which has only ever made one post, on February 27, 2014. It reads, "Please respect our no-photo-policy. No pictures, no videos, no media. #switchoff Thank you."

The dancers of Berghain, in its upstairs Panorama Bar and its downstairs sex club called Lab.oratory, have the freedom to experience what the editors of *Aperture*'s 1974 "Celebrations" issue called "the climactic affirmations of life's events and feelings." Their brains are temporarily freed from the dopamine-hit spiral that comes from taking and sharing smartphone imagery. Many Berliners make visits to Berghain a regular part of their weekend. They head to the club for a while, then go back home to rest and restore before returning to the club for its closing hours into Monday morning. In this era of presumed documentation of everything, these key cultural and countercultural happenings remain unrecorded.

This image-free zone points against the presumption of universality in photography because photographs of clubs cannot express what it means to be in *that* club. Universality falsely claims that all is said and done. What interests me are the possibilities in images that are often taken before or after a night of clubbing. *London Olympics* (2012) by Wolfgang Tillmans is an image of the artist himself and three other male figures, on and around a bed, in daylight. They are all wearing clothes: leather jackets over shirts and T-shirts, ripped jeans, sneakers. Going-out clothes. The three others are unaware the photograph is being taken; Tillmans has his camera pointed at what appear to be mirrored wardrobe doors. Tillmans is on the bed, wearing sneakers. His leg is blurred in the foreground, the camera focused, instead, on what the mirrors reflect. In *London Olympics*, we see the connection and community among those who go out. We see their lives outside of the club: their world.

This sense of human interactions also turns up in Nan Goldin's photographs: She doesn't show us Misty and Jimmy Paulette on a dance floor, but in the back of a New York taxi, in daylight. Or, Jimmy Paulette on the back of David's bike, also in daylight. In doing so, she exhibits no interest in projecting nightlife depictions of impossible perfection, a notion that can lead to smug and incorrect thinking—this was the best night ever, nothing can ever be as good again. Goldin captures what is true: This is what we did. You can do it too.

An atmosphere of shared lives is also found in the work of Liz Johnson Artur, whose images of PDA, the radical queer London party, played a pivotal role in her 2019 exhibition, *If you know the beginning, the end is no trouble*, at the South London Gallery. Miss Jason, Ms. Carrie Stacks: the photographs are about people. Arranged on structures of bamboo cane, scenes of the PDA community took their place alongside those from

Goldin exhibits no interest in projecting nightlife depictions of impossible perfection. She captures what is true: This is what we did. You can do it too.

churches, from the street, from across the artist's life, from history to today.

Right now in London, I am greatly taken by the photographs of Roxy Lee, who is open to the possibilities of the individual. Lee has been documenting her community for the past few years, mostly at the queer rave Adonis, or at an after-party called The Shed. Lee has gentleness and curiosity. She is calm and welcoming and perceptive to what is around her, like the bead of sweat about to drip from the chin of Ms. Sharon Le Grand, or the rhinestones that spell out the word *Juicy*, just visible through the fog of sweat, across the butt of a human's bikini bottoms.

As I write about Lee's work, I'm trying not to use words that contain negatives, such as *unflinching*, because to say her approach is unflinching presupposes there is something to flinch at. These are humans breaking binaries and boundaries and doing so with humility and extravagance and seeking the permission of nobody. To my mind, Lee is not after the perfect image because what matters is the potential: that next weekend, and the weekend after, and next year, and in fifty years' time, these experiences can happen, and they all will matter.

And yet nightlife is always under threat. In the United Kingdom, licensing laws make it increasingly difficult to find party venues. This situation is exacerbated by what are known as "luxury flats," which are usually mediocre housing developments in neighborhoods of gentrification. These buildings are often in areas that previously had no residential properties, where parties could happen free from noise complaints. Those who buy luxury flats don't want to live next door to a club: they'll do all they can to shut it down.

It's now six days since the party. Writing this piece has taken me a while to navigate. And yet, the effect of the party on me is still the same, it still guides me—it was the humans I encountered,

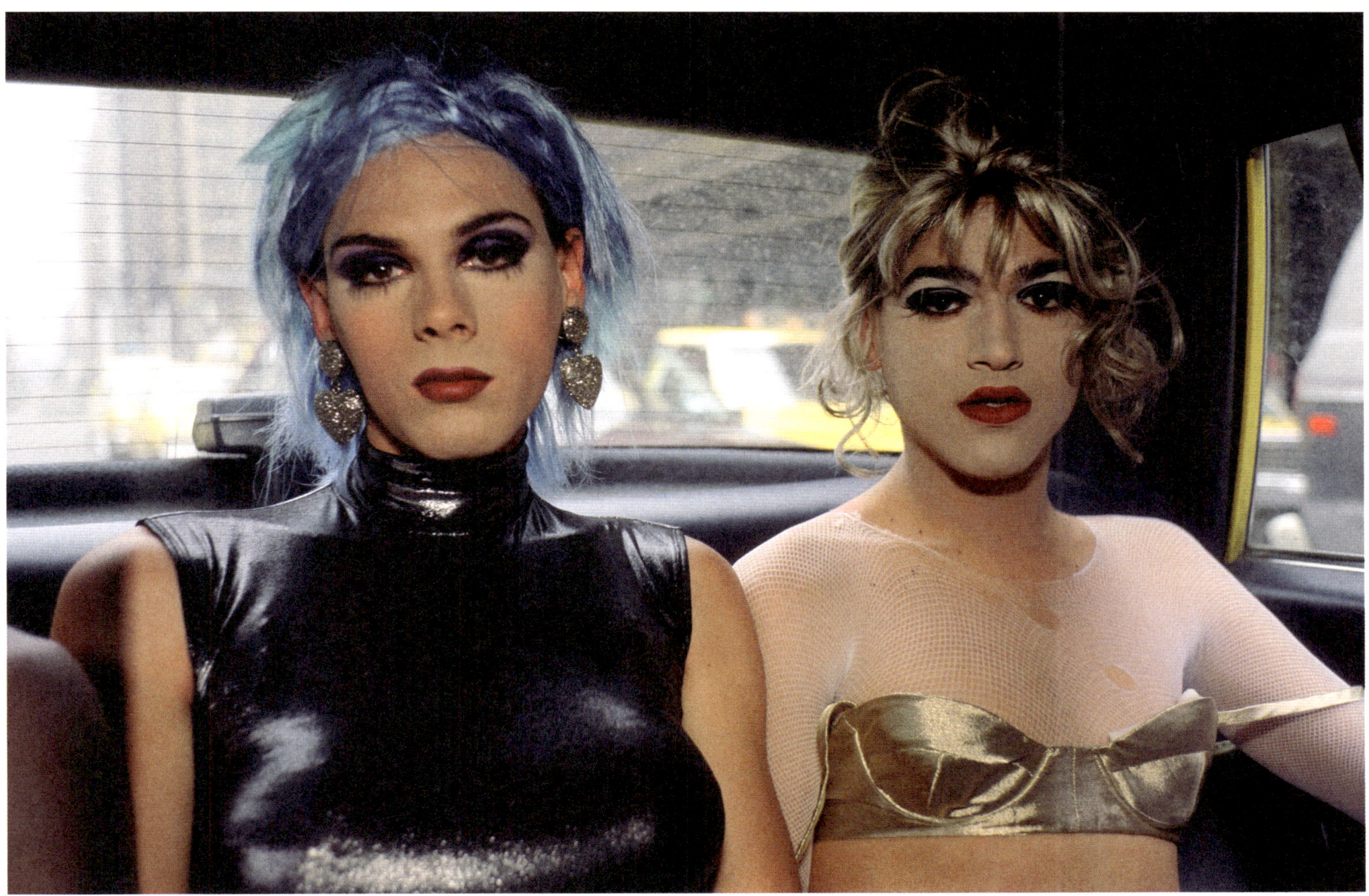

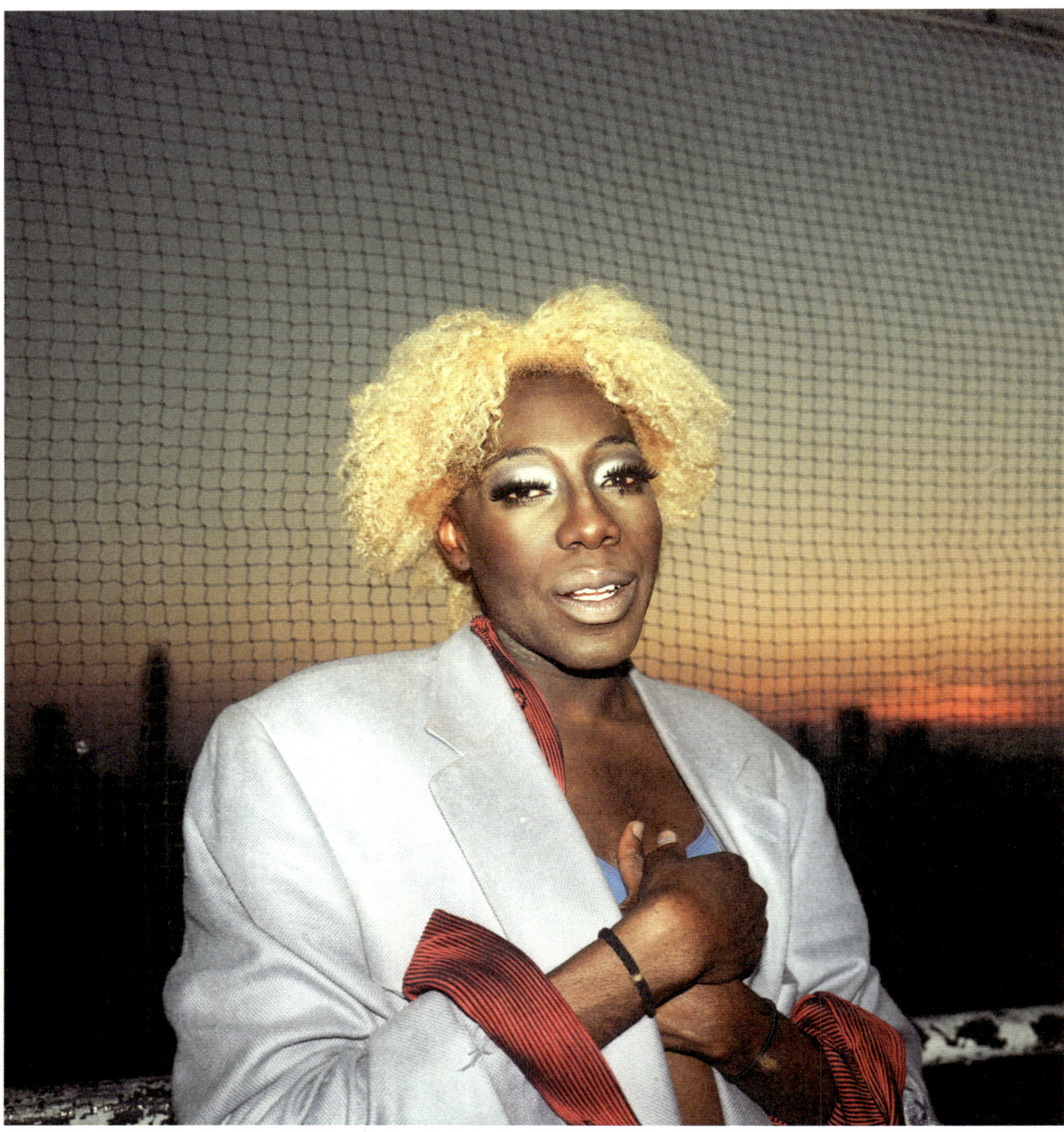

the conversations we had, what the humans revealed to me, how they were thinking about their own lives, how their thinking could encourage and energize my own.

I just counted on my phone's photography reel that I took 110 images on Saturday night and Sunday morning. But this number is misleading: most were failed takes of what turned out to be essentially six shots. Of these six, three were redundant attempts to capture the energy of the crowd. One was of a bottle of tequila, I do not remember why. But two were of a human: our host, the drag artist A Man To Pet. She always does at least three looks per night; I documented two of them. And there, in one of the images, someone walks between us, the blurred back of their head and their shoulder entering the frame. And behind them stands A Man To Pet with a crystal-clear, sharp, joyous, questioning connection in her eyes, her mouth in the kind of smile that has its own levels of meaning, and it was all that I need.

Charlie Porter is the author of *What Artists Wear* (2021).

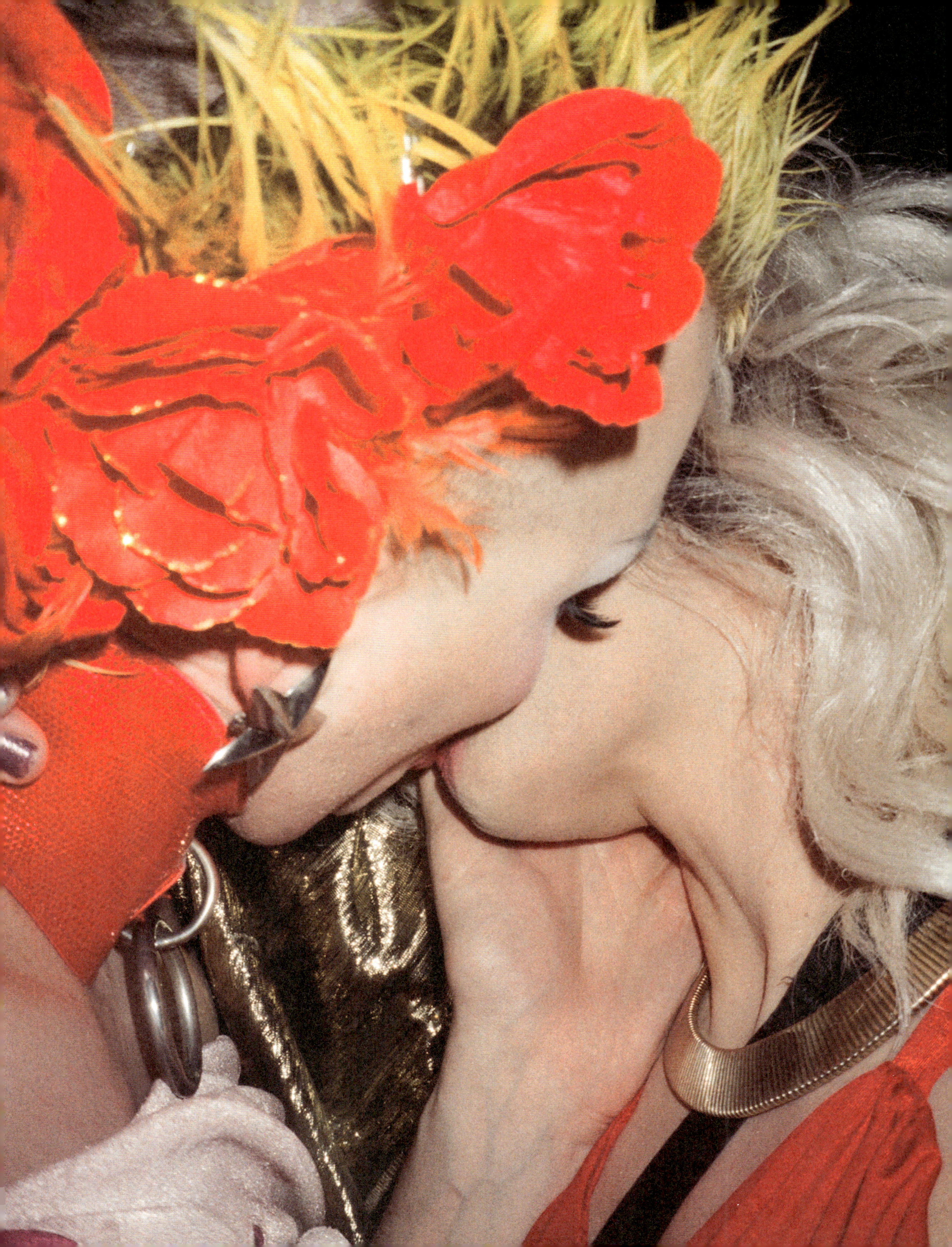

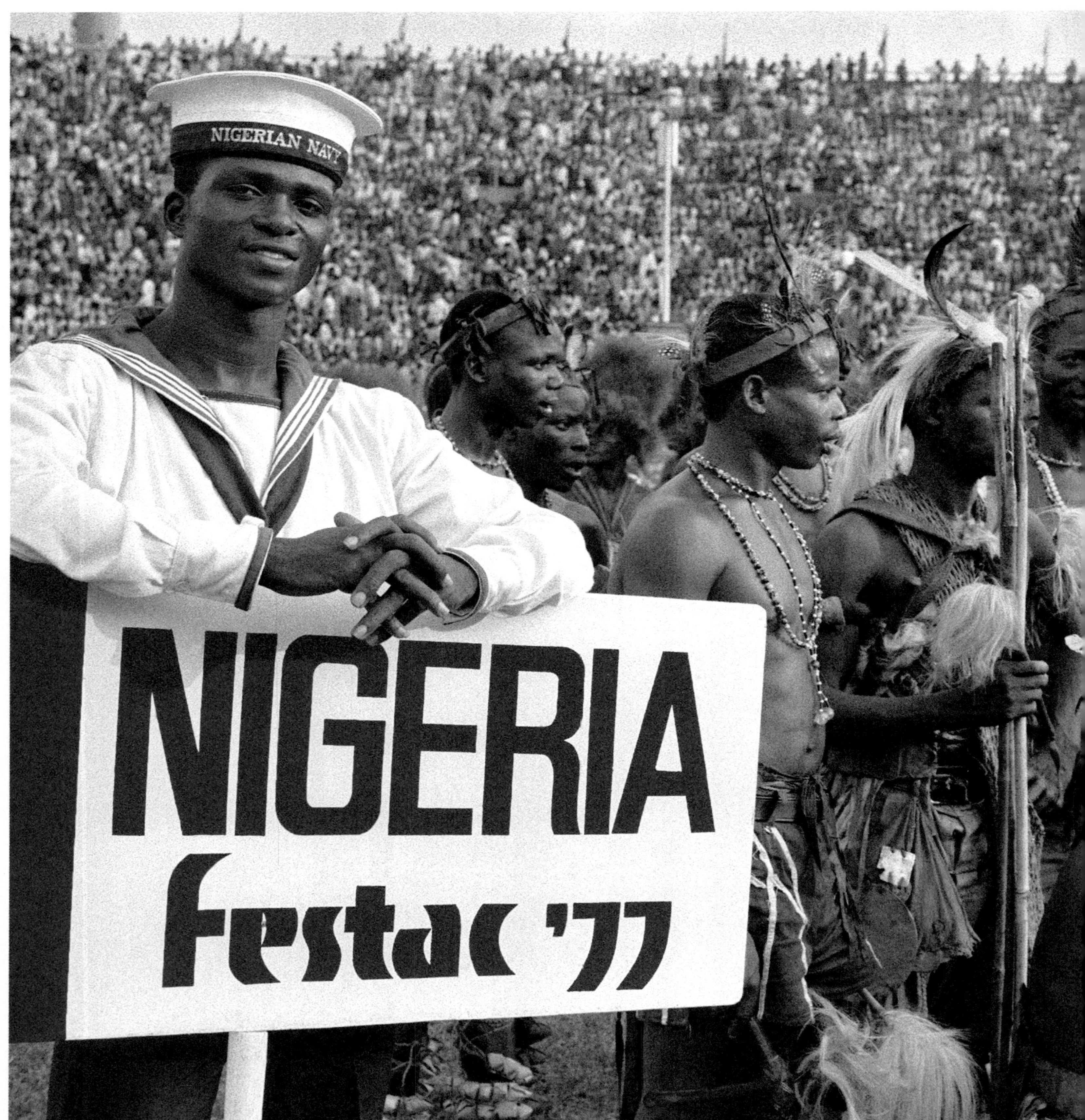

FESTAC '77, 1977

When the Party Came to Lagos

In 1977, when Marilyn Nance traveled to Nigeria for FESTAC, she discovered a euphoric reunion of the African Diaspora. **Anakwa Dwamena**

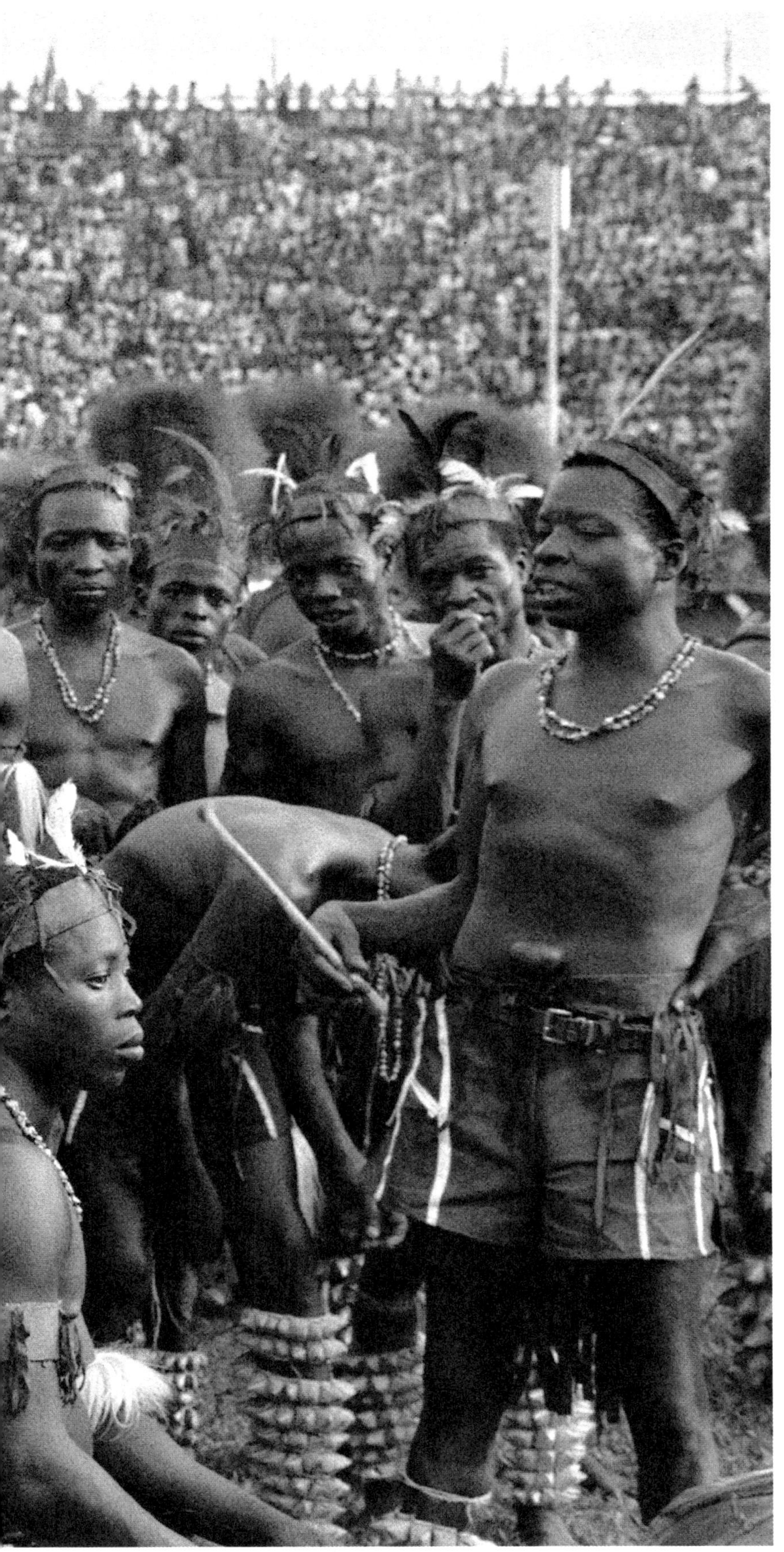

Marilyn Nance can't find Stokely Carmichael. She is compiling a bibliography for her forthcoming book, *Last Day in Lagos*, which documents her time as a photographer at the Second World Black and African Festival of Arts and Culture, or FESTAC '77, as it is popularly known. Nance has a lingering, unshakeable, urge to include a book by Carmichael. His life's work "sprung from being a young intellect to a civil rights worker to a Pan-Africanist," she told me recently. "My life, while much more humble, follows a similar trajectory." The Pan-African revolutionary, later known as Kwame Ture, attended the 1969 Pan-African Cultural Festival in Algiers, Algeria, where Eldridge Cleaver's Black Panther Party also held court. Combing through photographic archives, books, and his own writings, Nance believes that the radical lover of Black music and culture should have been at FESTAC '77. But it has never been easy to tell who was actually there, especially among revolutionaries always on the move.

Nance's and Ture's paths had crossed a couple of times before. The first time, in the late 1960s, Nance was a member of the Black Cultural Society at the Bronx High School of Science and the group invited Ture, an alumnus, to speak. The second time, about a decade later, was in West Virginia at the John Henry Memorial Blues and Gospel Jubilee. Then, there was an All-African People's Revolutionary Party event at Syracuse University, in the late 1980s. "If our paths crossed three times, then, why not at FESTAC?" she asks.

Over fifteen thousand artists, dancers, actors, musicians, scholars, activists, photographers, filmmakers, and other cultural workers from the extended Black family came together for a month in 1977 for FESTAC. Officially, it sought to "provide a forum for the focusing of attention on the enormous richness and diversity of African contributions to world culture." What makes one look back at FESTAC '77 with wonder is the sense that it was an extraordinary representation of arrival—a high point of exchanges, conversations, and overtures Black people had been making with and toward each other in response to the historic rupture of slavery. As early as 1859, Black abolitionists such as Martin Delany were scoping out possible sites on the African continent for free Blacks to return to. In 1900, W. E. B. Du Bois closed the first Pan-African Conference, held in London, by declaring "the color line" as the problem of the twentieth century. At the 1956 Conference of Negro-African Writers and Artists in Paris, Richard Wright declared that African Americans were in "the technological vanguard" among Black people and "would prove of inestimable value to the developing African sovereignties." These initiatives pulled together the creative and political energies of Black people all over the world to harmonize efforts in a collective liberation. Ten years later, Duke Ellington, Langston Hughes, and Alvin Ailey joined Wole Soyinka and Nelson Mandela at the 1966 First World Festival of Negro Arts in Dakar, Senegal.

FESTAC '77 was bigger. Nance, who attended and photographed this historic event, describes it as the Olympics, a biennial, and Woodstock combined. *Ebony* magazine declared that "for the first time in 500 years, the black family was together again." This was possibly the largest group of African American artists, over four hundred of them, to have traveled to the African continent together. Those on this "symbolic reversal of the transatlantic slave trade," as Nance has described the 1977 moment, included Stevie Wonder, Jayne Cortez, Betye Saar, Faith Ringgold, Paule Marshall, and Jeff Donaldson.

A photographer for the U.S. contingent, Nance made images of the great diversity of people at FESTAC. Getting there hadn't been easy. In 1974, she submitted her portfolio to the festival organizers to participate as an artist, sending, among other things, a photograph of her grandmother sitting at a lunch table in Alabama. In 1975, Nance heard back that her work was accepted. But the next year, she was informed that the number of attendants from the United States—herself included—had been cut. Discovering that there was a need for a photo-technician, she made a case to be chosen, especially since the photograph of her grandmother had been lost by the organizers. Nance called the offices of the festival's North American headquarters, housed in Howard University's art department, every day until they relented. There was no pay, or camera, or film. Just a ticket on Capitol International Airlines to Lagos and back.

With a similar spirit of persistence, Nance stayed for the full length of the festival rather than the two weeks she was allotted by the organizers, allowing her to see and document it in a comprehensive way. The resulting photographic archive remains one of the largest visual records of this monumental occasion, where the poet Audre Lorde "felt the earth move." A selection from Nance's approximately 1,500 FESTAC images will be collected in *Last Day in Lagos*.

At FESTAC, Nance was less interested in the contentious academic arguments around a definition of Blackness that had carried over from previous international gatherings. (The words *Black* and *African* in the festival's name were used to allow for the inclusion of North Africans who might not consider themselves Black.) Instead, Nance was busy in the streets and arenas, at cafeterias and parties, interacting with people and collecting on-the-scene photographic representations of the joy of recognition among participants from around the globe, of spontaneous relations being formed through identified commonalities, and of the forging of communities and collaborations. This trip was Nance's first time traveling outside of the United States, and, as the spirits of the ancestors would have it, all of Africa had come to meet her.

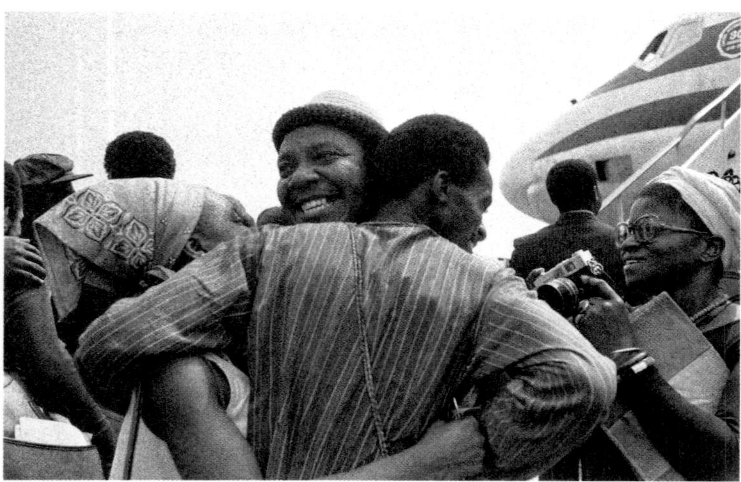

Mid-festival, the first contingent of FESTAC '77 U.S. participants greets the second U.S. contingent at the Lagos airport, 1977

What makes one look back at FESTAC '77 with wonder is the sense that it was an extraordinary representation of arrival.

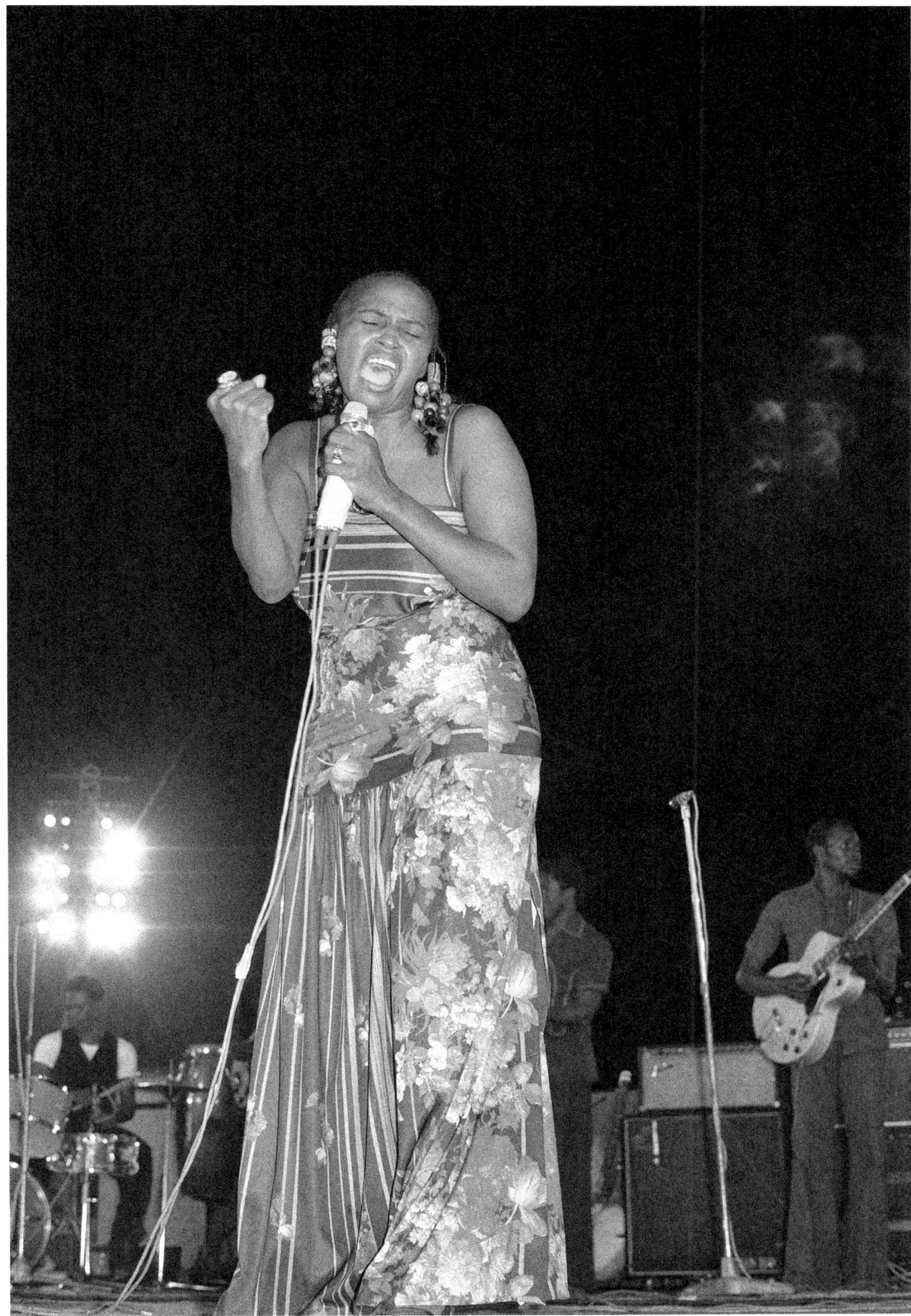

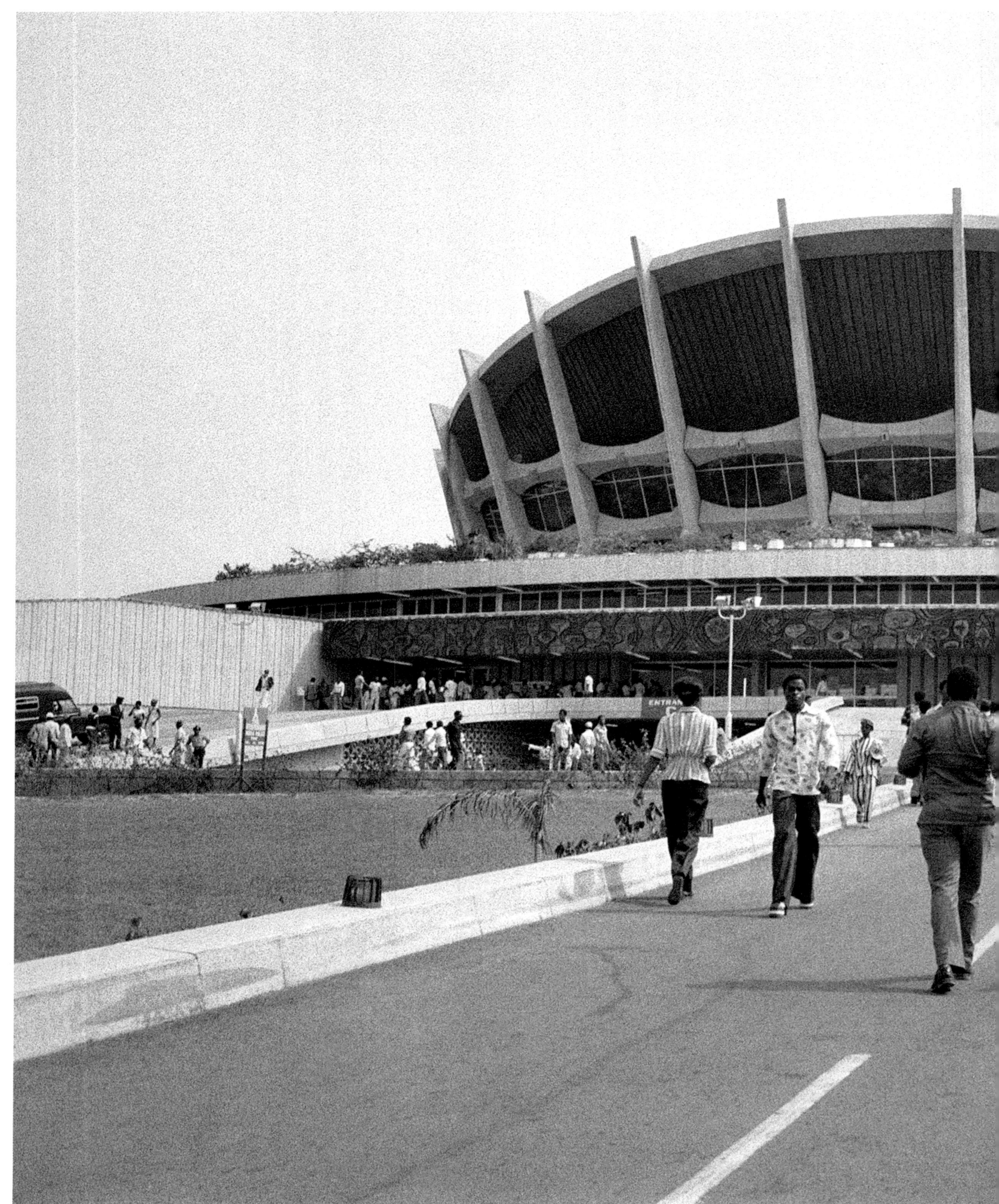

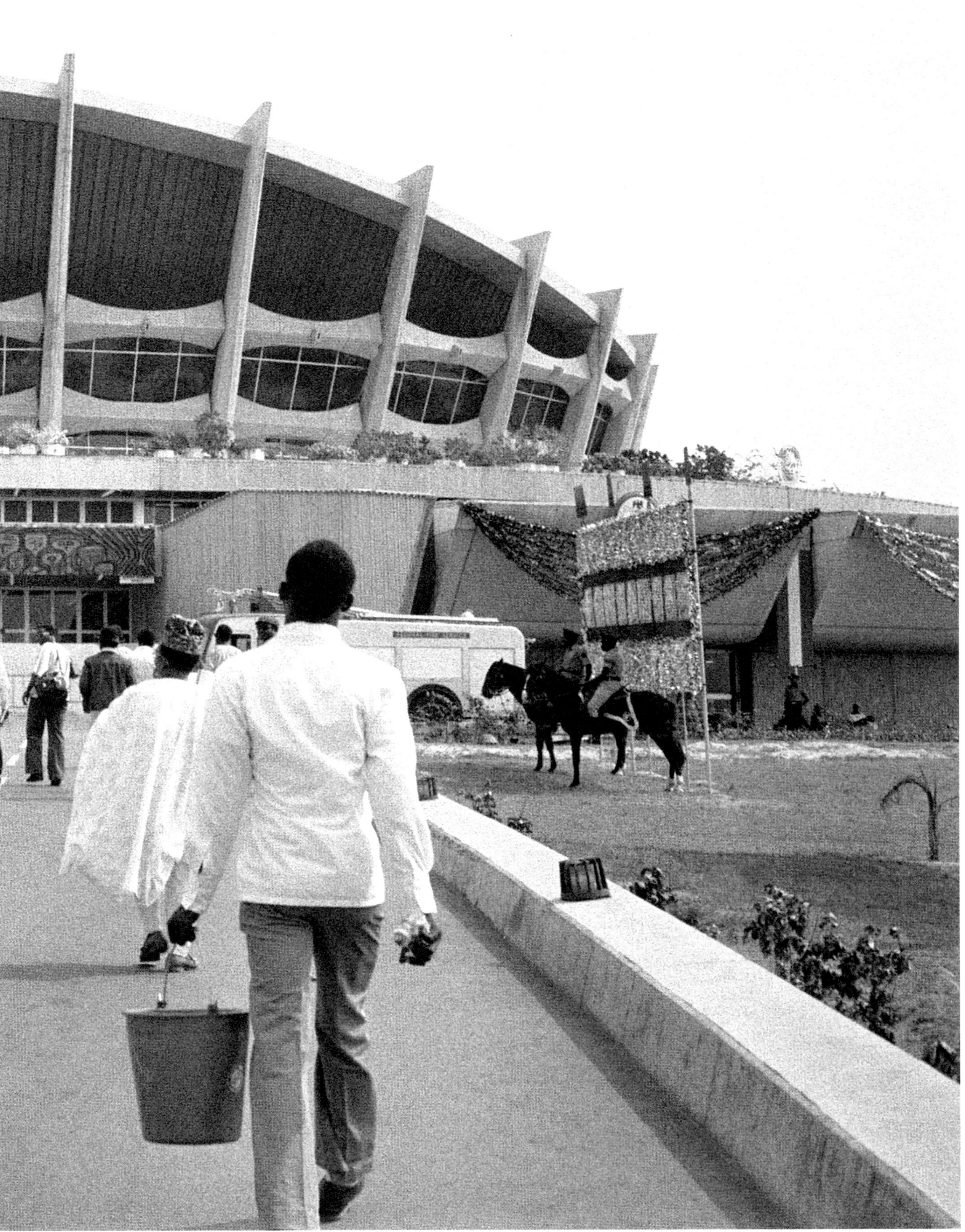

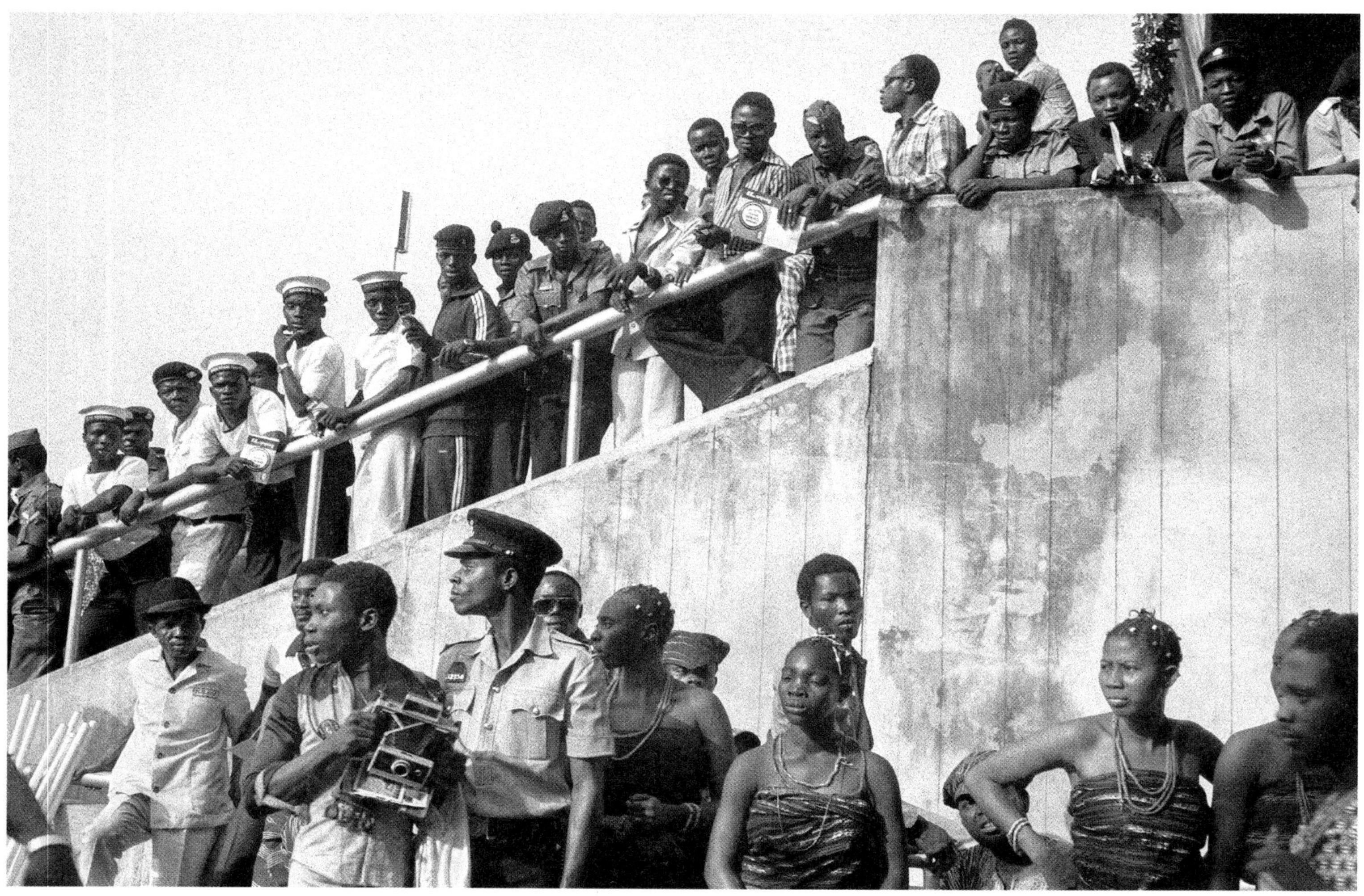

Seeing the faces of friendly folks from the other side of the world, Nance thought she recognized characteristics of her U.S. relatives and acquaintances—in the cadence of speech, in the pitch of laughter, in facial expressions. She had a desire to visually investigate Africanisms—the shared habits, tendencies, and proclivities observed wherever Blacks had been sprinkled. Nance had long thought of herself, although born in the United States, as African. Here, in Africa, she was seen as an American. She began to grapple with her place, and that of African Americans in general, in the larger Black diasporic family. "I got an understanding of the history of how we became African Americans," she says. "I knew it. But at FESTAC, you could feel it." Feeling complemented a political awareness of Blackness drawn equally from her African ancestry as from her political education and knowledge of history informed by the civil rights and the Black Arts movements. "I feel connected to other people," she says, "and my photographs document that connection."

Nance was born in Fort Greene, Brooklyn, in 1953. Her father and mother had left Wadesboro, North Carolina, and Birmingham, Alabama, respectively, as part of the Great Migration north. Her grandmother (who thought of herself as African and was most excited about Nance's "return" to Africa) was born in 1886. "Her father would have been born in the time of enslavement," Nance states, "meaning our family is only two generations removed from having been enslaved and one generation removed from sharecropping." As a child, Nance came to know family members primarily through photographs. Her mother would point out people and tell her their stories. At age eight, she received her first camera, a gift from her cousin that is still in her possession. Nance would graduate from New York University's Interactive Telecommunications Program, study graphic design at Pratt Institute, train in audio and film production at the Institute for New Cinema Artists, and earn a master of fine arts degree in photography from the Maryland Institute College of Art.

Arriving at FESTAC, at age twenty-three, with a wide multimedia skill set was beneficial. But a more important foundation for her work, then and later, is the political education on which Nance's craft is erected. Her mother's father was a labor organizer and only in adulthood did she realize that never crossing a picket line isn't a commandment everyone's parents held them to. From middle-school days, she remembers conversations with her sister about demonstrations demanding summer jobs for Black teens. In 1968, the year Martin Luther King Jr. was assassinated, she attended her first Black Power rally while in high school. Her formative years were suffused with the political energies of the civil rights movement and the creative energies of the Black Arts movement, which encouraged art with the purpose of awakening consciousness, forming community, and striving for liberation. "I really believed in all African people," she says, "because that had been my training, my political education." Nance immersed herself in the recordings of the musician and activist Rahsaan Roland Kirk and the teachings of Malcolm X, participated in Black cultural rallies, and went to see plays by Amiri Baraka and Ed Bullins, who served as the minister of culture for the Black Panther Party. "FESTAC was a triumph of the Black Arts movement," Nance explains, "because in the Black Arts movement, there was always a reference to Africa."

In Lagos, and in true Pan-African style, Nance roamed from one contingent to the next. Language could be a big barrier. Nance recalls a lot of smiling, staring, and dancing as ways of communicating. At the lunch table, you might find Indigenous Australians across from you, musicians from Burundi to your left, and North African intellectuals to your right. "'Who are you?'

and 'Oh, look at you!' were the ethos," she says; physical presence
was the currency of exchange. Tagging along with Nance through
her photographic archive is a wild ride. We see not just Lagos
but journey also to Ile-Ife and Benin City. We feel the blistering
afternoon sun; squeeze into a rehearsal of Sun Ra and his Arkestra;
and dance with Stevie Wonder and Miriam Makeba at Fela Kuti's
nightclub the Shrine.

With either her Canonet point-and-shoot or Miranda
Sensomat cameras ever present, Nance navigated this month of
encounters by quite literally being in people's faces. This immediate
nearness and proximity, almost making her invisible to her subjects,
gives the viewer a strong illusion of being present on the scene.
In one image from the opening day ceremony, the frame includes
no action from the festival but is zoned in on the crowd. Standing
on the ground level is an eclectic collection of observers—women
wrapped in their traditional cloths, beads draped gently around their
necks; a fedora-wearing man with a tailored shirt and trousers; a
young photographer with a pinkie ring, firmly holding his folding
camera; above, on a staircase and landing, facing the photographer,
are naval men in white shirts and sailor caps, assorted security
men in their starched uniforms, and a group of general onlookers.
The photograph is filled with people, yet there is a sense that you
are interacting with each person on their own terms, sharing their
perspective—wondering what has caught their attention as the
rich and active atmosphere of the festival has drawn everyone's
gaze toward a different direction.

"While her images of FESTAC '77 have left an indelible mark
on how we understand the festival visually," Oluremi C. Onabanjo,
an associate curator in the department of photography at the
Museum of Modern Art, New York, says, "I feel FESTAC '77 also
left its own mark on her, as a formative experience in her life as a
photographer and adult." Onabanjo, who is the editor of Nance's

**Nance's archive remains one
of the largest visual records of
this monumental occasion, where
the poet Audre Lorde "felt the
earth move."**

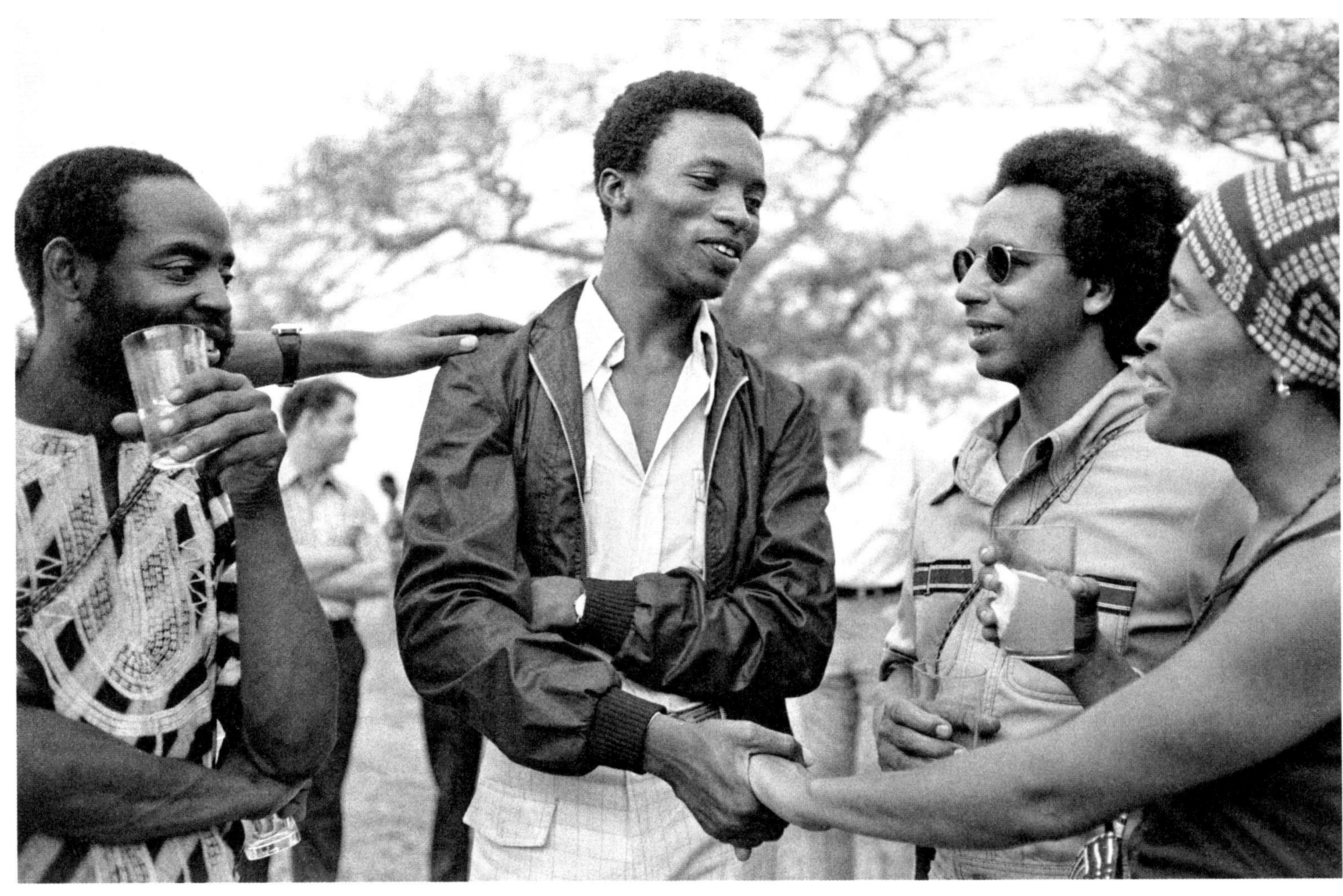

**Her focus on connecting people
and histories corresponds to
the African practices of festivals,
where it is believed that all
generations come together.**

forthcoming photobook on FESTAC, traces a special attention and
interest in bodily expression in Nance's later work—of the intimate,
the sensual, the quiet—back to FESTAC. As Nance states, "It is
what is in your heart and in your mind that makes the images."

An "undying love for the people," a phrase Nance borrowed
from Kwame Ture, is the spirit that inspires her photographs.
Attending FESTAC intensified Nance's commitments to the
principles and values of the Black Arts movement. In her coverage
of anti-apartheid activism in New York and the vulnerable, ecstatic
scenes at the Oyotunji African village in South Carolina, there
remains that interest in interchanges of ideas, people, and events
found at FESTAC. As Onabanjo explains, Nance's photography
after 1977 "witnesses an amplified scope of vision as to the various
transnational spiritual, cultural, and political experiences . . .
while showing a finely attuned sensitivity of the place of African
Americans within this global context." She points to Nance's
1980 images of the Black Indians in New Orleans; her work
as a producer on the 1985 film *Voices of the Gods*, directed by
her husband, Al Santana; her image *Three Placards* from 1986,
with the faces of Malcolm X, Martin Luther King Jr., and Elijah
Muhammad on placards at an anti-apartheid rally in Central
Park; and the place of Yoruba culture in her installation *Egungun
Work* (1994).

Nance is a self-described "digital elder" who seems to bring
her archival practice to all her interactions. Perhaps this approach
reflects back to her childhood of "meeting" family through photo-
albums. In a wider sense, her focus on connecting people and
histories corresponds to the African practices of festivals, where
it is believed that all generations—the living and the dead—come
together. *Last Day in Lagos*, then, is a festival of its own, a feast for
the creative imagination that introduces today's generation to their
artistic ancestors.

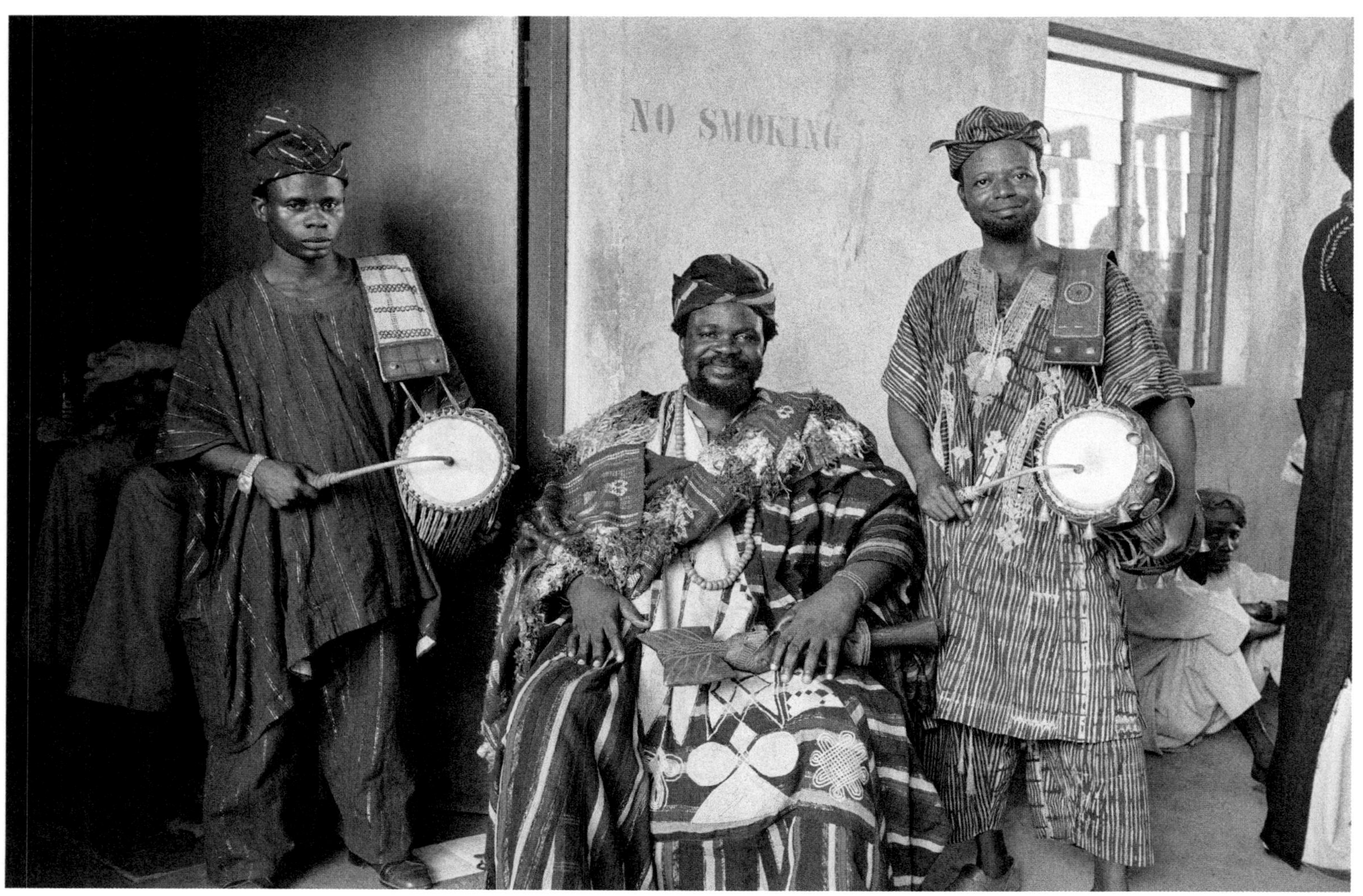

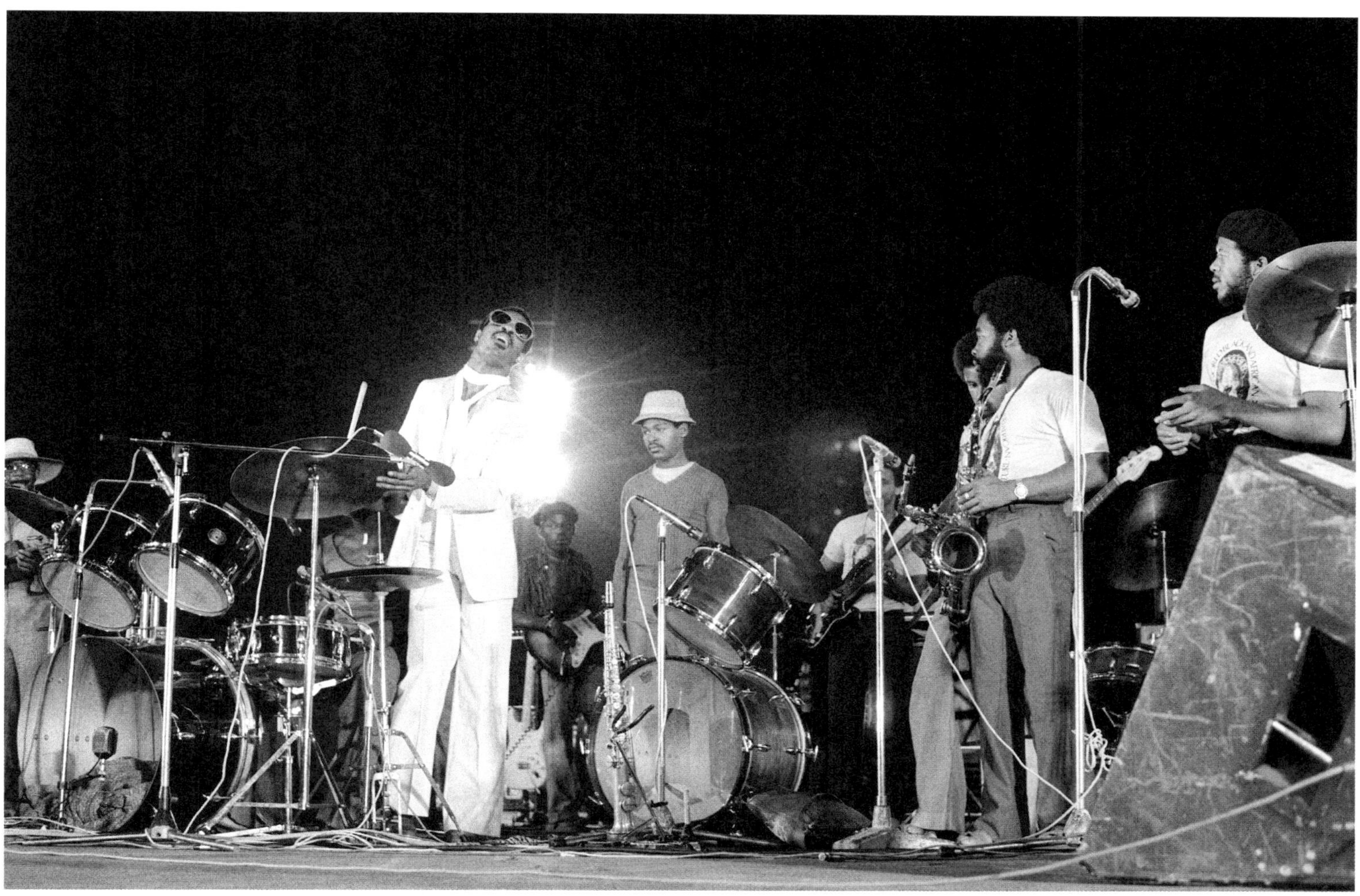

For Nance, the images are "visual medicine," a reminder of mutual joy preserved for the future. The making of *Last Day in Lagos* led Nance to rediscover other FESTAC goers. In the process of creating the book, Nance found mementos—address books, cloths, notes, letters—that fueled her desire to bring together what she refers to as the FESTAC '77 fellowship. Despite the event's historic nature, on returning, participants found little interest in telling others about their time in Lagos. In March 1977, Kay Brown, of the Black women artists collective Where We At, organized an open house in Brooklyn for participants to share photographs and stories. The following month, the Studio Museum in Harlem hosted a reception honoring U.S. participants. But there was no organization or space created to hold FESTAC archival materials or oral histories. Until relatively recently, interest in the work and experiences of the Black artists who were there has been relegated to a handful of academic articles and discussions. Memories of the festival, outside of the participants and their personal archives, persist in some memoirs and biographies. In 2017, the curator Dominique Malaquais organized the panel "FESTAC '77 and Other Pan-African Festivals" where participants, including Nance, spoke. Nance's images are also found in the 2019 book *Festac '77: 2nd World Black and African Festival of Arts and Culture*. In 2021, the Museum of Modern Art, New York, acquired twenty of Nance's photographs. When I ask Nance why the sudden uptick in interest in FESTAC, she throws the question back to me. "I was ready in 1977 but there was no interest, so we had to go on living," Nance says. "My job was to make the images. I did the work. I kept the work. I respected the work. I just had to live long enough and wait until the right time came around."

These days, Nance is occupied with "deep sleuthing" online. She's tracked down, connected with, and even spoken to some of the people she's identified in the photographs. Whether or not she finds Kwame Ture in her archive, she is determined that the legacy of the Black Arts movement is not lost to history. U.S. participants at FESTAC spanned generations, from members of the Harlem Renaissance to their creative descendants. For Nance, this is American history, Black history, world history, and art history that she won't allow to be forgotten. "I'm interested in making sure that someone knew that I was here," she says. "To be a Black person in America is to always be disregarded, to never be thought of as an intellectual, or an artist, or a collector." If FESTAC, in the shadow of a civil war, military coups, and political instability, and lacking the technology and degree of connectedness we have in the world today, could be planned and executed successfully in the 1970s, imagine—Nance's archive seems to tell us—what the future could hold.

Anakwa Dwamena is a writer based in Accra, Ghana.

Jamie Hawkesworth

Wandering from Antarctica to Beijing to the British Isles,
the photographer creates a dreamscape of everyday encounters.
Alistair O'Neill

Around the World

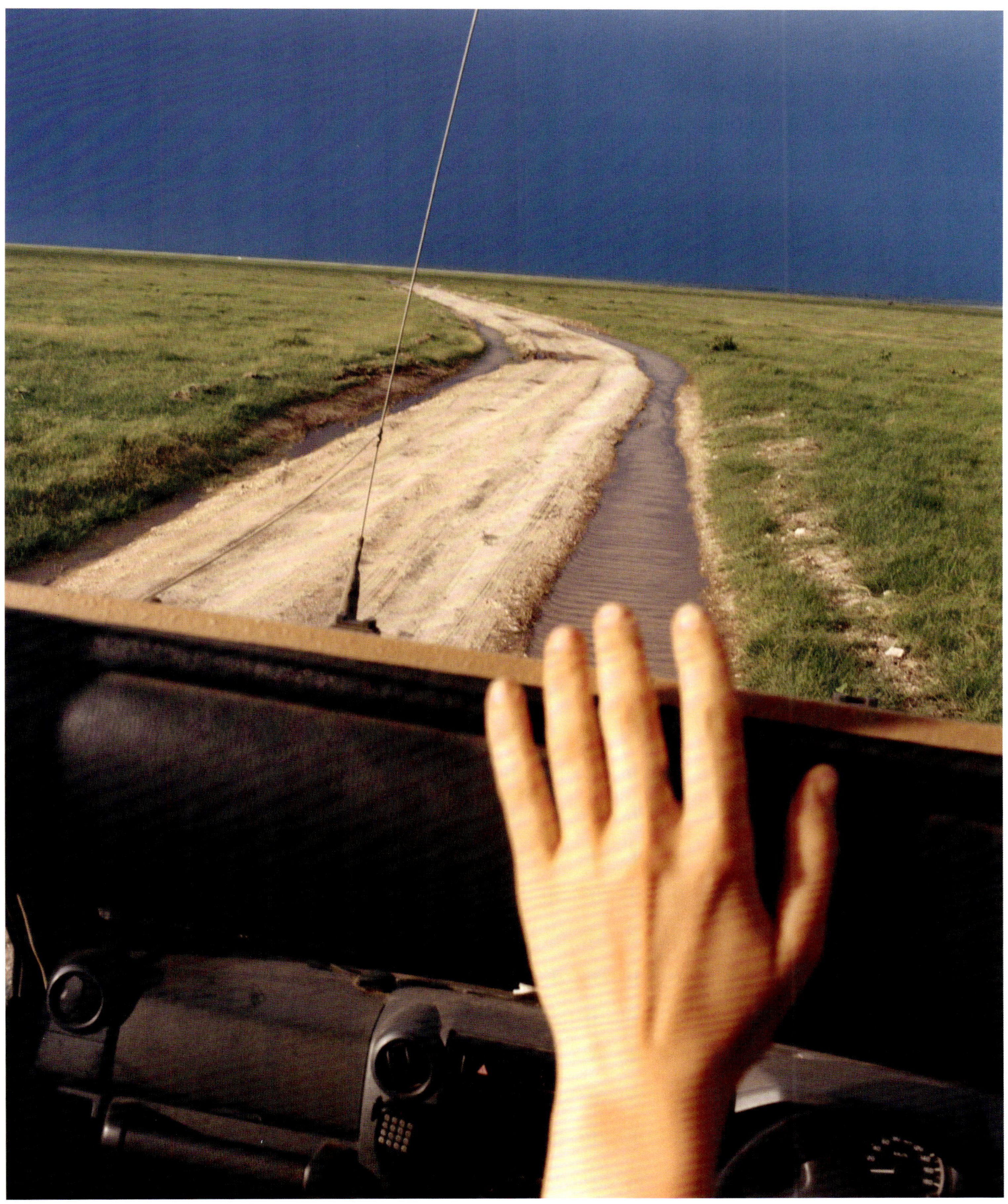

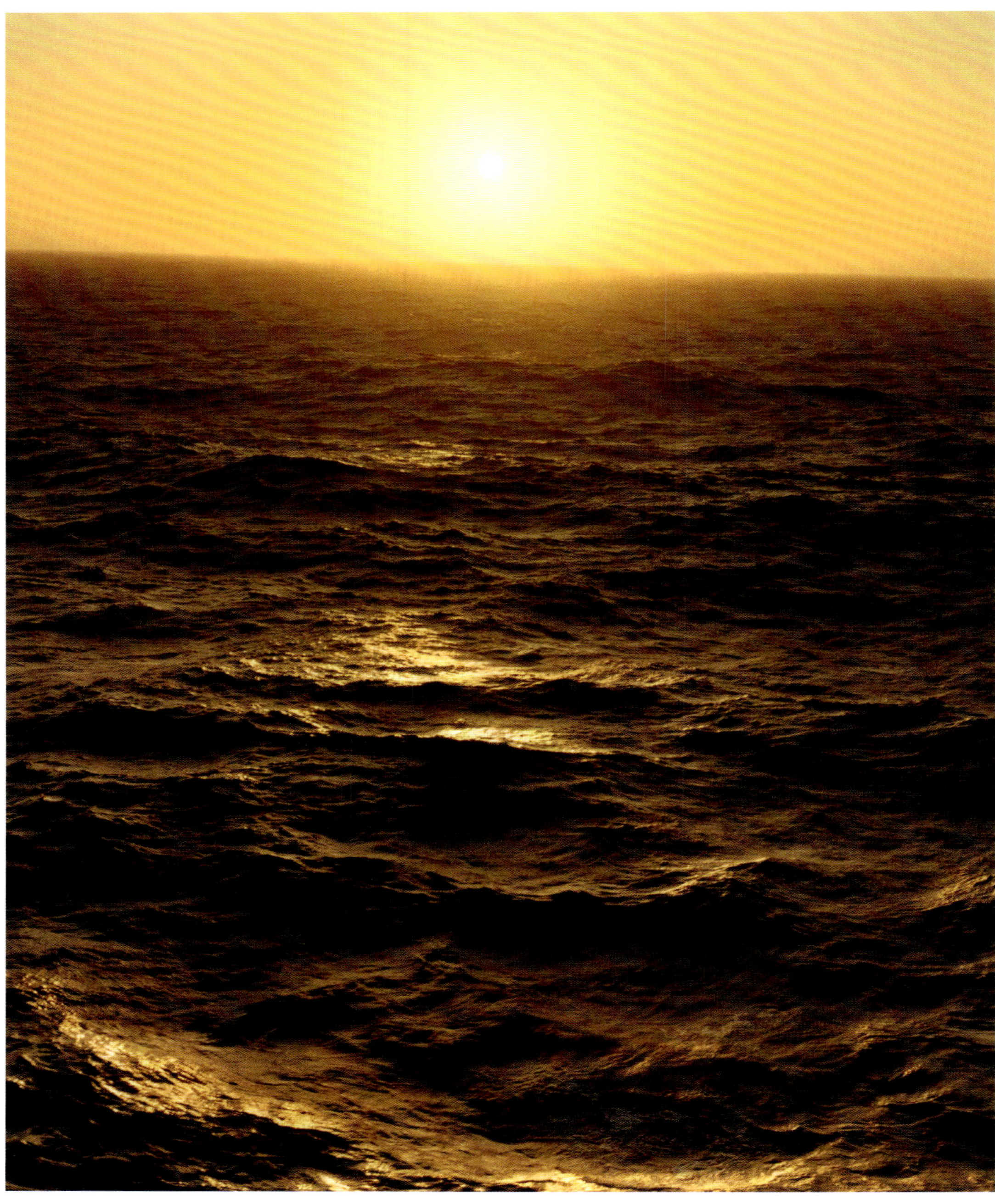

A boy watches as Jamie Hawkesworth passes the couchette the child's family is riding in on the Trans-Siberian Railway as it runs from Moscow to Beijing. As his parents play chess, the boy hangs upside down from his upper berth, poised and perfectly still as he addresses Hawkesworth's lens. The scene evokes the strange comfort that travel sometimes produces when, close to one's nearest in small surroundings, the world unfurls on the other side of the window.

Since making his name in fashion photography, Hawkesworth has used any available space in his work schedule to go on trips to places he hasn't visited before. This desire arises from his wanderlust about the United Kingdom, the island nation he lives in, and the vastness of the lands that lie beyond. But rather than being a means to establish himself as a travel photographer, the trips have served as opportunities to simply take photographs of people in the places he finds them. For Hawkesworth, it's not so much about his journey, or destinations visited, but about the journeys of those he meets along the way: the world is the means to illuminate an upside-down boy as sunlight shines through the train's window, to make us think of his view of the world in that topsy-turvy moment.

The pictures in this issue of *Aperture*, the majority of which are published here for the first time, are a selection of photographs taken on many of these trips. Together, they form a tender portrait of people around the globe. We are shown a checkerboard of cities—Detroit to Kerala, Los Angeles to Mumbai—and we travel along fantastical routes: Jamaica, Sweden, Mongolia, the Netherlands, the Democratic Republic of the Congo. The work, made between 2009 and 2021, is illustrated without titles, so we don't learn the specifics of locations or when they were visited. Hawkesworth is not interested in a grand tour. Instead, we see an accumulated, and fragmented, picture of the world as it appears in the twenty-first century: the ground is dusty, the buildings are sun bleached, the sky is mostly cloudy, and it rarely rains. And in the midst is all humanity—a riot of dyed hair, tattoos, colorful mass-produced clothes—going about its business. Traces of older orders of society persist in certain Indigenous dress styles or in the layout of arable land. But what accrues, image by image, is the remarkable consistency of how individuals present themselves.

The more we see of Hawkesworth's imagery, the more we seem alike in our multitude of differences. But this is a fiction the work raises, collapsing time and space, cultures and continents into a set of faces addressing a camera. In this process, it differs from the documentary universality found in initiatives such as Edward Steichen's exhibition *The Family of Man* (1955), in which he curated a collective photo-essay about human experience.

Hawkesworth, by contrast, gives us a dreamworld from a single viewpoint about quotidian existence. The historian Ludmilla Jordanova, who has written about *The Family of Man*, has observed that the ordinary people who are the staple subjects for such photography projects "see through photographs because, since there are so many of them, they have long ceased to be remarkable." What is left to them is to inhabit images that draw attention to the "selective artistry of photographs," which they, by and large, fail to profit from. Viewed today, Hawkesworth's work largely represents a prepandemic world; part of its charge lies in how it allows us to wander in places now less easily traveled. This body of work, which follows Hawkesworth's celebrated photobooks, *The British Isles* (2021), *To the Antarctic* (2021), and *Preston Bus Station* (2017), suggests new territory for the photographer.

Hawkesworth was born in 1987 in the English county of Suffolk. He first studied forensic science at the University of Central Lancashire (founded as the Institution for the Diffusion of Useful Knowledge in 1828) before shifting to photography, having been taught to use a camera to document mock crime scenes. After failing the law exam element of the forensic-science program, Hawkesworth decided to reject the objectivity of forensics and learned to use a camera according to a creative set of concerns. "It was a bit of a whim when I switched to photography, but within a week I just completely fell in love with it," he told me when we spoke last autumn. "For the first time ever, I could use my hands to play around with something and make something."

In 2010, a year after graduating, Hawkesworth spent a weekend in Lancashire in northern England with his former tutor, the writer and curator Adam Murray, photographing young people at Preston Bus Station, a key example of British brutalist architecture. The portraits were published that year in a newsprint pamphlet titled *Preston Bus Station*, one of the first publications of the collective Preston is my Paris, founded by Murray and the photographer Robert Parkinson. In 2012, hearing that the bus station was threatened with demolition, Hawkesworth returned to Preston for a month to document it again, taking photographs and making a film. Every day, he studied the people who arrived at and left the terminus according to the timetables of the numbered bus routes, along with those who loitered all day hidden in plain sight. The large plate-glass windows of the station showed him how light moved hour by hour, illuminating the details of appearance in all manner of journeymen. The project became a pictorial symbol for local campaigners trying to save the building, with the pressure group Gate 81 securing a site-specific installation of Hawkesworth's images in the bus station. The opposition forced the local council to abandon its redevelopment plans, and the building became a Grade 2 listed building (a building warranting preservation as being of architectural significance) only a year later in 2013.

This formative undertaking taught Hawkesworth how to negotiate a portrait. "Growing up," he says, "before I got on the phone to call someone, I would always have to practice what to say because I was quite shy. When I started to approach strangers, I'd be incredibly nervous and knew that person was also probably nervous, so it was very awkward, which I found really exciting." Hawkesworth adds, "I very quickly learned how to talk to someone, how to use my camera under pressure, how to conduct myself so that person feels comfortable—all these millions of things in such a simple exchange." He began photographing with a Mamiya RB67 with a 127mm lens, which he continues to use, as it was "always about trying to keep things basic." His focus lay in the nature of the encounter over and above the securing of the picture: "I always said to myself, If I hold on to that excitement, then the pictures are always going to feel honest."

The other contributing factor to Hawkesworth's aesthetic style is his practice of developing and printing his own work.

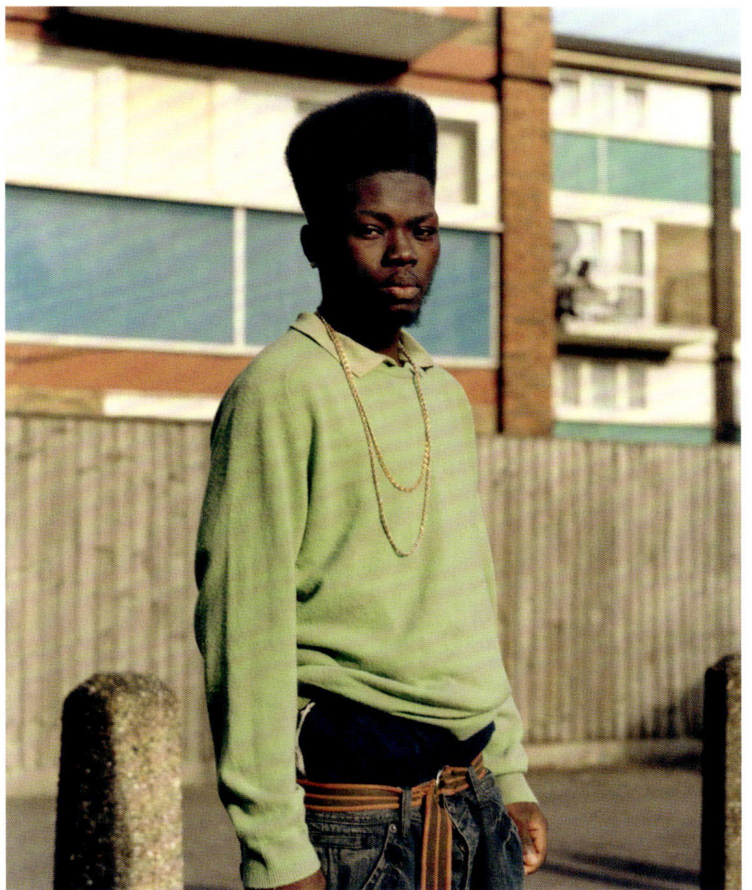

Hawkesworth is not interested in a grand tour. Instead, we see an accumulated, and fragmented, picture of the world as it appears in the twenty-first century.

Hawkesworth's wanderlust is as much about dreams as it is about exploration.

"The biggest thing that I got from the darkroom," he explains, "was that once, by mistake, I opened the door a fraction and it brought this warm glow into the picture." He turned the mistake into a stylistic feature, infusing the subject matter with a different disposition: "It was a huge part of my printing, particularly at the beginning with a project like Preston Bus Station, a very cold space. When I came back to the darkroom that technique would help me to warm up the photographs, making them feel a lot more optimistic than they were in reality. It felt celebratory of the place rather than it being a freezing cold bus station—which it was." The project brokered a different framework for photographing people, perhaps not in the documentary tradition, but one more analogous to the contemporary art model of participatory practice, or the design model of codesign, both of which flatten out hierarchies between artists/designers and audiences/consumers through open collaboration in creation and development.

News of the *Preston Bus Station* pamphlet came to the attention of Julie Brown, director of M.A.P, a fashion-image agency. She made contact with Hawkesworth to request a copy and signed him at their first meeting. An ongoing collaboration with the designer JW Anderson across a number of seasons and projects soon followed, with Hawkesworth participating in *Disobedient Bodies*, the exhibition Anderson curated at the Hepworth Wakefield, in 2017, for which Hawkesworth photographed 123 local schoolchildren in key examples of twentieth-century and contemporary fashion designs.

Hawkesworth's desire to resist being categorized was brought into sharp focus by the agency. "I remember them saying that they wanted the website to have my personal work in one section, fashion in the next section, and documentary here, and I was always really confused," he says. "Why would you separate any of it?" Hawkesworth is disinterested in such divisions. "I've always just been plodding along, doing portraiture, traveling around the country, and then an interesting fashion project will come up, and I'll treat that in exactly the same way, same camera, same printing, so I never really separated anything."

Hawkesworth's photographs of India, Kashmir, and Bhutan taken in 2019 made the Japanese fashion designer Junya Watanabe nostalgic for Asia in the midst of lockdown. For his Spring 2022 womens wear collection, usually shown at Paris Fashion Week but this time staged in Tokyo to a remote audience, Watanabe presented the models in front of large projections of Hawkesworth's images of golden deities, monks, and mountain peaks to frame a collection that incorporated collaborations with Chinese, Thai, Nepalese, and Japanese artists and craftspeople living in Asia and around the world. It's a poignant statement about connectedness and isolation, with both the visuals and the clothing allowing the eye to travel. Watanabe knew of Hawkesworth's reputation through his fashion editorials in *Vogue* (U.S. and U.K.), *Love*, and the *New York Times* as well as advertising campaigns for Alexander McQueen and Holland & Holland. That Hawkesworth's foothold in the space of fashion is matched by the photography he produces beyond this category is why a designer such as Watanabe finds the nonfashion/fashion intersection of his portfolio appealing.

Indeed, ordinary individuals with distinct personal style permeate Hawkesworth's most recent book, *The British Isles*, a three-hundred-page publication that collects the photographs Hawkesworth has taken on trips around the United Kingdom. Hawkesworth printed from the negatives in his darkroom in Shoreditch, London, over a sustained eighteen-month period. *The British Isles* arose out of him setting himself small journeys, he says, "where if I hadn't been to a place, I'd just go and see who I'd come across. Just really that simple." Keeping his observant eye on what he witnessed allowed him to perceive often-overlooked details. What the trips were not about was cataloguing a nation and a country. "When I went to Scotland, I never thought, Oh, for

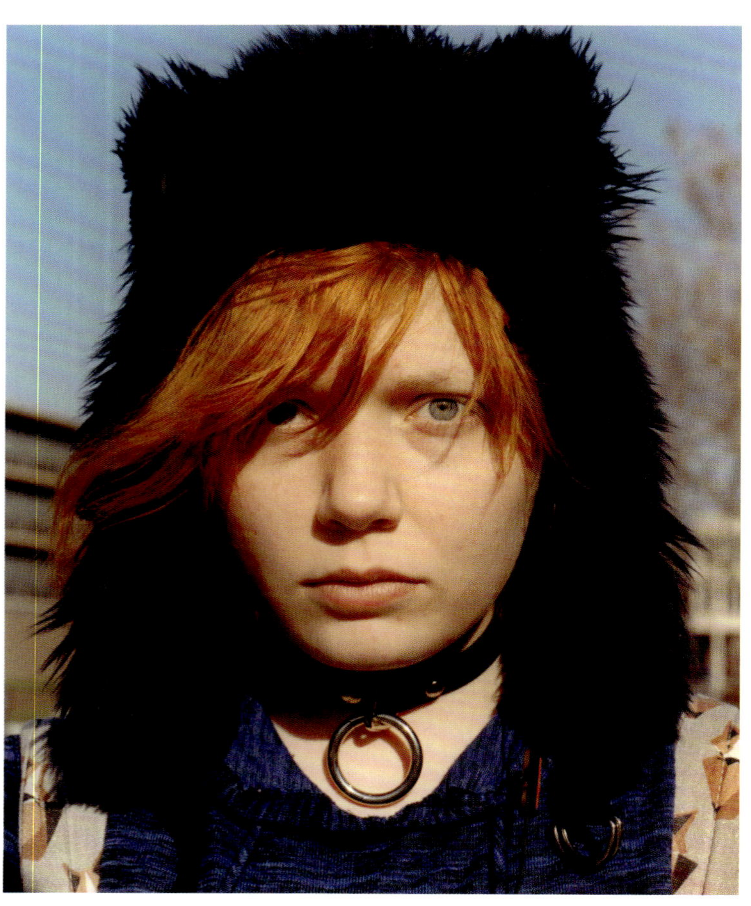

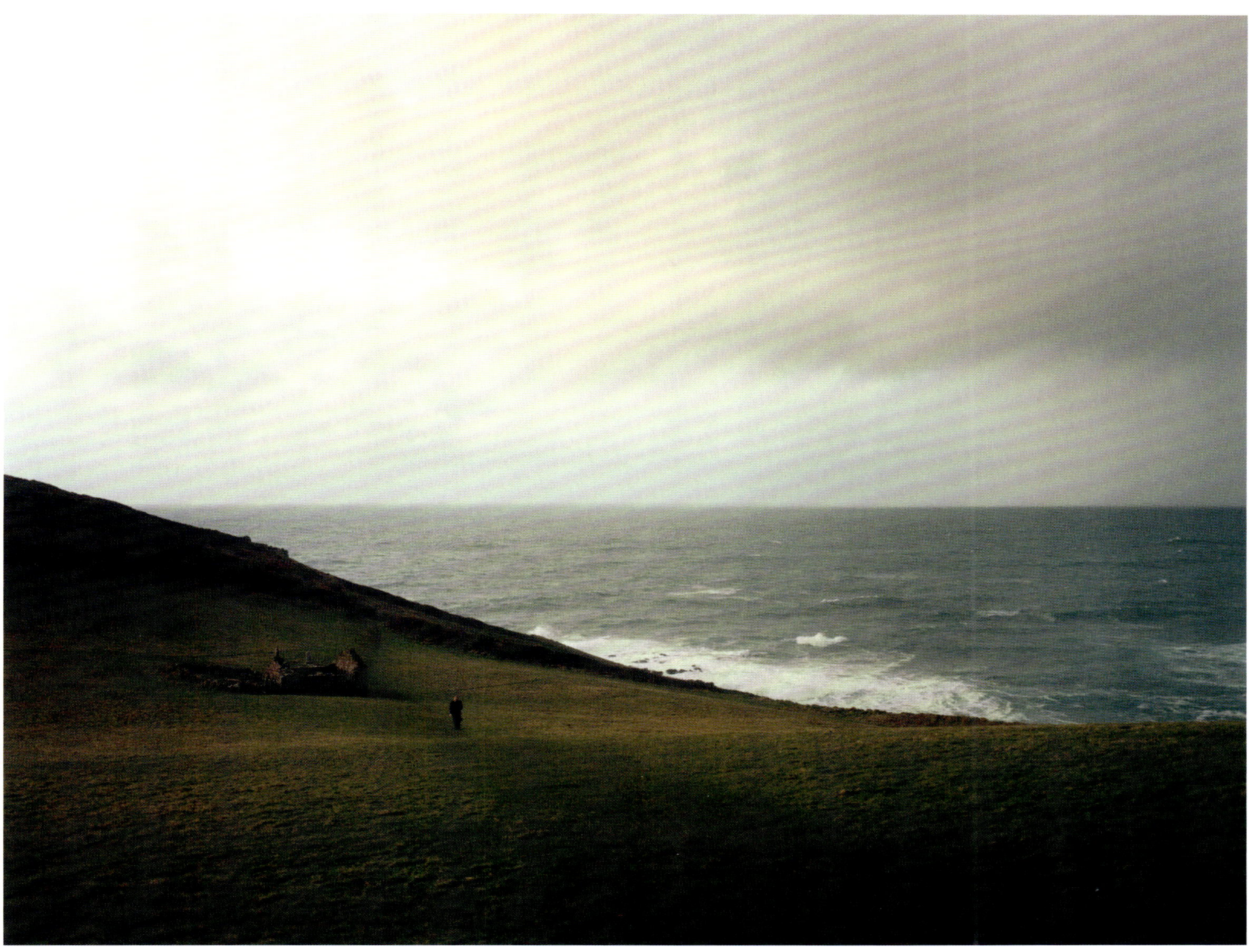

the next three weeks I'm going to explore the identity of Scotland, or what it is to be Scottish. I never had the idea to document Britain, it just sort of happened."

When thinking what to call the publication, Hawkesworth remained very conscious of the word *Britain* in a climate of Brexit, devolution, and disunity. The title deflects a political position, merely raising "all of the little islands that I went to, plus all of the mainland." The book contains no captions, so the lack of place names or dates produces a rounded experience of a people and land redolent of subtle seasonal transitions and temperate climate. At the book's heart is a sequence of portraits of pupils at Christ's Hospital school. They look like extras from a Harry Potter movie, but their uniforms are, in fact, unchanged from the school's inception in the City of London in 1552. The private school is now in East Sussex, but it upholds its tradition of offering scholarships to academically gifted children from disadvantaged backgrounds. And it's here that we find the just model for the country Hawkesworth was searching in, a paragon for social equity distinct from the current British government's rhetoric of "levelling up" economic disparities as the country recovers from the pandemic.

In Hawkesworth's own education, his first year studying forensic science was where he learned to use a camera to document evidence. The course involved simulated crime-scene houses where "you are actually searching for the evidence to then photograph as it hasn't been marked for you—you have to find it." Was dusting for fingerprints that different from photographing people he hadn't met before? "It is very similar in that you're running around

trying to find something, and then you photograph it," he says. Hawkesworth's photographs uncover as much about his subjects as the setting he finds them in, revealing faces and places, and the unseen connective tissue that binds one to the other.

Hawkesworth has worked in fashion, documented global communities, and detailed uninhabited regions, but he is unusual in resisting the trope of the glamorous photographer-explorer typified by Peter Beard, or maybe even Patrick Lichfield. In his unassuming manner and in the gentle nature of the images he produces, he has no need for a safari jacket to signal his ego or his photographic output. This is not to suggest he is unaware of such precedents. In traveling to Antarctica, he downloaded a copy of Werner Herzog's documentary about the polar region, *Encounters at the End of the World* (2007), onto his phone. He explains that when you sleep on the ice, "you dig a hole, and you sleep in the hole in a special sleeping bag, and that was where I watched that documentary." Hawkesworth's wanderlust is as much about dreams as it is about exploration. I also get the feeling Herzog would be pleased to know of Hawkesworth's viewing experience.

Alistair O'Neill is professor of fashion history and theory at Central Saint Martins, London.

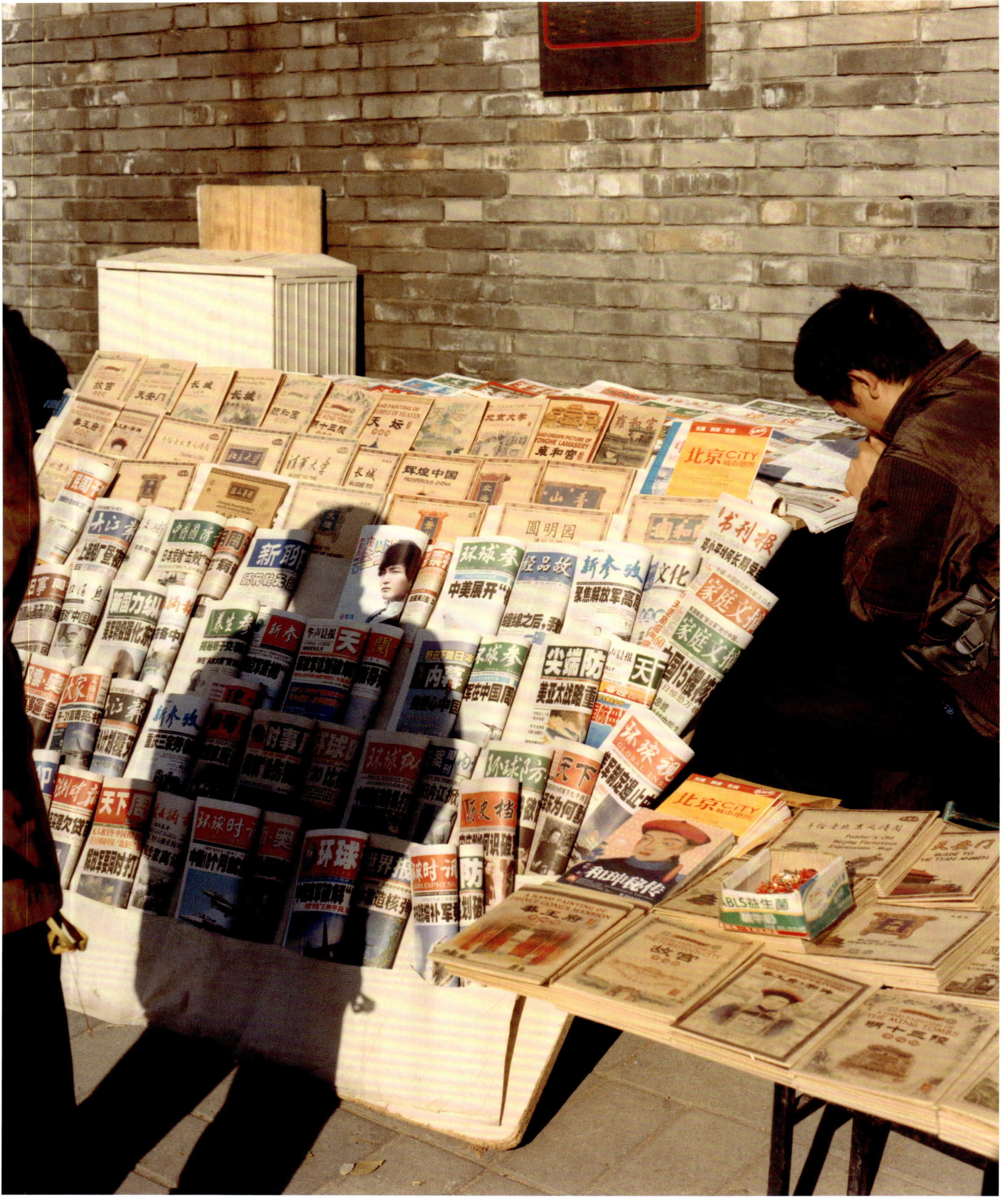

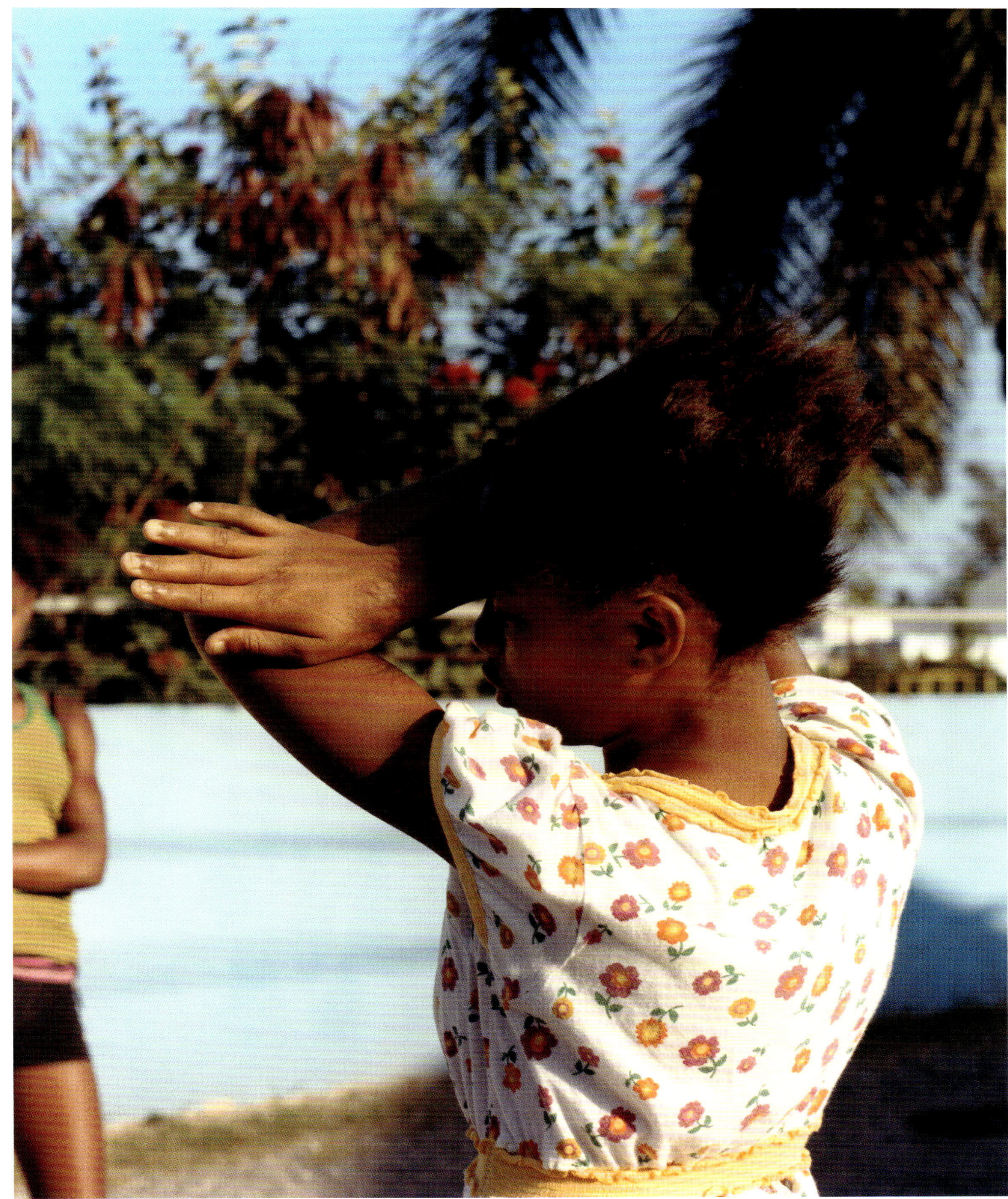

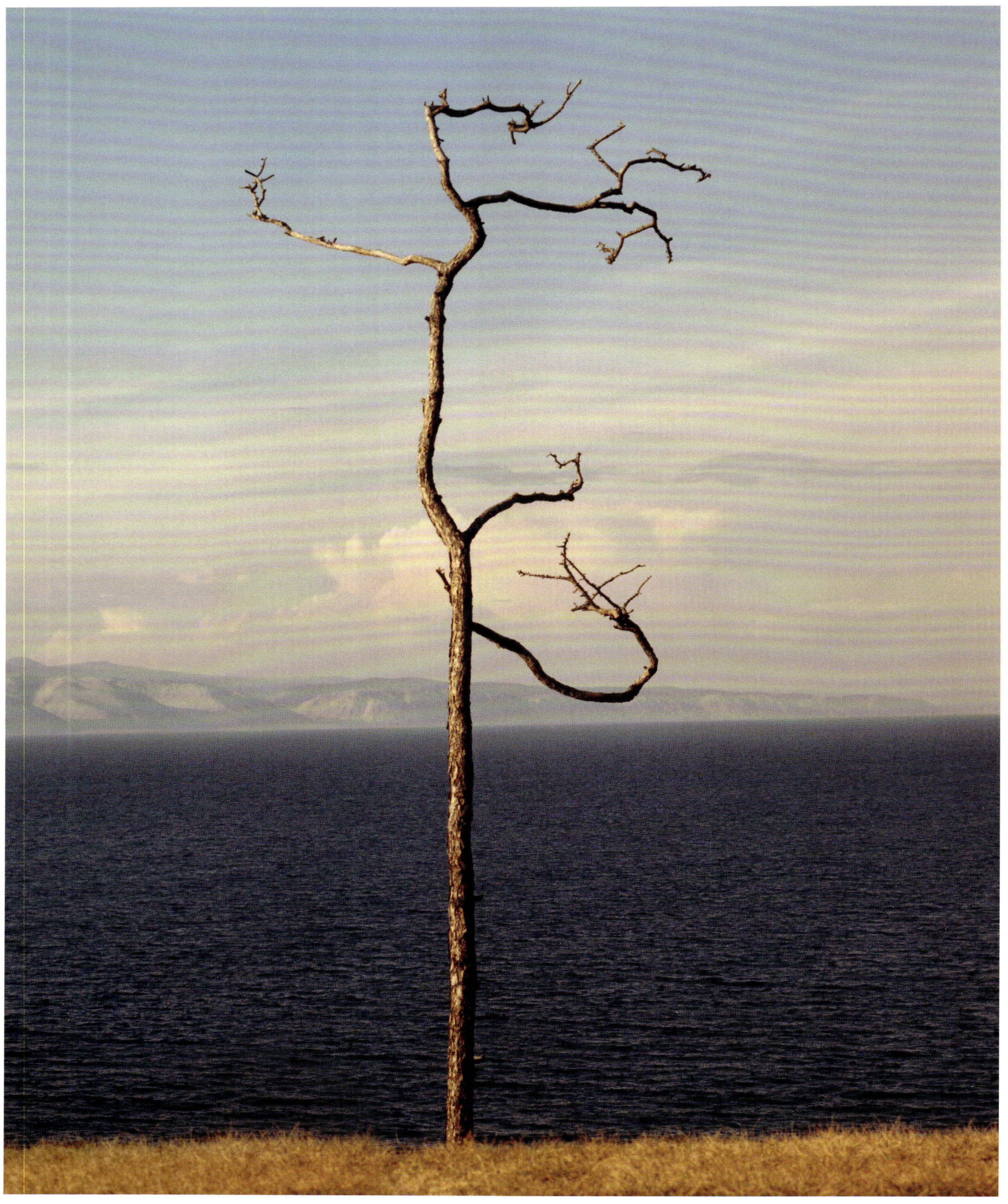

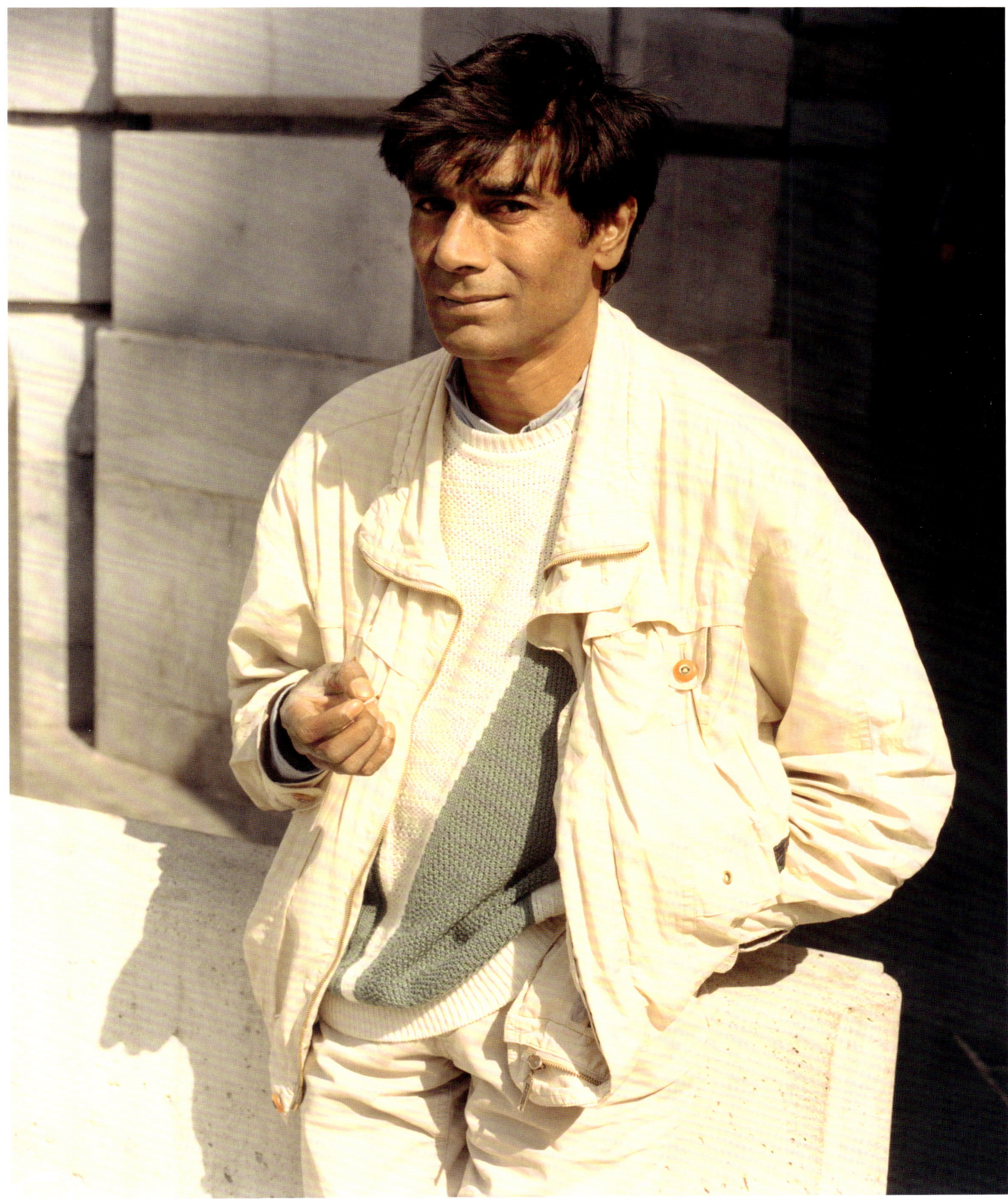

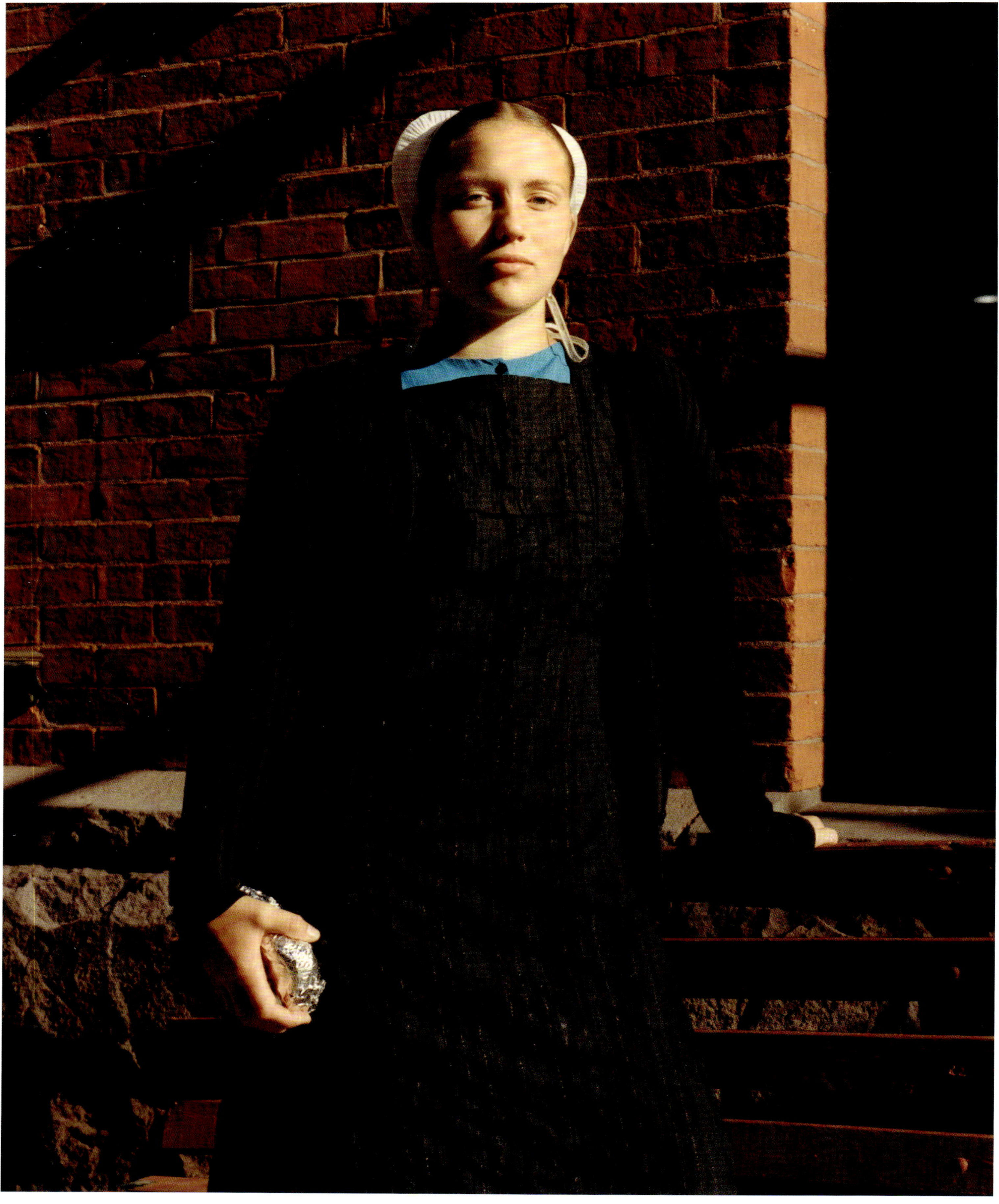

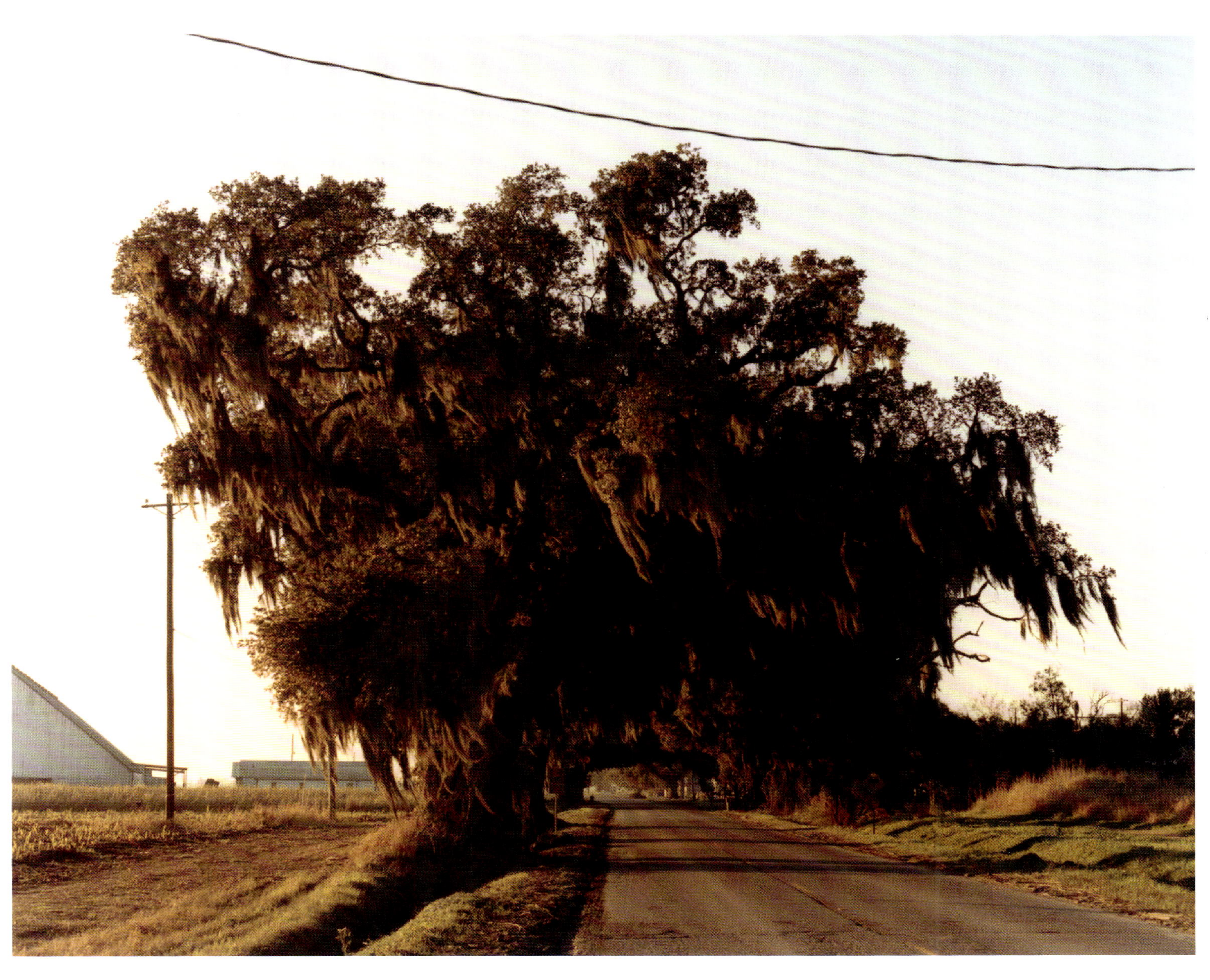

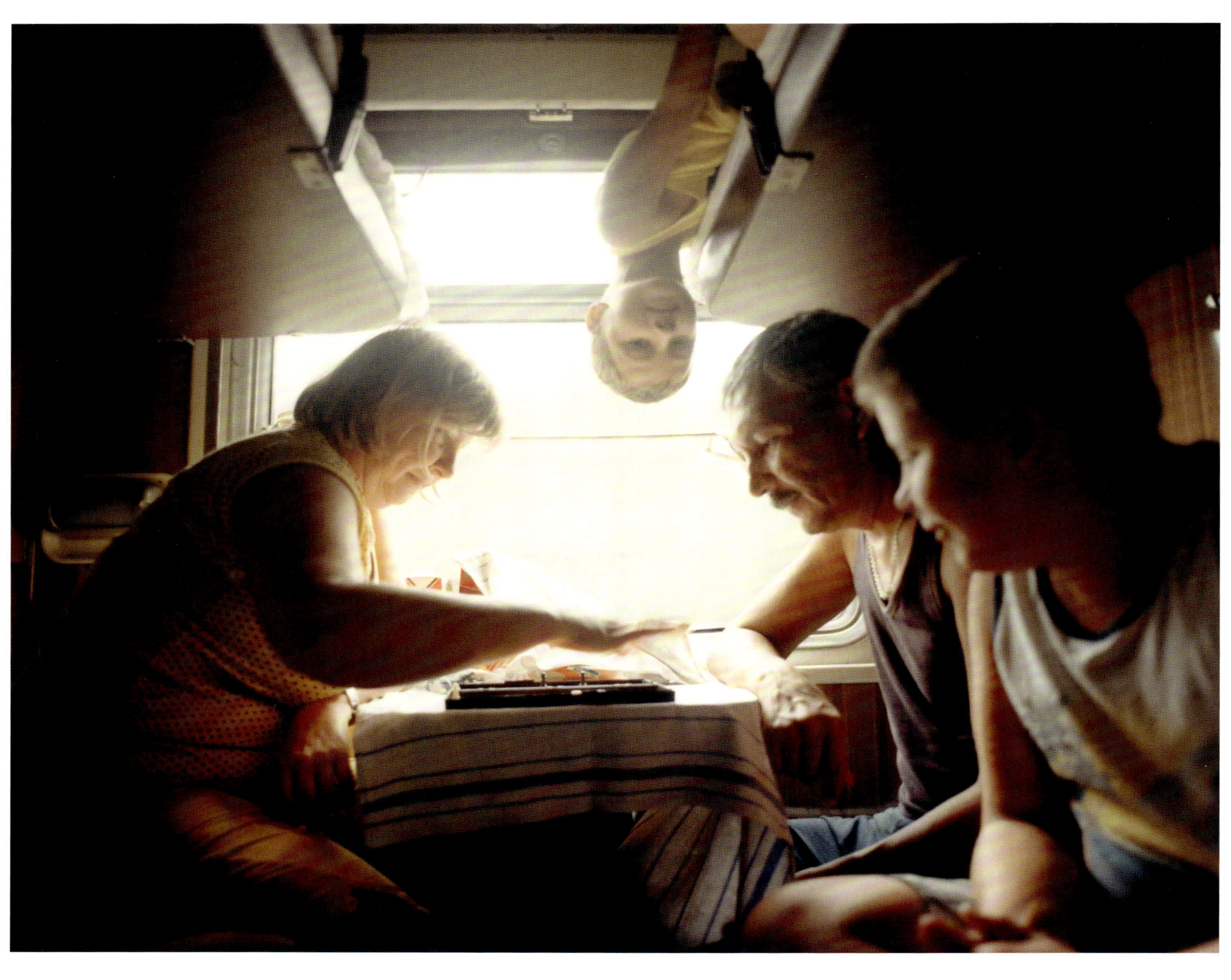

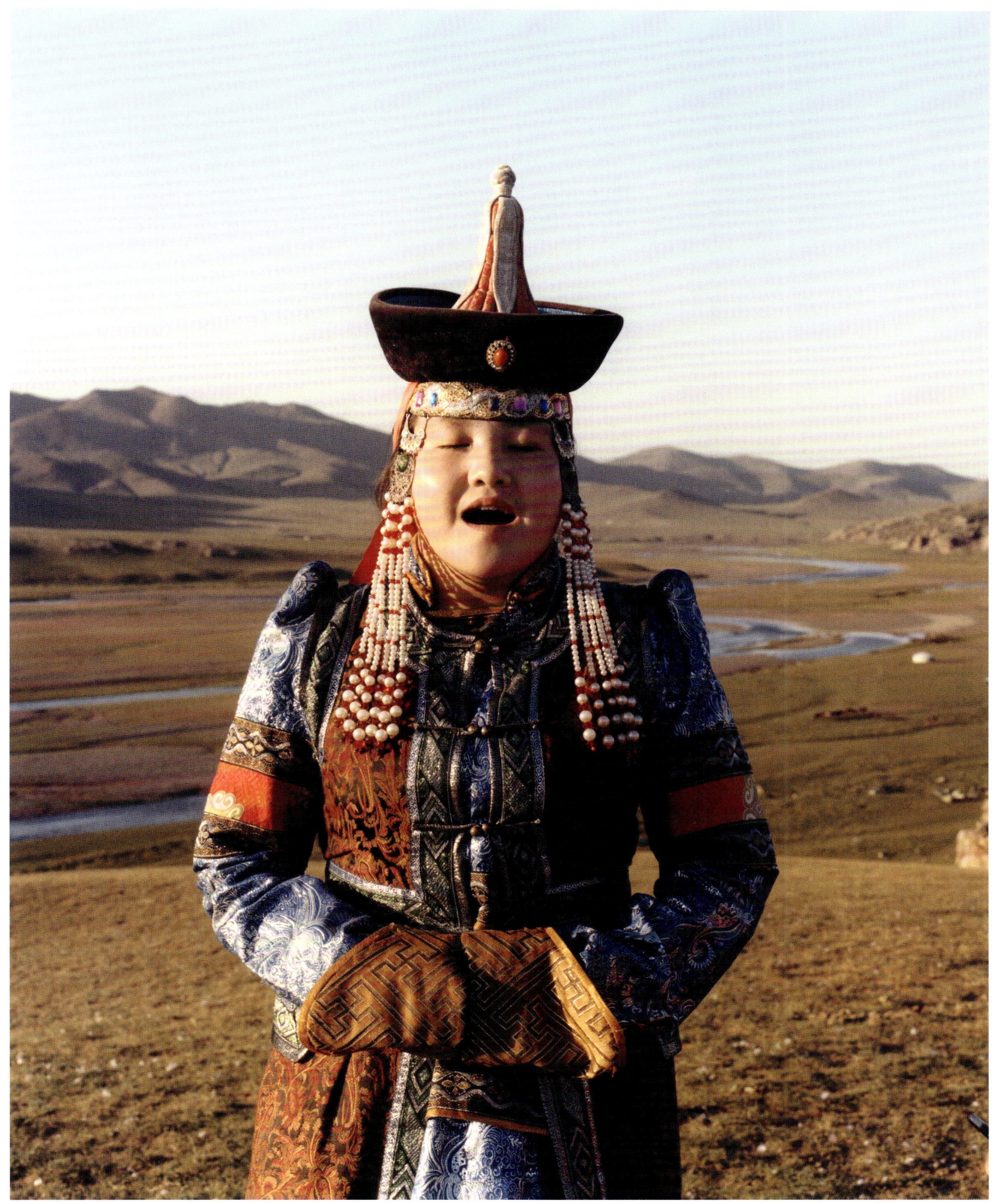

All photographs *Untitled*, **2011–21**
Courtesy the artist

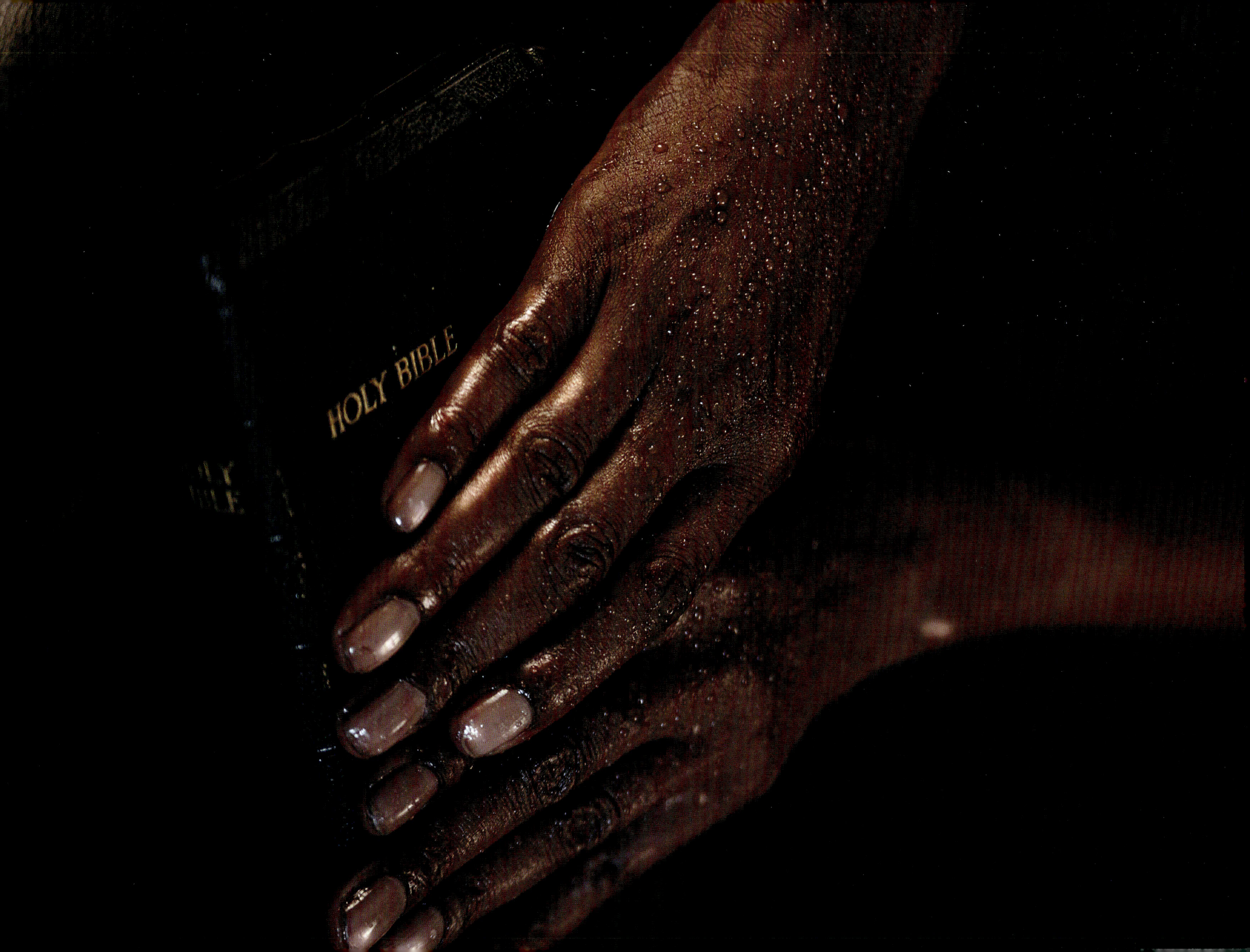
HOLY BIBLE

Celebrated for his striking portraiture, the young multimedia artist conjures visions of spirituality, queer presence, and the ghosts of history.

Shikeith's Black Uncanny

Tiana Reid

The artist Shikeith, born in Philadelphia, in 1989, as Shikeith Cathey, now goes by just his first name. But that does not mean that he is without antecedents, without family, or without history. With interdisciplinary work spanning photography, installation, film, and sculpture, Shikeith's practice is in conversation with a rich canon of Black queer men—the documentary poetics of Marlon T. Riggs, the editorial sensibility of Joseph Beam, the ceremonial politics of Essex Hemphill, and the cutting lucidity of James Baldwin.

While Shikeith's artistic universe addresses a number of masculine literary, musical, and cultural figures, his first universe, if we can call the vexed enmeshments of home a universe, was one of women. "I grew up in a household with my mother and my grandmother," Shikeith told me recently on Zoom. He is from North Philadelphia but now lives and works some three hundred miles west, in Pittsburgh. North Philly, as it is called, is "kind of known for being the more volatile area, the more impoverished

area in Philly," Shikeith explains about his upbringing. "It was an environment that had limited resources, a place where, because of that, we had to utilize our imagination a lot as children."

His maternal grandmother was a singer and a poet. "I got a lot of my creative skills from her," he says, noting that she was very spiritual. "Among regular Black shit that people would expect," he adds, hesitating, hers was a very "odd house." He goes on to tell the story of how his childhood home was haunted by ghosts, including one named Tom, who his grandmother would lock in the basement for hours at a time. "Once, the pastor came over to the house, and the ghost took a glass of water and dropped it on the ground," he recalls.

Shikeith's short but active career has been touched by this familial gift: a Black uncanny, an awareness of hauntings, a surreality, a speculative nature. The titles alone of Shikeith's recent solo exhibitions—*Feeling the Spirit in the Dark* (2020) at the Mattress Factory Museum of Contemporary Art, in Pittsburgh, and *Imagining Flesh Through Shadows* (2019) at the Alexander Brest Museum and

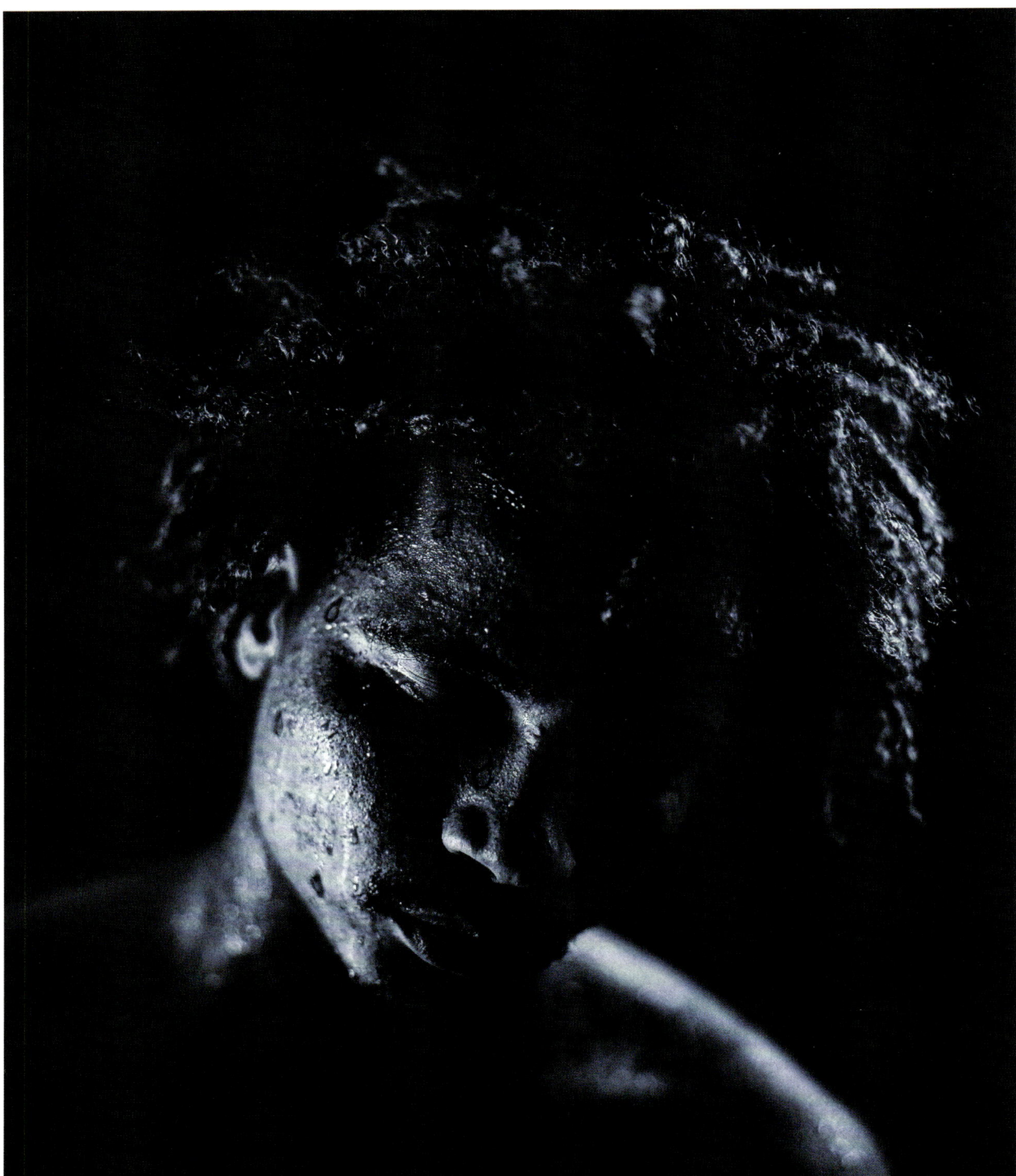

Gallery in Jacksonville, Florida—speak to Shikeith's interest in spiritual errancies. His work was also presented in *Ceremonies*, a 2021 online exhibition at the Yossi Milo Gallery, in New York, where he is represented.

The artist's full-color portraits of Black men, from 2020, some of which will be included in a forthcoming monograph published by Aperture, are luscious stagings of the body—a thick black cloak, hands perched over a Bible, a Madonna figure, sweat bubbling up on the surface of skin, do-rags and chains transformed into ornaments—all sparkling under Shikeith's photographic light. In the image *O' my body, make of me always a man who questions!* (2020), a topless man appears to be floating underneath the four summoning hands of two men dressed in pastoral suits. Despite the languor of the clipped body, the way the main subject's back is arched and the muscles around his ribs are protruding also suggests physical tension. A possession. Something clandestine. Shikeith's

Black uncanny, his aesthetic unhomeliness, indexes those feelings of strangeness and alienation attached to the intimate and the familiar. Though his work has been canonized in a quicksand of cultural highlights ("Black gay photography") and though there is rescue and relief in his practice, his art does not fit squarely into the optimism sanctioned by much discourse around representation.

Shikeith's ability to balance opulence with sparseness and excess with measure has been honed by a steady flow of commercial commissions. A few years after graduating, in 2010, from Pennsylvania State University with a BA in integrative arts (an interdisciplinary degree that aims to blend the creative and the professional), he moved to New Haven, Connecticut, earning, in 2018, an MFA in sculpture from the Yale School of Art. Since then, Shikeith has been a frequent contributor to the *New York Times*, where he has photographed a number of subjects including a *T Magazine* fall fashion cover, the models Samuel Atewogboye and Mohamed Cisse for a spread on spring suits, and an exuberant cover for *The New York Times Magazine* featuring Lil Nas X to accompany Jazmine Hughes's profile of the electric Black gay pop star for a 2021 cover dubbed "Hot Boy Summer." Whether the images are fashion editorial or commercial portraiture, Shikeith says: "I think about them as extensions of my fine-art practice, meaning that I'm wanting to embark on assignments that contribute to a larger archive of material that I'm creating." He adds, "When I first began making photographs in high school, I primarily focused on fashion because I was inspired by Tyra Banks's *America's Next Top Model*. That was literally the reason why I picked up a camera in the first place. So, it's really nice to be able to come back around years later and contribute my own visual vernacular to the fashion landscape."

When Shikeith and I connected in October, his work life was a little hectic, particularly leading up to the Performa Biennial, in New York, where he showed *notes towards becoming a spill*, a commissioned, four-act "experimental opera" that blends modern dance and gospel songs. Shikeith and his crew spent the week before the two-night presentation prepping at a "residency" at the Rockaway Hotel in Queens. As did his film *A Drop of Sun Under the Earth* (2017) before it, *notes towards becoming a spill* evokes the writings of Audre Lorde. "I am essentially creating a biomythography that talks about the process of disentangling oneself from a lot of the ephemeral presences that continue to haunt Black queer men—particularly those that are connected to racism and homophobia," he tells me a few days before the Performa debut. "It's going to be set against the Atlantic Ocean in Rockaway Beach."

It is rather revealing that Shikeith says the opera is set "against" the Atlantic, and not on, with, or beside the ocean. *Against* signals opposition. For Shikeith, the water is both a model of boundlessness and spillage and a history of terror and ruination. In a video created to promote and contextualize the Performa Biennial commission, he talks about the Middle Passage as a site of devastation but also one of escape, referencing the enslaved jumping overboard, sometimes en masse: "This word *spill*—which, for me represents a sort of freedom, a way of existing unpoliced and not constrained to the confines of any one particular forum—is very queer, a queer shape."

In Shikeith's photography, sculpture, and installation, we also bear witness to the psychic life of sexual subjection—what it means to be looked at, the subtle traumas of being perceived despite the elation of mutual recognition. In his video installations such as *to bathe a mirror* (2018) and *#Blackmendream* (2014), choreography and documentary performance narrate Black queer masculinities and desires. The opera, then, is an occasion for an altogether new sensorial experience: the smell of the salty ocean, the twenty-piece gospel choir led by Rashad McPherson, the movement of the dancers choreographed by Morgan Bobrow-Williams, their sheer costumes by Carlos Soto. One of the seeds Shikeith planted for the opera was a 2019 installation of the same name at Atlanta Contemporary, which used materials including paint, soil, mud, and audio recordings. "In that installation, I painted the room haint blue, which is a particular shade of blue that I use in my work. It comes from the Gullah Geechee who live along the coasts of the Carolinas and Georgia, the Low Country," he says. "They created this shade from the indigo crop, using the paint to protect their interior space with the blue color of water to ward off evil energies from entering. They believed that haint blue was ghost tricking. Ghosts can't cross water."

Haint is one letter away from *haunt*. And *blue* one letter away from *blues*. Connecting these two ideas—blue and hauntings—is key to experiencing Shikeith's artistic practice. In a 1983 interview with the scholar Nellie Y. McKay, Toni Morrison, speaking on the

This page: Found photographs from the artist's archive, undated

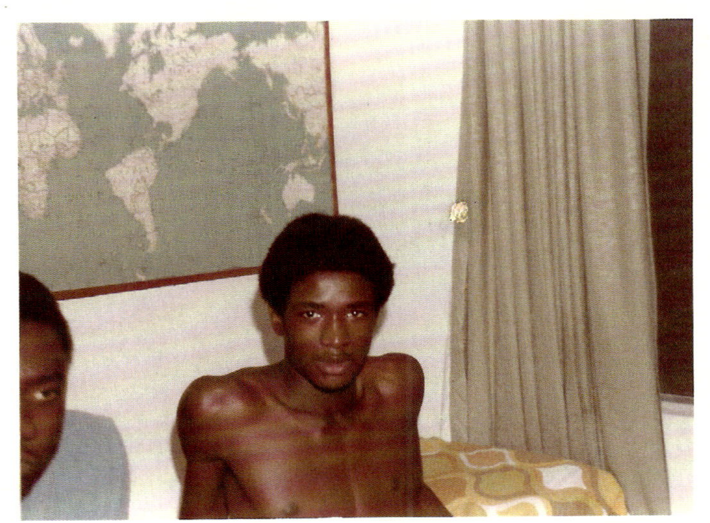

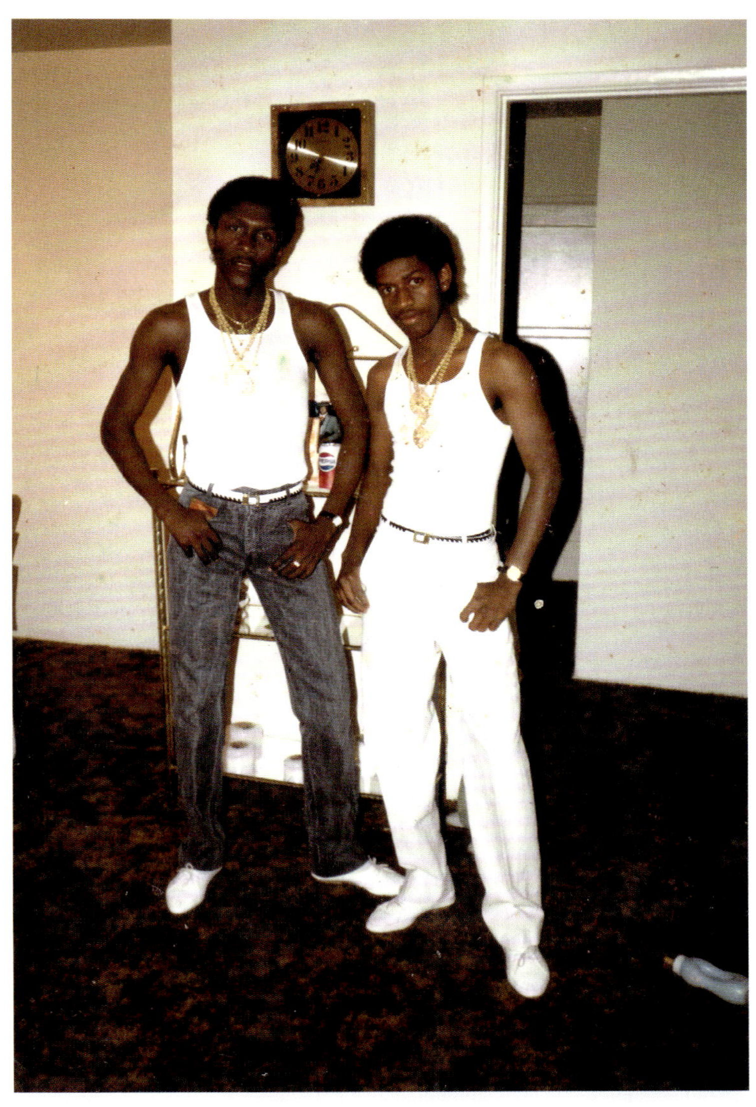

Shikeith's portraits are also self-portraits of a man whose eyes keep fluttering, whose self is irretrievable.

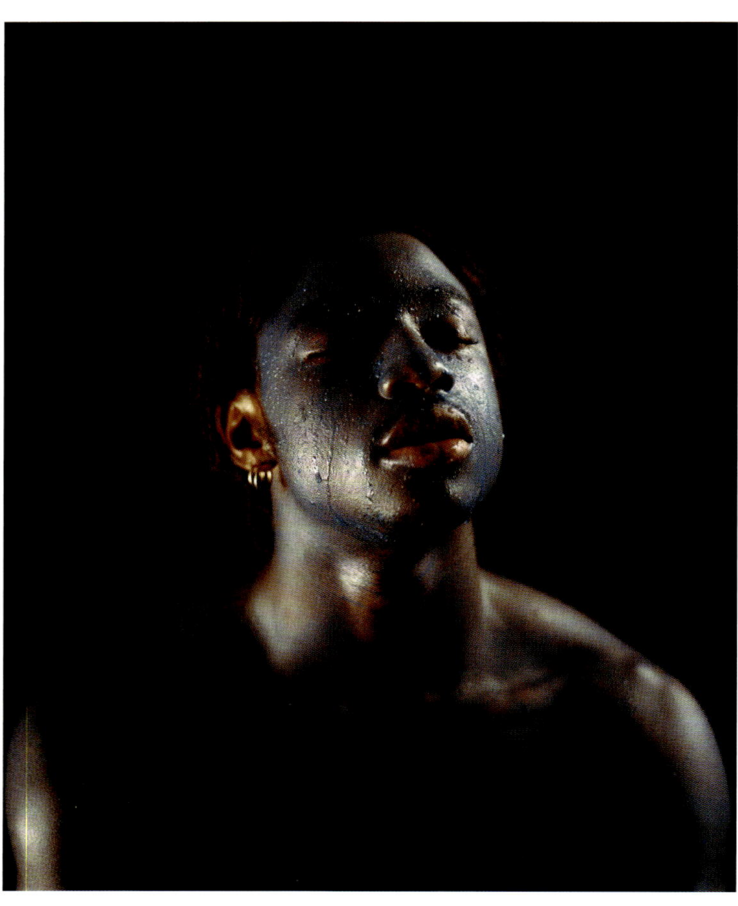

The smoke made the night blue/I have walked in the rain, 2020

heterogeneity of styles (plural) of Black art and Black literature, diagnosed a sign of the times: "Some young people don't want to acknowledge this [supernatural element] as a way of life. They don't want to hark back to those embarrassing days when we were associated with 'haints' and superstitions. They want to get as far as possible into the scientific world." Perhaps this has changed since the early 1980s, and Shikeith is one example of an artist who invites the ghostly in, who acknowledges what has been left behind, what lingers, what is unknowable.

The opera, oceanic and spiritual, marks a turning point in Shikeith's career as he actively tries to renew his established practice. Shikeith is best known for formal portraiture, crisp images of Black figures executed with conceptual clarity, but his perspective is an intense, enveloping, and often experimental style. In *The moment you doubt whether you can fly, you cease forever to be able to do it* (2014), which you might have seen as the cover of Danez Smith's 2017 National Book Award Finalist *Don't Call Us Dead*, two Black men are in flight, hands linked, reaching and floating away on a black balloon. "I think [Shikeith's work] speaks to innocence, to vulnerability, to healing, and to friendship and love in a way that is super beautiful, and also super bare, and literally naked, without reaching toward a hypersexualized view," Smith told *Gulf Stream Magazine*. "There are so many penises and they never feel sexualized, they feel vulnerable."

Shikeith's recent work, he says, attempts to obscure what was previously more readily available. "I don't want things to be so easily consumed anymore," he explains. "I want to withhold." He juxtaposes his own photographs with archival images of Black men that he sources from an antique shop in Pittsburgh and from eBay. "I would seek out images that felt very queer or at least were depicting Black men in very intimate encounters." Where the queerness of some of these photographs lies, of course, is complex, if it can be located at all. But they are queered through Shikeith's arrangement and attention. "I lay them out like they're family photographs in my house, so they're just chilling on the mantels," he says. "And people are like, That's your grandpa? No—just the things that I've collected and want to cherish because they were out there sort of lost." In his grandmother's home, there were so many images of loved ones, family, extended family, ancestors, plastered all around the house. "I grew up in a home where photographs were stacked everywhere, not an inch left of space," he remembers.

Still, it would be oversimplifying to mark Shikeith's new direction using archival images as a clear-cut distinction to identify what came before as easy to digest. After all, since early on, some of his subjects have refused the capture of the photographic gaze. In *Kris* (2019), the figure is subtly slumped over, head bowed down, eyes closed, glistening with sweat. In *A Missed Prayer* (2017), two Black men embrace. In the foreground, the man is turned away so that the viewer can see only the back of his head, his ears, the nape of his neck, his shoulders. "Only God Can Judge Me" is splayed in large cursive lettering from his left to right shoulder. But behind him, a man crouches, sitting knees to chest, peering over, hiding but valiantly confronting the camera's gaze. In *Brush your Blues* (2017), the back of two heads, necks intertwined, almost form the shape of a heart. And in the forty-four-minute documentary film, *#Blackmendream*, nine men speak—about a range of issues including anti-Blackness, masculinity, and emotions—with their backs to the camera. About a minute in, white typewriter-style lettering appears on a black screen, reading: "This work expresses my, and our, apprehension to be."

With Shikeith's distinctive noble vividness—clean edges, detailed visual contrasts, a confrontation, averted gaze, backs turned—a complexity emerges, marked by a deepening relationship between the photographer and the photographed. His approach

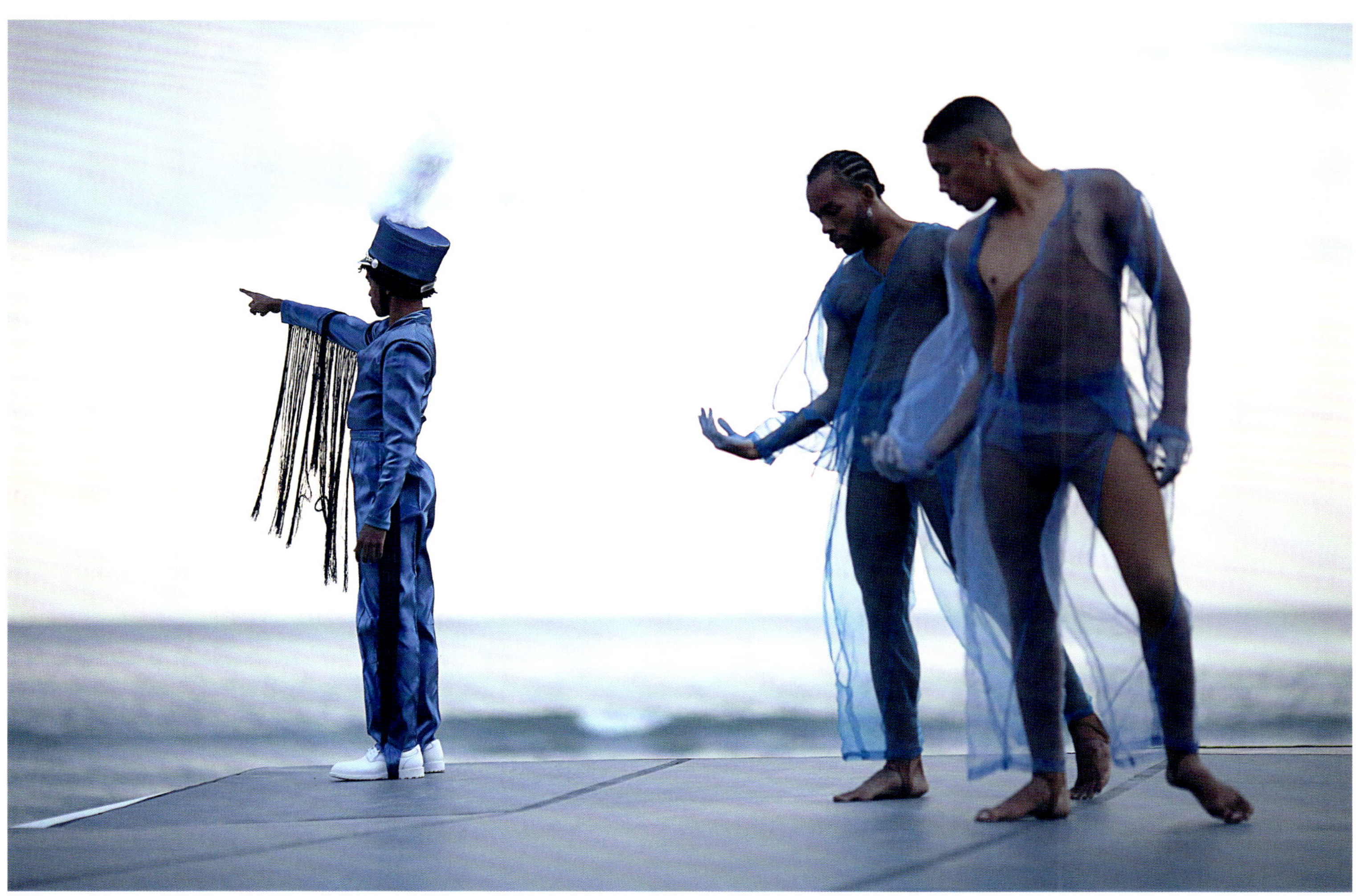

begins with composition through sketching but extends well
beyond the time of the sitting. "For the most part, the people in my
photographs are people I've photographed for years, since 2012 and
forward," he says. "I'm really interested in this progression. I change
as an artist; they change as individuals. The one big goal in my head:
to capture these people over time."

Perhaps, then, Shikeith's portraits are also self-portraits of a
man whose eyes keep fluttering, whose self is irretrievable, troubling
the distinction between who you're really taking a picture of when
you take a picture of someone else. He fashions a corpus saturated
with liquid relation. As depicted across his oeuvre, spill threatens to
undo any "us" that has formed. Desire spreads like ripples. Intimacy
crashes like waves. History is already here. History haunts. Mixing
ghosts and oceans, he constructs a way of making art that intensifies
that one-letter difference between *haint* and *haunt*, between *blue*
and *blues*. Ghosts are both welcome and in need of warding off.

These past two years, Shikeith's life has been like the ocean—
nothing constant but the ebbs and flows. "I am just surrendering
to my life and not letting the Capricorn in me try to control
everything," he says, laughing. At the beginning of the pandemic,
he lost the grandmother who had taught him so much about art
and spirituality. Amid grief, he is also trying to prioritize fun and
openness—eating, dating, unfamiliar experiences. "I just want
to follow a feeling," he states. And we're all following him now.

**Tiana Reid is a postdoctoral research
associate in the department of English at
Brown University. Her writing has appeared
in *Art in America, Bookforum, Frieze,
The New York Review of Books,* and
*The Paris Review.***

This page:
*O' my body, make of
me always a man who
questions!*, 2020

Opposite:
Kris (In Blue), 2021

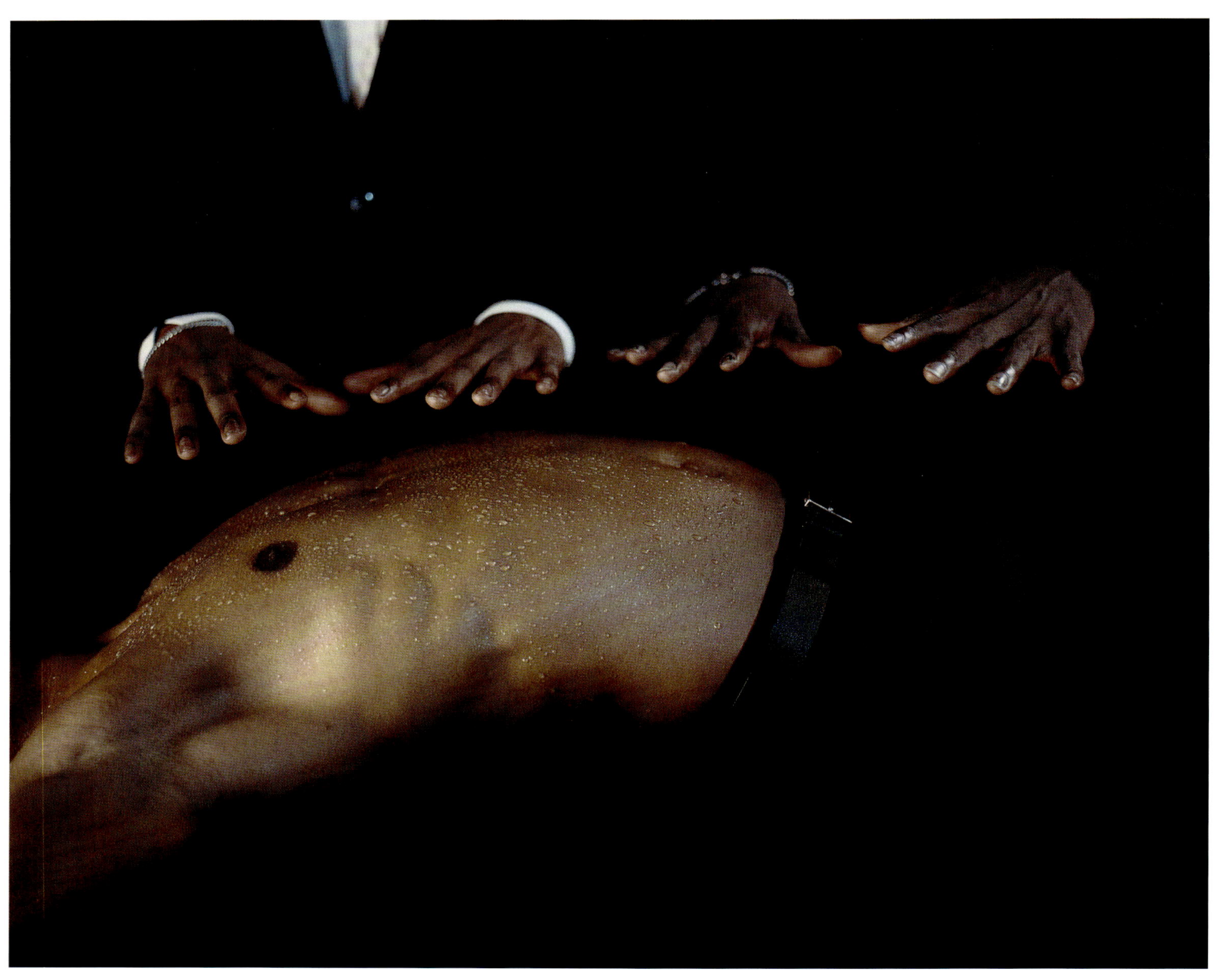

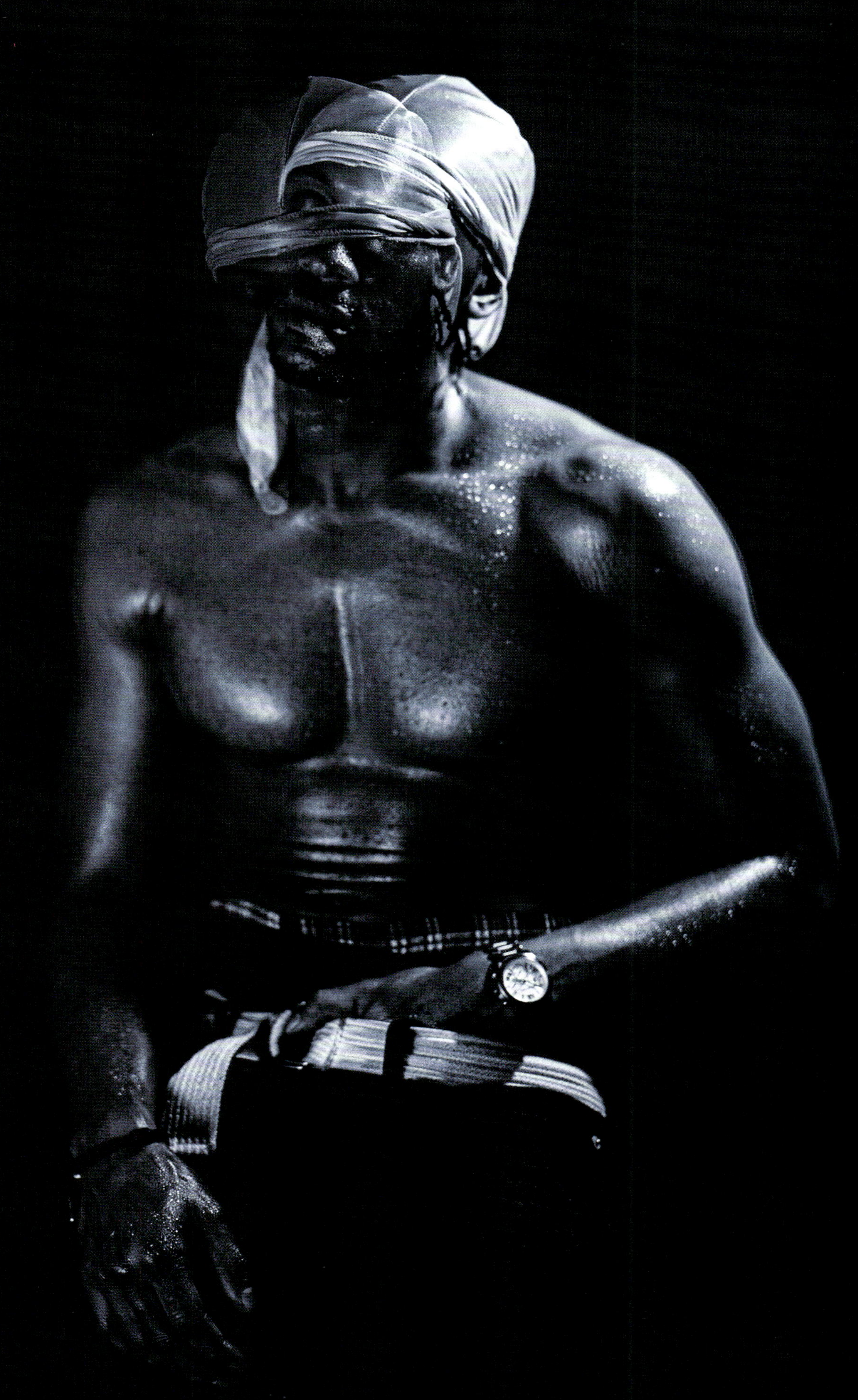

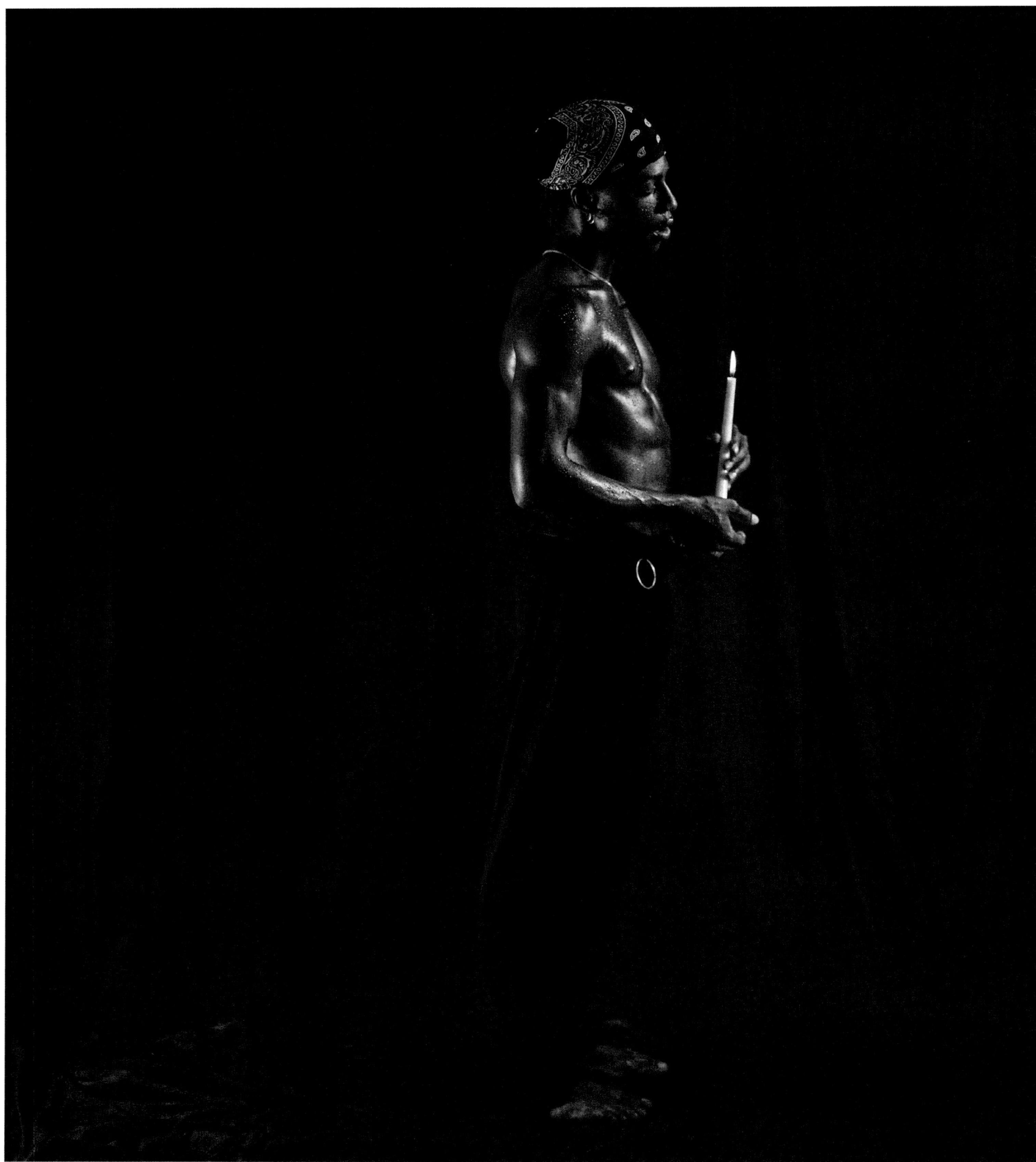

This page:
Oche (with candle), 2021

Opposite:
The Adoration (never knew love like this before), 2020
Unless otherwise noted, all photographs © the artist and courtesy Yossi Milo Gallery, New York

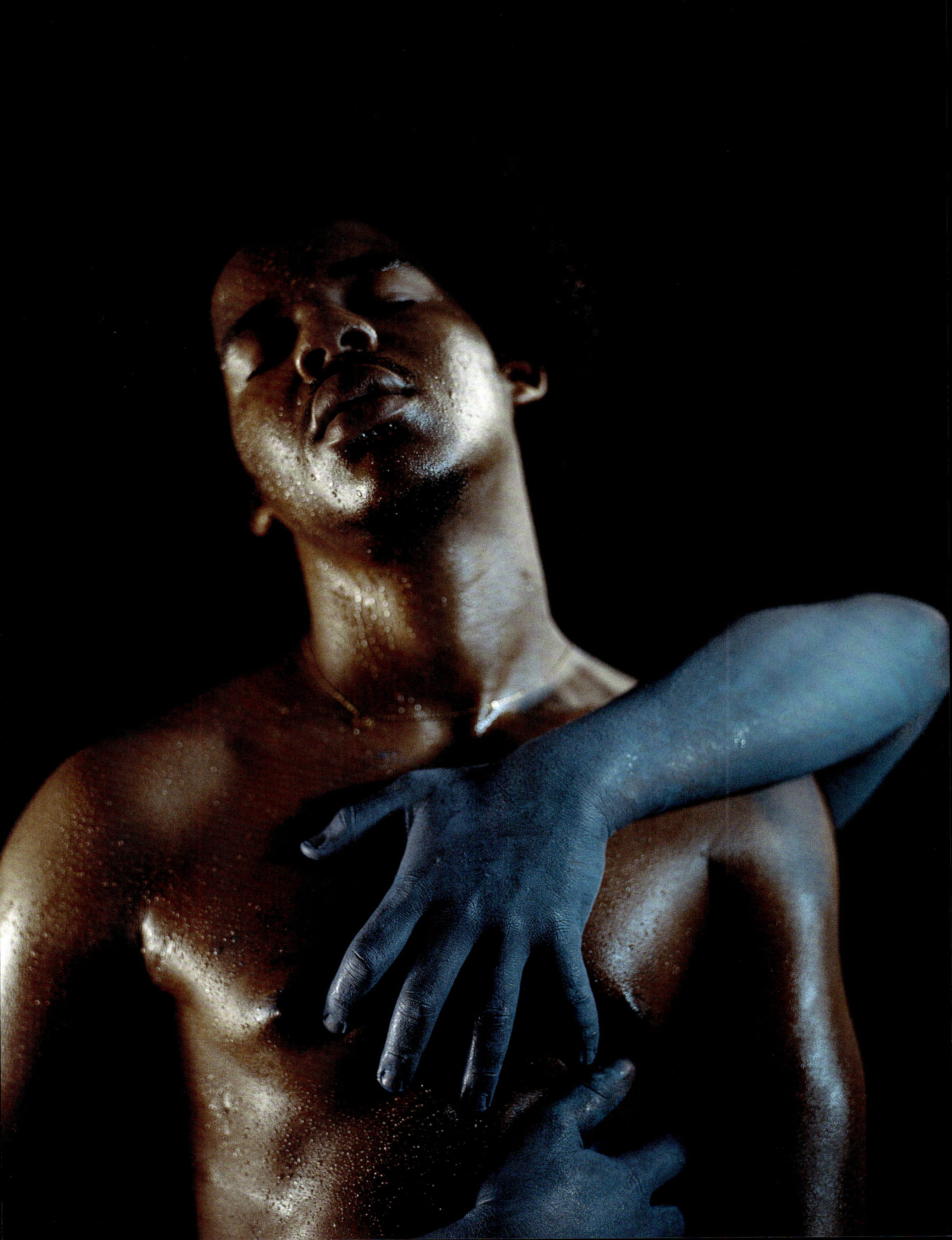

Heinkuhn Oh
Itaewon Story

Harry C. H. Choi

Behind the gleaming Namsan Tower that stands imposingly at the center of Seoul rests Itaewon, a compact quarter in which locals, artists, U.S. soldiers, drag performers, Muslims, gay men, transgender people, sex workers, and expats from around the world have long coexisted. The district's history is thorny: when the U.S. army established a base in the area in the years following the Korean War, it garnered a reputation as an untamed, foreign terrain where GIs and Americana ruled. Soon after, the neighborhood became a territory for outsiders of all kinds, offering refuge for those who did not belong anywhere else in the city. Seoul's inadvertent dip into multiculturalism thus began under the mythical, Cold War–inspired pretext of U.S. armed forces safeguarding democracy in South Korea—a nation that remains largely ethnically and culturally homogeneous to this day.

That gritty, crude version of Itaewon is extinct now for the most part, as relentless gentrification replaced small businesses with shiny but sterile coffee shops and restaurants. A glimpse into its past is nonetheless possible in the images of Heinkuhn Oh, who ventured out into the streets of Itaewon in 1993, shortly after studying photography in the U.S. at the Brooks Institute and Ohio University. As with his preceding series *Americans Them* (1990–91), which captures the raw, unglamorous lives of lay protagonists across Louisiana, Ohio, and Kentucky, *Itaewon Story* is tinted with a documentary outlook, curiously tapping into the disparate lives of individuals unfamiliar to the photographer. But if the earlier project portrayed rural America from the perspective of an outlander from the Far East, *Itaewon Story* locates the feeling of estrangement within the bounds of Oh's hometown. Its impetus perhaps originates with the mavericks who meandered the cramped streets between brothels and the nearby Seoul Central Mosque as well as Oh's own experience encountering his offbeat childhood neighborhood as a returnee from the United States.

Yet there is little distance between Oh and his protagonists in *Itaewon Story*. Theatrical as they might be, the characters of the series are photographed, in black and white, at moments of candor with minimal pretension, producing an unapologetic take on the traits of the locale. One image, *Jiyoung in the Itaewon Barbecue Ramen House*, features a young trans woman immaculately made-up, wearing a dark dress and a light-colored off-the-shoulder crop top, chuckling in the corner of a run-down restaurant whose walls are filled with graffiti. In another, Twist Kim, a forgotten movie star who made a living performing late-night shows in local bars and clubs, stands cheekily on the street with enough flair to land him on the cover of a fashion magazine. Astutely but affectionately, Oh's camera seizes these releases of fleeting freedom, only made possible in the corners of seedy Itaewon.

Oh's series thus resonates with other artistic endeavors to represent the marginalized and the vulnerable, including contemporaneous projects from the United States, such as *Hustlers* (1990–92) by Philip-Lorca diCorcia, that were shaped in the wake of the culture wars in the late 1980s and the early 1990s. Nonetheless, unlike counterparts across the Pacific, with *Itaewon Story*, Oh resists the temptation to politicize the identities of the individuals depicted—almost naively so, perhaps because there was no public sphere to accommodate discourses on identity at the time in South Korea. The series instead serves as a tender reminder of these Itaewon denizens' existence, capturing a certain childlike sensibility of the young artist. Oh's images demand that we remain curious about those strangers, foreigners, and outsiders around us, that we let them freely roam, showing us who they are.

Harry C. H. Choi is an art historian and curator based in San Francisco and Seoul.

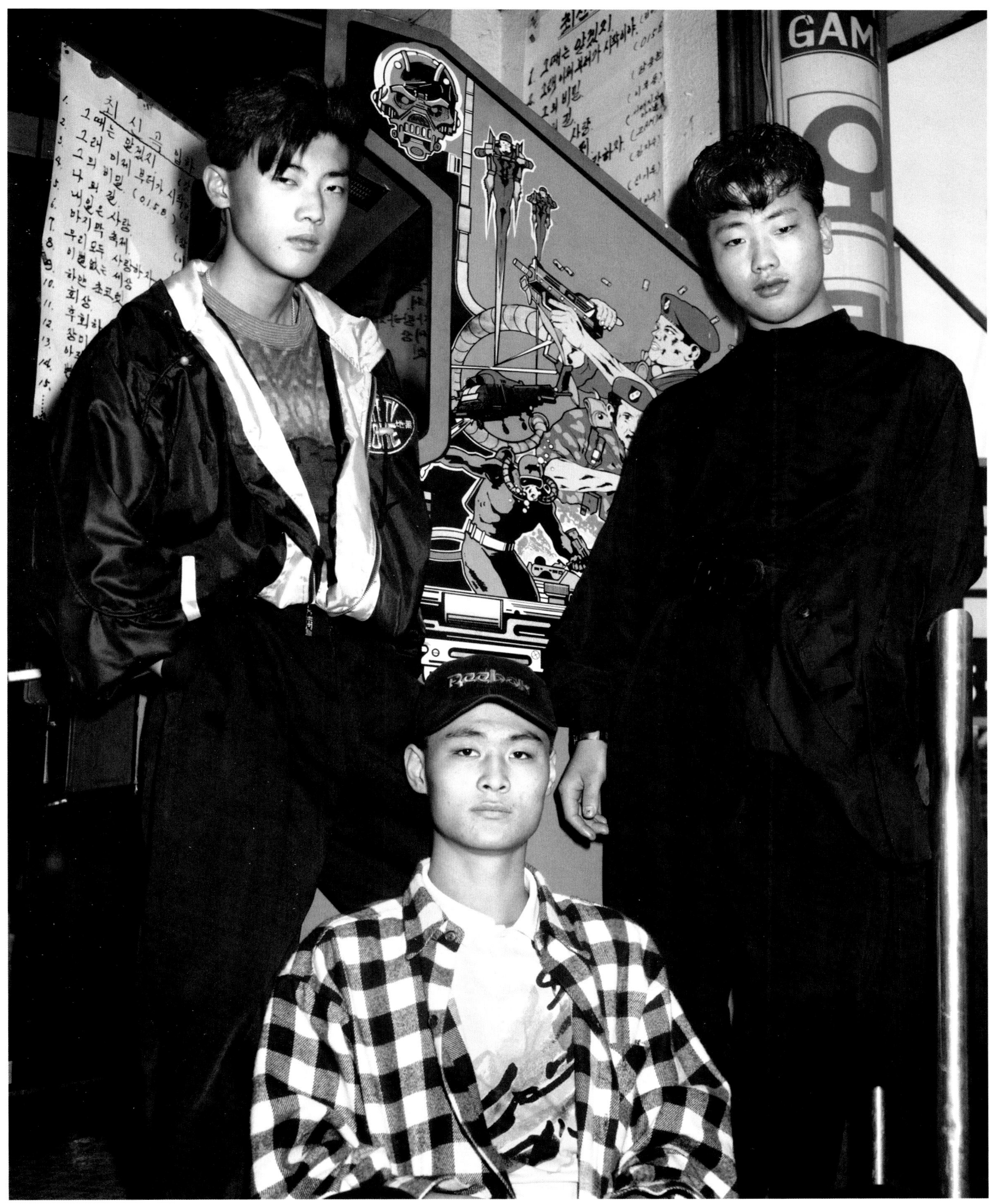

Kowon, Bowon, and Changgyu, Waiters, in Front of Bogwang Karaoke, May 1993

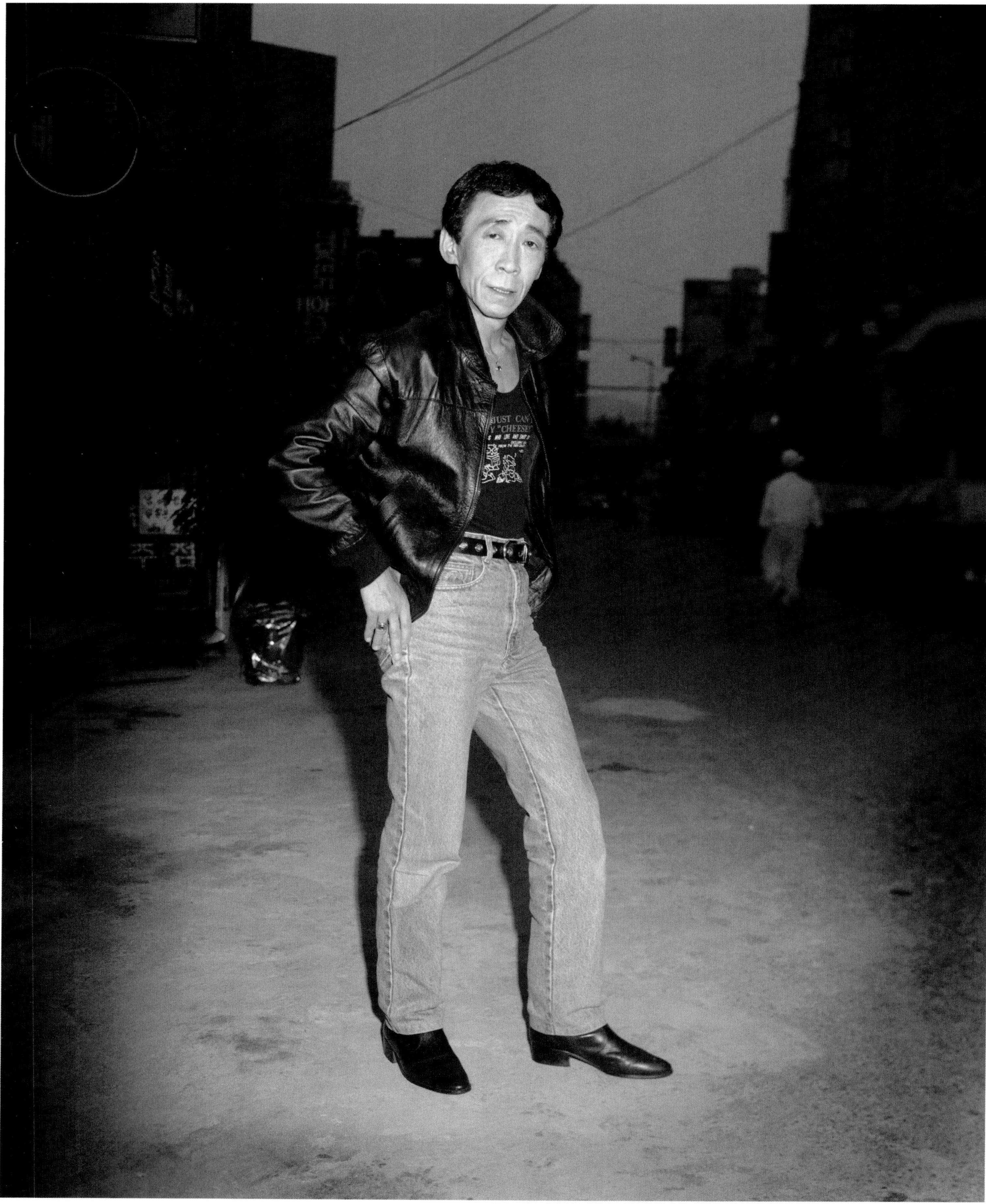

*Twist Kim, Actor and
Singer, March 1993*

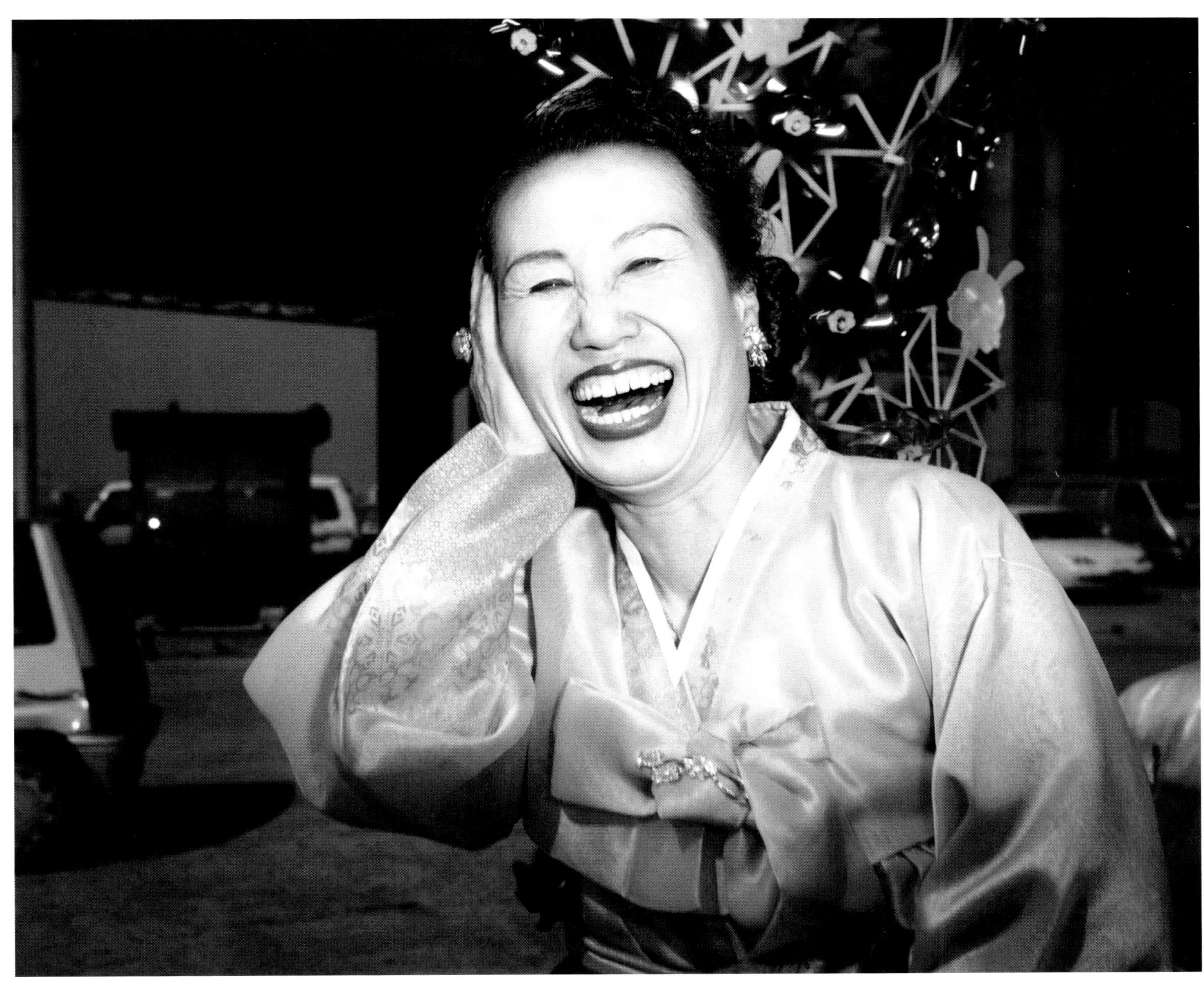

Background Actress,
June 1993

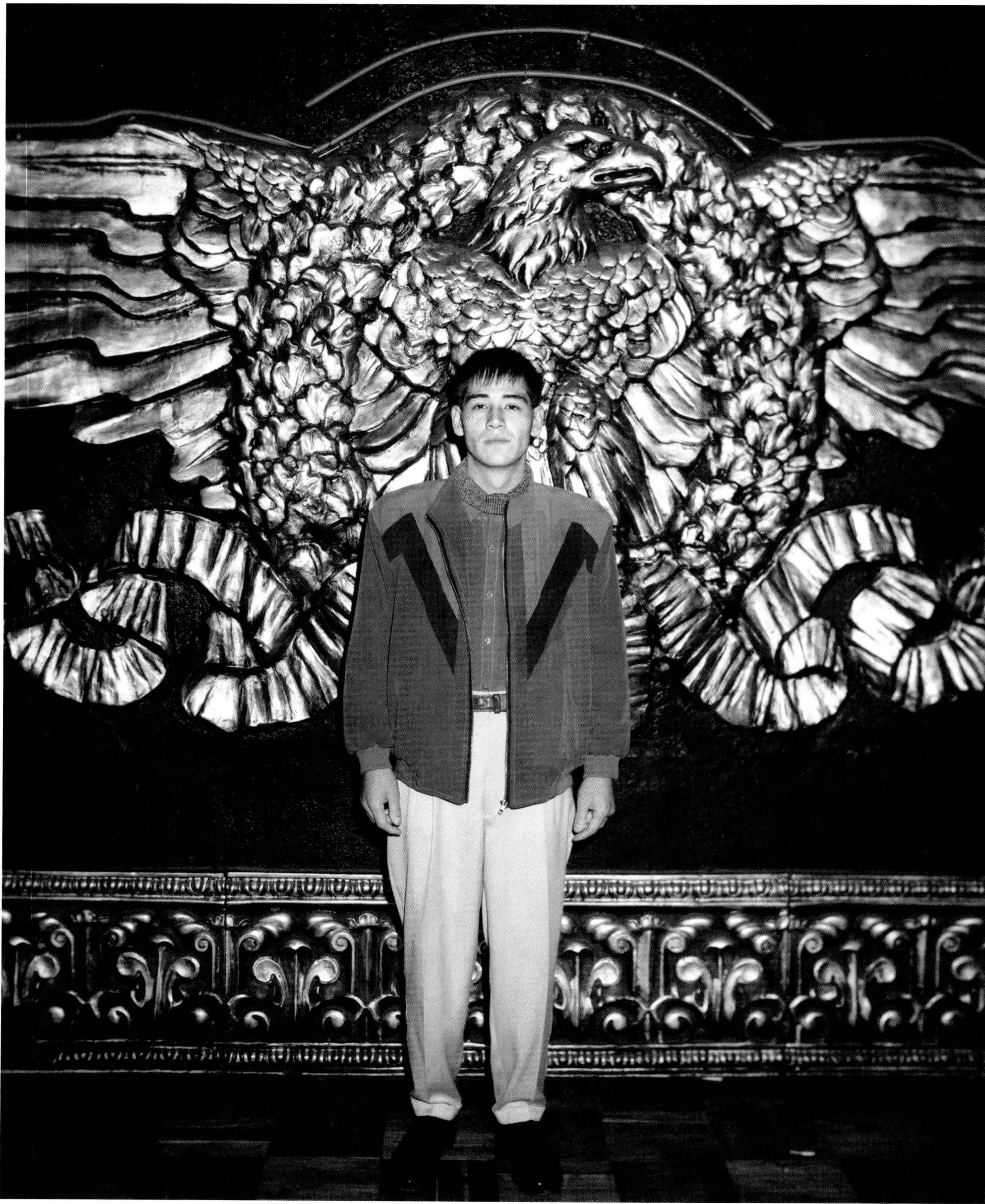

*Youngbok Han, GI Club
Waiter, on the Dance Floor
of King Club in Itaewon,
February 1993*

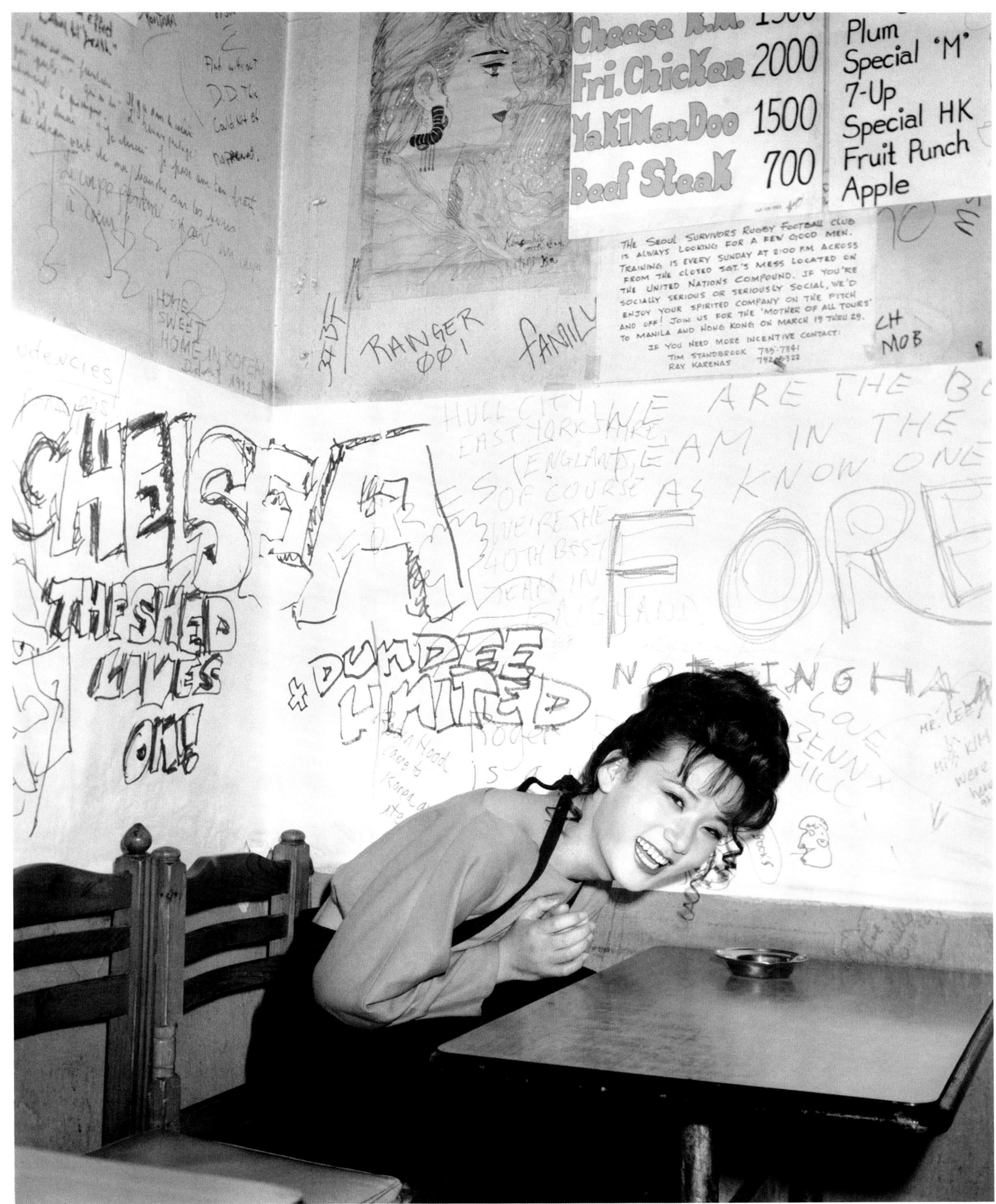

*Jiyoung in the Itaewon
Barbecue Ramen House,
February 1993*

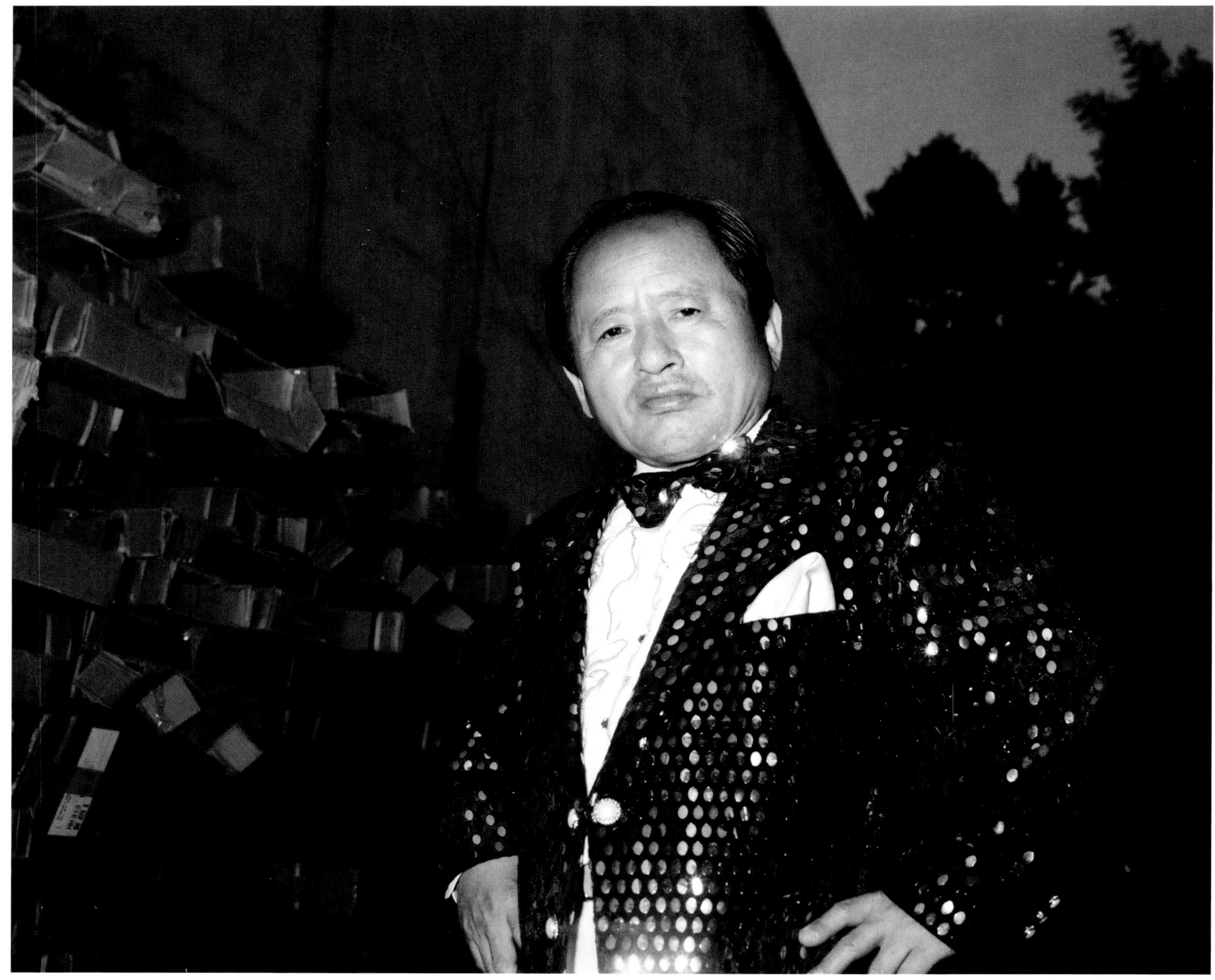

Bulyi Kim, Actor,
in a Backyard behind
Tae-pyoung Theater,
March 1993

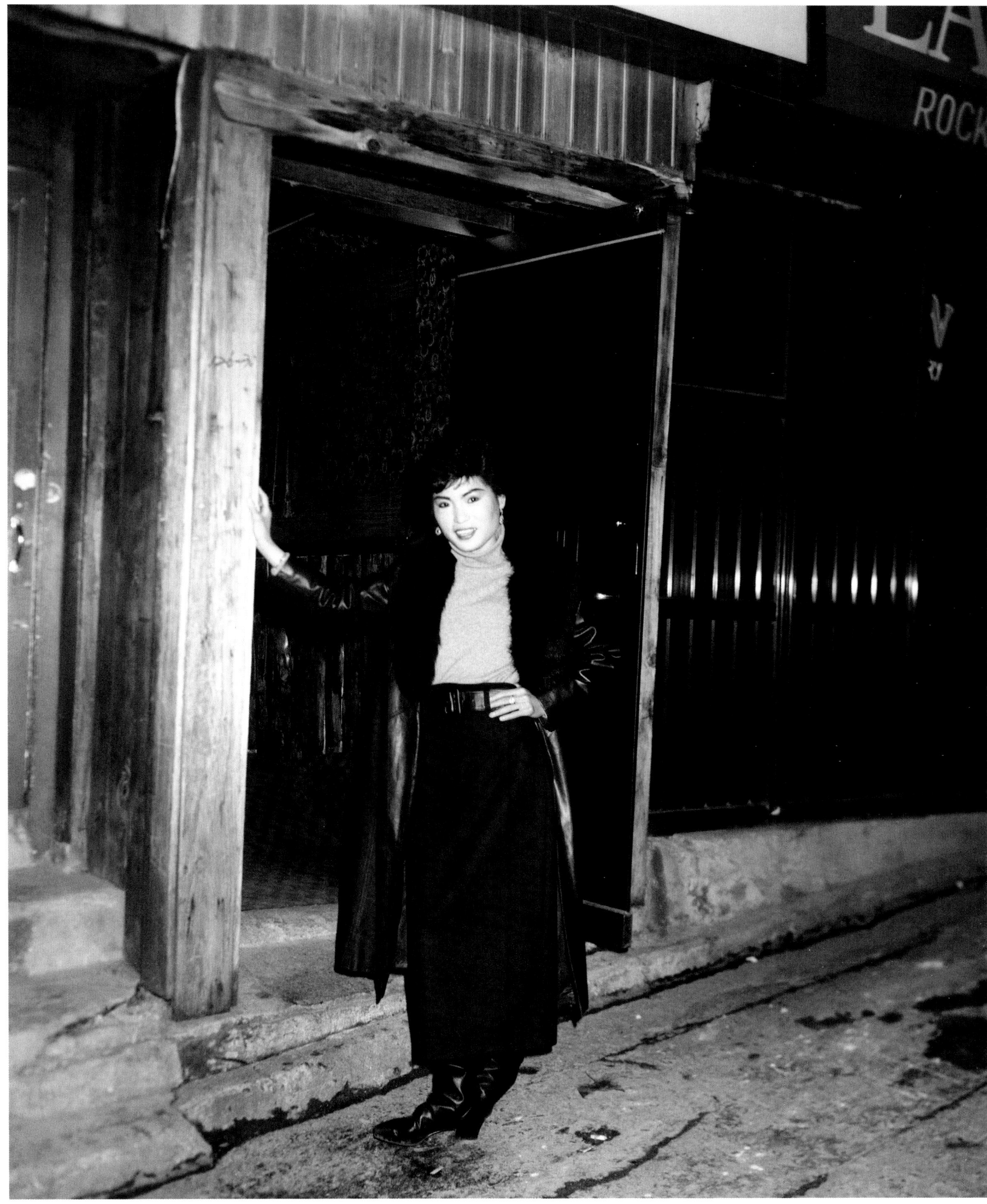

Some Lady on the Hill of Lucky Club, **January 1993**
All photographs courtesy the artist

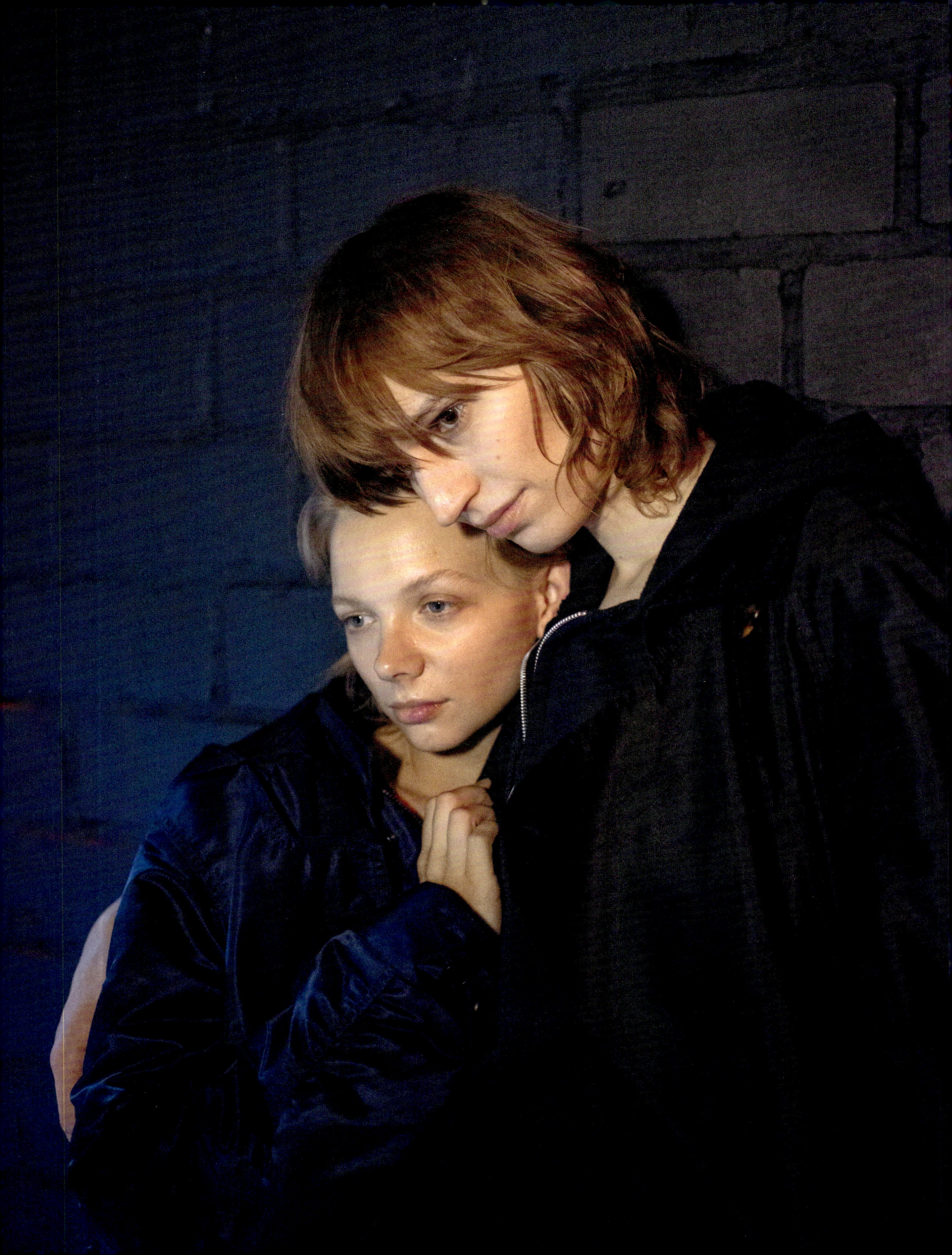

Tobias Zielony
After the Fall

A Conversation with Kimberly Bradley

For more than two decades, the German artist Tobias Zielony has been tracking people in marginalized communities, and the spaces they occupy, through the lenses of both still and motion-picture cameras. Treading a blurry line between documentary and fiction, his images primarily capture youths whose often-challenging milieus elicit a yearning for self-determination and varied forms of self-representation. Zielony infiltrates, even joins, his subjects' worlds—subcultures he finds around the globe, following his own curiosity, intuition, and instinct—to reveal the lesser seen layers of society.

Some of Zielony's early photographic series depict protagonists caught in webs of poverty in places such as Canada and California; later series see him diving into nightlife subcultures in Eastern Europe and Asia. Beyond still photographs, Zielony has also produced videos, including *Vele* (2009–10), an eerie, abstract look into a mostly abandoned, monumental housing project on the outskirts of Naples, and *Hurd's Bank* (2019), a fourteen-minute film based on oil smuggling off the coast of Malta. Last fall, while in Poland, Zielony spoke to the critic Kimberly Bradley about the strangeness of a mid-career survey exhibition, *Tobias Zielony: The Fall*, held in 2021 at the Museum Folkwang in Essen, Germany, and the difficulty of celebration in the midst of an ongoing global pandemic.

Kimberly Bradley: **This issue's theme is "celebrations"—but you've said your work isn't celebratory, which makes this interview a bit of a challenge! Still, your recent retrospective could certainly be seen as a celebration of your oeuvre thus far: around four hundred people attended the opening last June, a small miracle during a pandemic. How did the exhibition come together?**

Tobias Zielony: I was invited by the curator Thomas Seelig, and we decided to look back at the past twenty years of my work. It's really about going back and coming full circle, starting with early series such as *Car Park* from 2000 and *Curfew* from 2001 to *Vele* about the Scampia neighborhood in Naples. The other point was to have about half of the exhibition space devoted to videos, including *Al-Akrab* (2014) and *Big Sexyland* (2006). It was tempting to mount a big photography show, but we decided to add black-box spaces with projections and screens as well; in eleven or twelve rooms, the choreography went from bright to dark in a kind of topography that suits my work, which is so much related to night and darkness.

KB: **True, many of your photography series were made at night with protagonists from sex-work or club-culture contexts. But why include so much video?**

TZ: Video has become a crucial part of my art, and the videos are related to the photographic still images, meaning they use animation and stop motion. *The Fall* was a look at a long period of my work, but also about the relationship between still and moving images and everything in between.

KB: **What was it like to assemble such an exhibition in your late forties? Retrospectives are interesting for artists, like you, who are not that old. It must be intriguing to be in a position to reflect on what you've done so far.**

TZ: It did make me *feel* a bit older, but we mostly avoided the term retrospective. Let's say it was a *mid-career* retrospective. And we tried to keep it from becoming too retrospective-like: One way was how we designed the space, which had a kind of makeshift quality, using a lot of cheap materials. The other was hosting workshops that activated the exhibition and made it feel current and present. And the third is the catalog, which isn't a huge brick of a book, like so many are, but rather a series of shorter volumes with essays written by young writers, none older than thirty-three, not necessarily interpreting my art, but . . .

KB: **Adding to it, augmenting it. Some of the essays are almost literary, responding to specific series in your oeuvre.**

TZ: Personally, I think that many photography shows are boring. You come into a big white space and have small or medium-size images along the walls and a big vacuum in the middle. We also tried to present my works that are not the typical photographic series; ones that are more

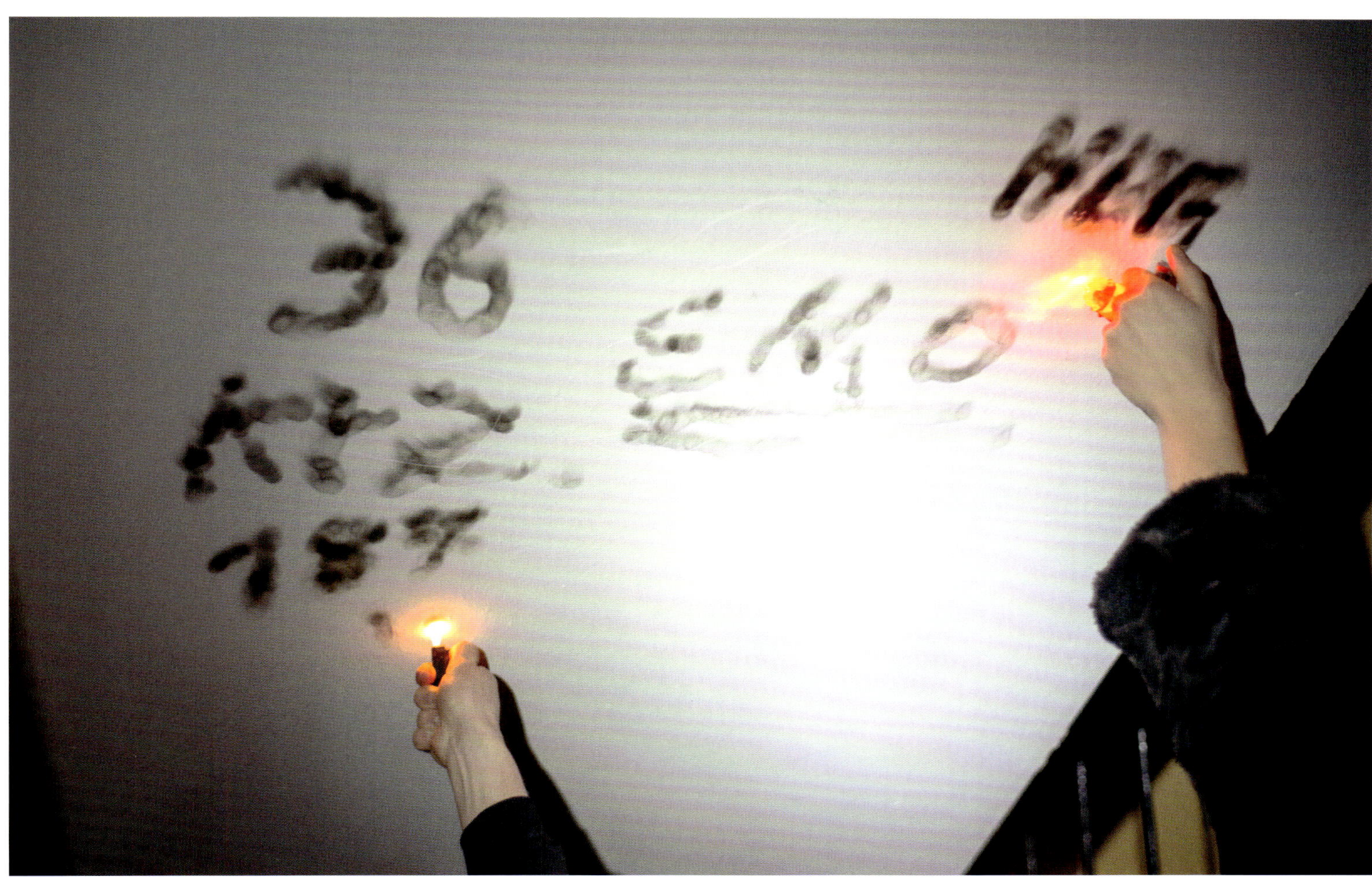

installation based or somehow extend into the rooms.

KB: ***The Citizen* from the German pavilion at the Venice Biennale in 2015 is one example. Starting in 2014, you followed and photographed groups of refugees and activists struggling for recognition and human rights in Hamburg and Berlin; then you activated newspapers in countries such as Uganda, Cameroon, Nigeria, and Sudan to publish the images of these people with stories of their difficulties. In Venice, these images were shown not as framed portraits but in newspaper format, installed on vertical structures.**

TZ: For *The Fall*, we created a different way of presenting *The Citizen* that worked well, with vitrines and the large layout images at varying heights on the wall, going high up. It was a condensed, more accessible version of this project. The focus was clearly on the original newspaper articles, which we showed under glass for everyone to read.

KB: **Could you talk about *The Fall* (2021), your recent body of work?**

TZ: So *The Fall* is the name of the overall exhibition and the book series, but it is

The Fall was a look at a long period of my work, but also about the relationship between still and moving images and everything in between.

also the title of this new piece that became an installation. The title came from the beginning of the pandemic—it's about me falling down a skate ramp while I was photographing, but also this feeling of general catastrophe or emergency. In the main room of the exhibition, we built a kind of wooden stage, or ramp. That was the venue for the workshops, which were all about the idea of falling—falling and standing up again. On the walls were forty-five large inkjet color prints starting at 50 centimeters by 70 centimeters, with the largest being 80 by 120 or so. They all differed in size and are like copy-shop prints, overlapping and forming this kind of frieze along the walls. It had the feeling of something impermanent. The layout, this kind of layering, was a reference not only to the stop-motion films I make, but also to the way we use and perceive social media. Each time we add an image on Instagram, another moves further down. It's a constantly evolving and self-rewriting archive.

KB: **The images include portraits you were commissioned by the French magazine *Numéro* to make of Berliners born after 1989, and photographs from the industrial Ruhr region in Germany, and even the basketball player Dirk Nowitzki's last season with the Dallas**

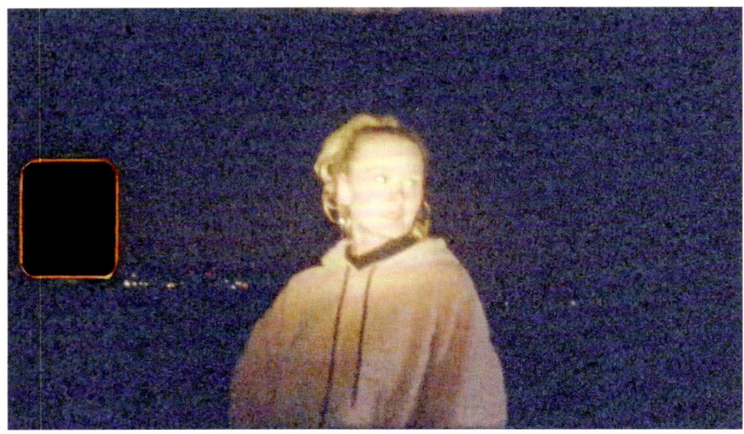

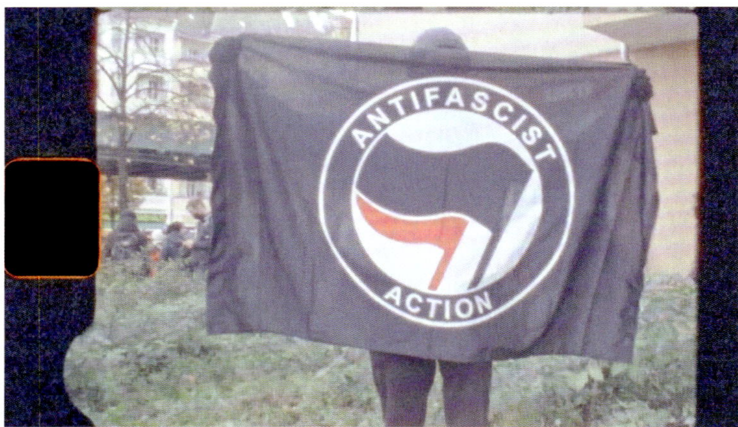

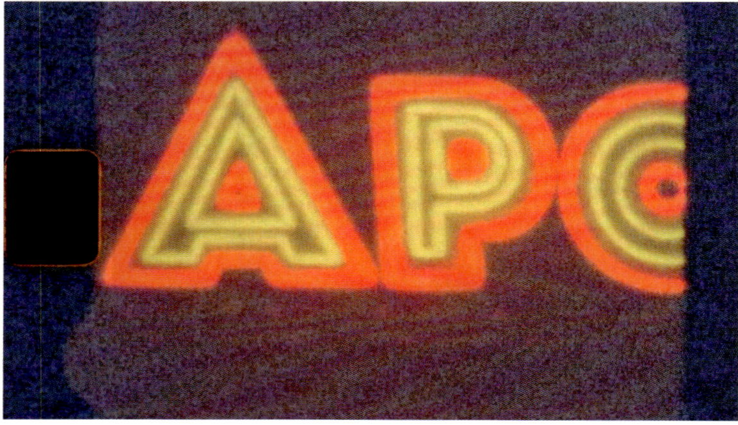

Stills from *Apollo*, 2021.
Digitized Super-8 film,
9 minutes, 23 seconds,
color, no sound

There has always been an aspect in my work that looks into what connects people in very different and often faraway places.

been an aspect in my work that looks into what connects people in very different and often faraway places.

On the superficial level, that could be sportswear, or poses related to an increasingly globalizing pop culture. On a deeper level, we are witnessing the fall of the neoliberal model. It has a more personal archive aspect as well: my nephew and brother are both pictured. It was beautiful to see pictures that normally would be single images not connected to any series, and I could edit them in. There was a long, almost meditative process during the lockdown in which I arranged the images on my studio wall, but there is no coherent narrative. It has the feeling that the narrative is never-ending, or it's just updating itself. Maybe that's what I was trying to achieve.

KB: **Much of your work is not just about the lines between documentary and self-representation but also indirectly critiquing media representation. You chose to include a Super-8 film as part of the installation.**

TZ: There's a screen standing on the floor with transferred Super-8 footage, and all of the scenes in the film, *Apollo* (2021), are running backward. I made it almost a diary of 2020. It ends with New Year's Eve 2020–21, with fireworks, but the fireworks fly backward, and skaters fall but then stand back up, and the water cannons suck in water. In it are also demonstrations in Berlin against COVID-19 restrictions. Are we going toward the future or back in the past? Are we going into a *better* future or something else? In this sense, the Super-8 film is anything but nostalgic.

KB: **This idea of falling and standing up reminds me of the essay by Joshua Gross, one of the writers in the first volume of the exhibition catalog. He refers to the opening scene in Werner Herzog's film *Heart of Glass* in which a character talks about tumbling deeper and deeper but then falling upward. He also references the writing of the philosopher Marcus Steinweg, with Gross stating that "falling can have a subversive power." I sometimes wonder if, in your work, you're searching for a kind of liberation from social oppression.**

TZ: I'm from a generation that's torn between having this upbringing in West Germany as a child where there was still the idea that the world is getting better,

Mavericks, which you did for a book project about him. But also portraits from recent trips. It's far less discrete than your other series in terms of context or location.**

TZ: The piece covers the past two or three years, with some exceptions. Archival material or work I've done for projects that have not yet been shown in art spaces—but much of it has been seen on my Instagram account—are also a part of it. The images come from diverse places: Korea and Japan, Germany, Malta, Palestine. For the first time, it brings together pictures from various contexts. So, it's not a series about a specific place or a group of people. It felt liberating to break out of this strict organization. It's more like a diary. And, of course, there has always

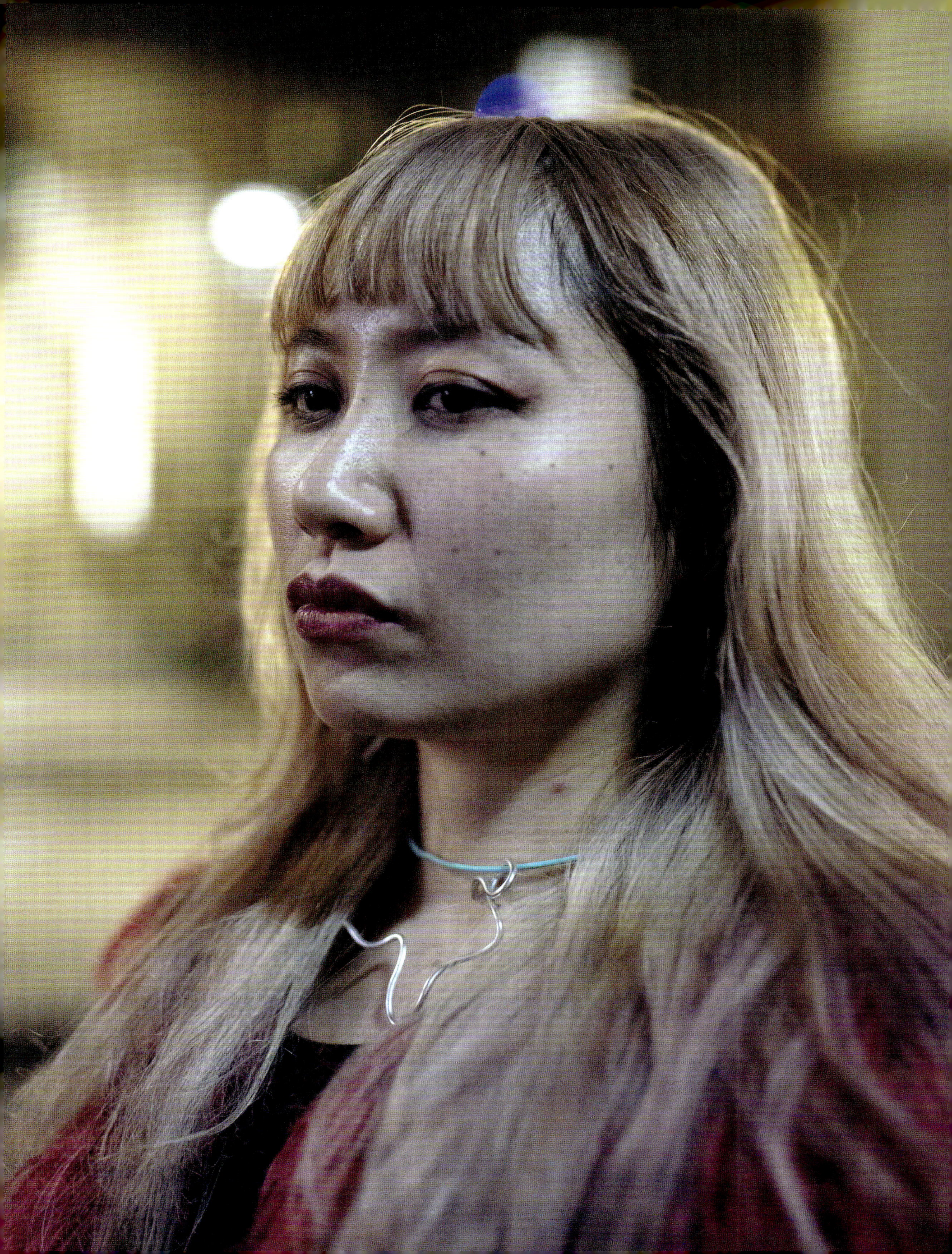

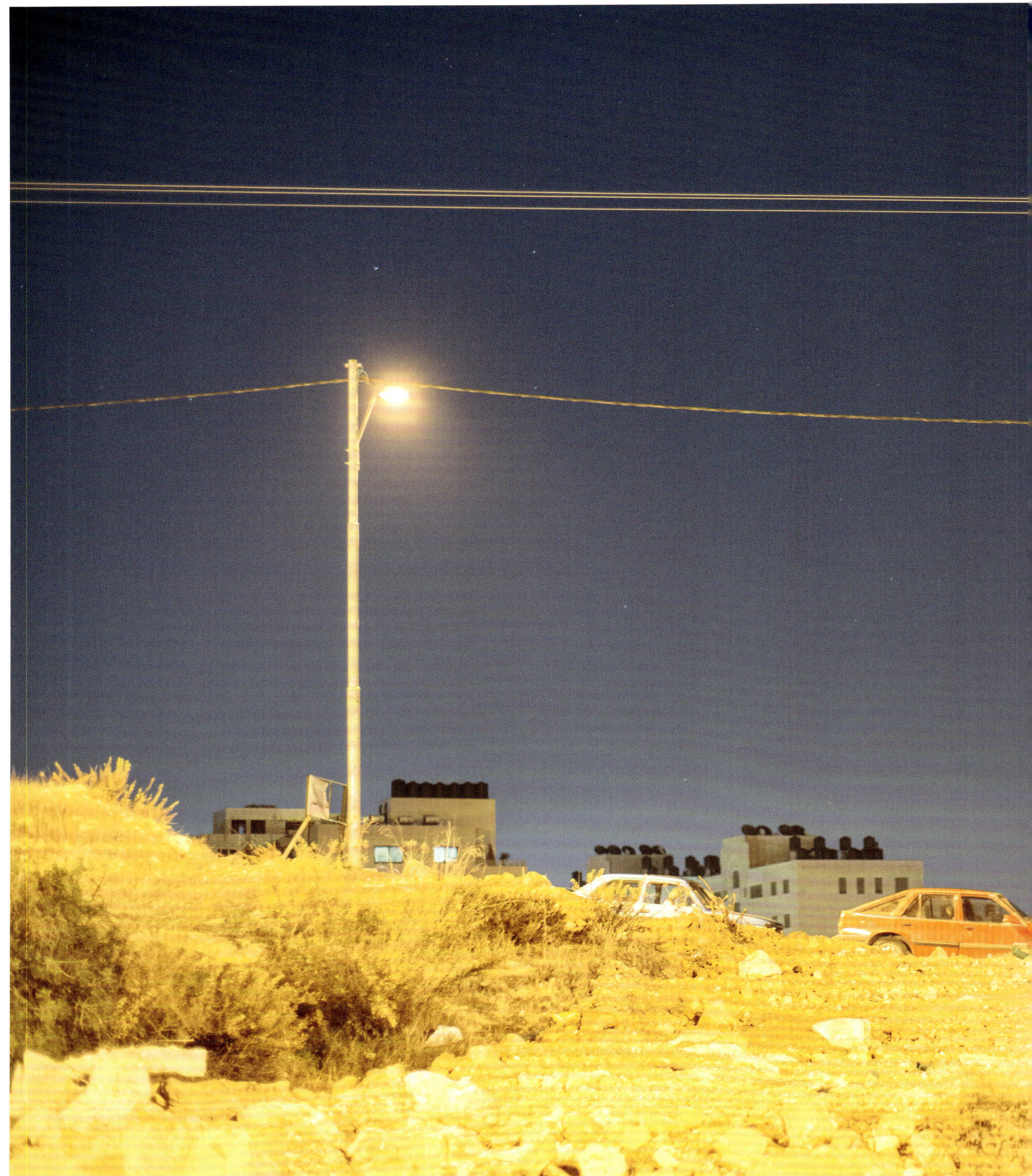

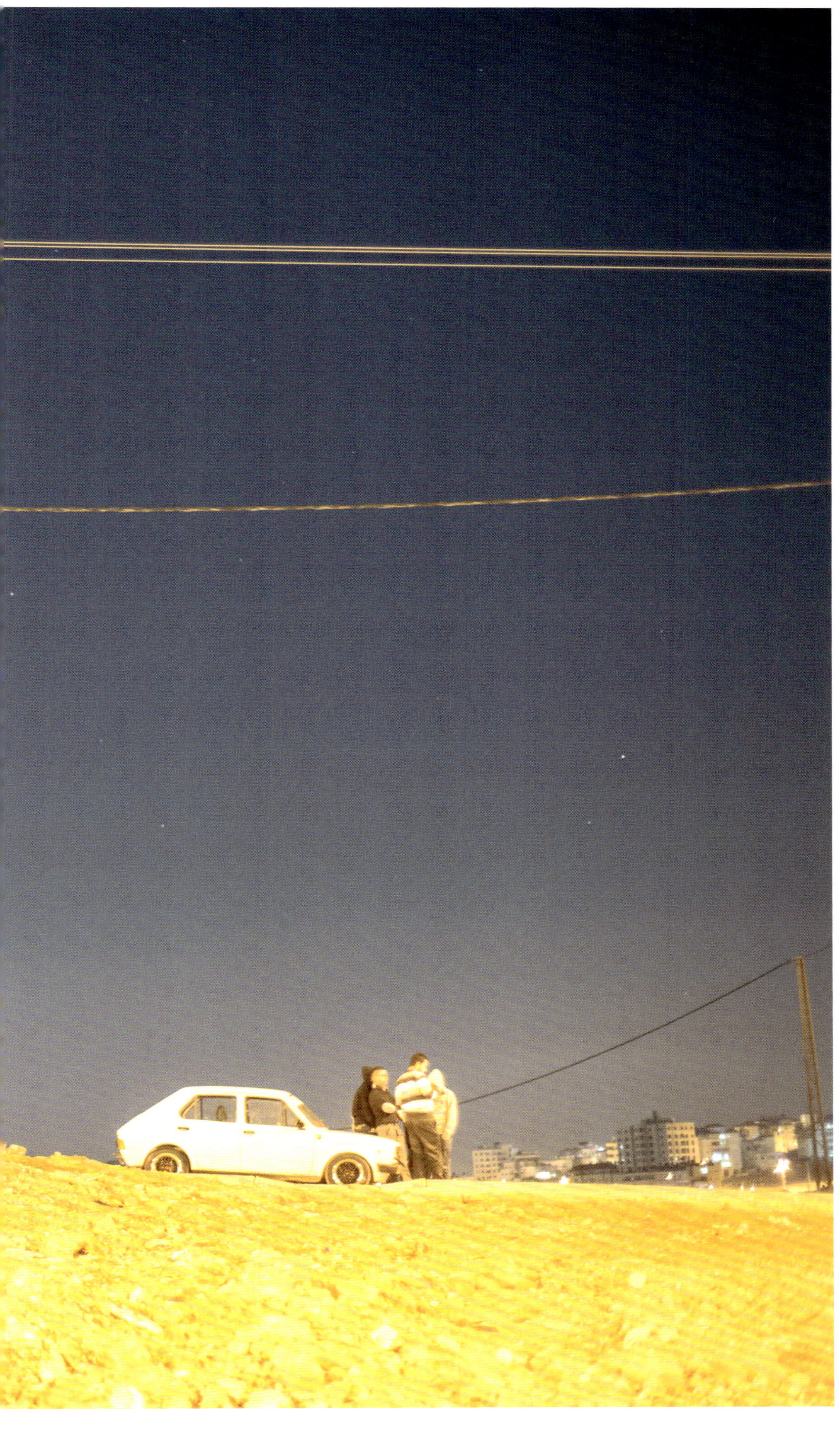

and we're all safe, and our parents are happy, and we have good politicians. There was a short period when a large part of the population thought that things were okay. Maybe it was just an illusion from the beginning. But, then, we were hit hard, of course. The punk movement was one of the voices to declare there was no future, and then turned destruction or negation into something subversive or liberating. I am not sure if that's really the case, but I grew up feeling that it's good to rebel and oppose. That's what we see happening right now. As a teenager, I worked at punk concerts, and, sometimes, my job was to be onstage and throw people back into the crowd. I appreciate this kind of feeling that it's okay to struggle or to fall. And, it's also important to help other people out.

KB: **Gross also mentions the "depressive hedonia" concept from the cultural theorist and philosopher Mark Fisher in his 2009 book *Capitalist Realism: Is There No Alternative?* It's not about the inability to achieve pleasure, but rather the inability to do anything but pursue it. There's some celebration within the hedonism implied here.**

TZ: People see my work and often say, "Oh, it's depressing" but it was never depressing for me. I maybe even felt it to be more like something liberating. We've spoken before about the boredom that I try to capture in these social groups, but once you're immersed in a "bored" state of mind or lifestyle, this lack of events might become enjoyable or hedonistic. But it has some more problematic aspects. Mark Fisher is between those poles. Of course, now we can say pleasure-seeking is very much related to neoliberal capitalism, or of leaving people not in the workforce out of the picture; it turns them into pure consumers. It's not so easy to celebrate that, but from my perspective, it was more about looking at the subversion or rebellion—of not doing what you're supposed to do.

KB: **I wonder if there's anything to celebrate right now as we head into another pandemic winter in Europe, and the continent is faced with increasing political upheaval. You're in Warsaw at the moment, talking to locals about the political situations there, exploring a potential project. Politics are unstable, but there's a strong sense of solidarity among the people. Could you talk about works in progress?**

TZ: There's one project in Bitterfeld-Wolfen, Germany, where the ORWO film factory used to be, which I can't speak about quite yet but involves unemployed people from the factory, older people. And then I'd like to be more in Poland, if possible. The general situation in Poland is similar to that in other European countries where there's a turning toward a weird control of the media. There are threads that are alt-right and neofascist, and there's toxic masculinity, but there's also a very neoliberal kind of direction. At the same time, in Poland, there's a lot of resistance from the people. One aspect I'm interested in is the forest on the border with Russia, where migrants are trying to enter from Belarus through a wooded area. I don't know if I'll follow up, but that's also why I'm here talking with people involved in a movement to protect the same forest. There are fights between environmentalists and the logging companies. A new project could come out of this. I'll see.

KB: The earliest phases of your work are quite similar to those of investigative journalists, even if your methods thereafter are different.

TZ: I talk to people, and I find out what's going on as well as I can, and go along with that, and then try to link local communities or grassroots movements. It could also be a party culture: some of my series focus on club kids and techno. But this happens within a bigger framework that also relates to things on a level that makes sense in places outside Poland. I went to an outdoor performance of a queer collective and also accompanied a friend to a demonstration as well as the workshop preparing banners for the event. I had my camera with me but that is not the most important part.

KB: I've been asking one question in almost all the interviews I do lately: Are you optimistic or pessimistic about the current global situation?

TZ: I am actually quite pessimistic. I'm not opening the door and thinking, Oh my God, the world is going to explode. But if I'm pragmatic, I don't see a good ending. Major crises will be coming up soon in terms of climate change but also politically. I worry about the ignorance that's governing public discussion, about how politicians chase this minority of cynical, nonempathetic, toxic people. In the United States as well as in Germany, Austria, and Poland, for sure, these people have this feeling that now is their time to speak up for revenge against

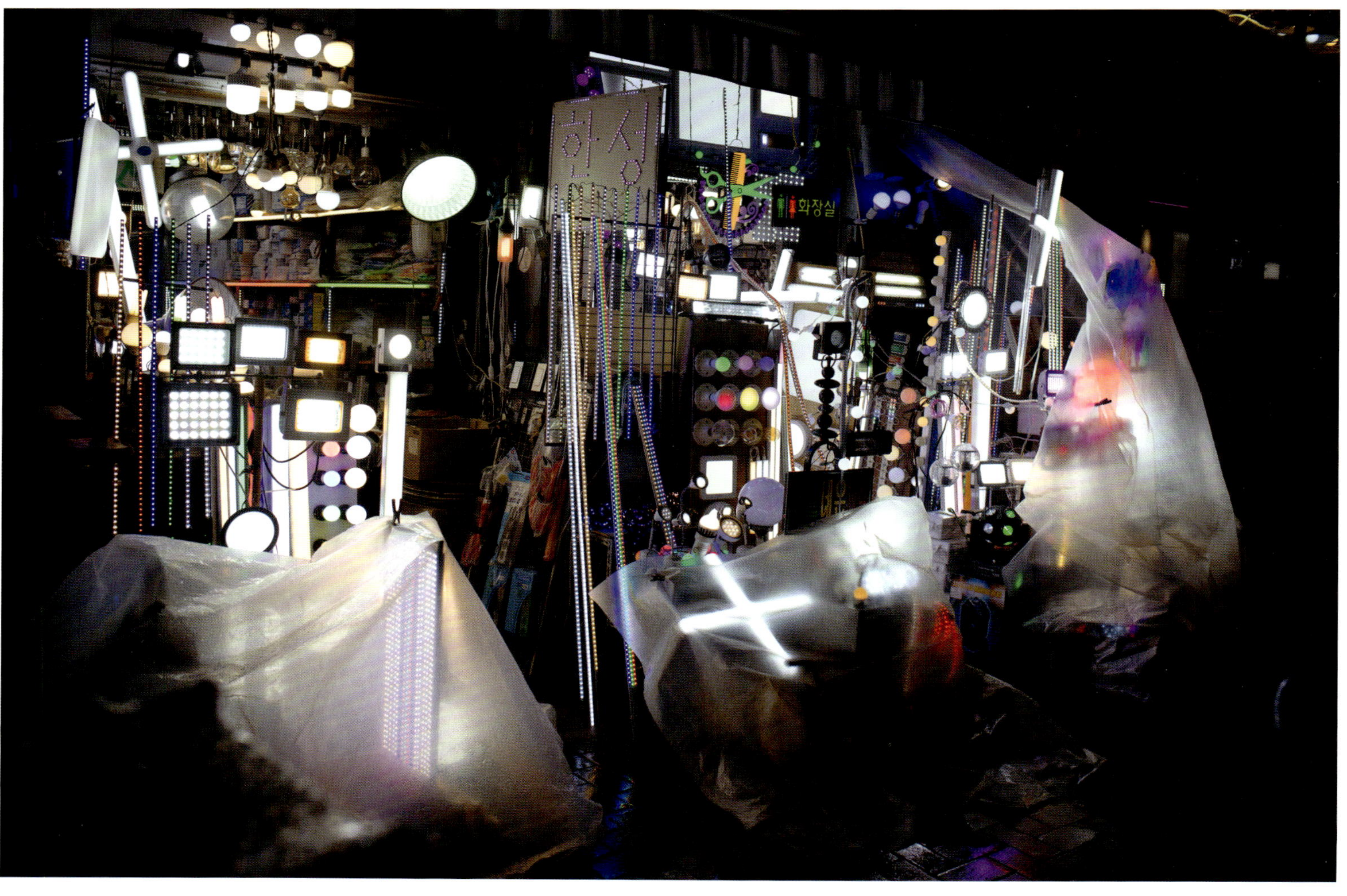

From my perspective, it was more about looking at the subversion or rebellion—of not doing what you're supposed to do.

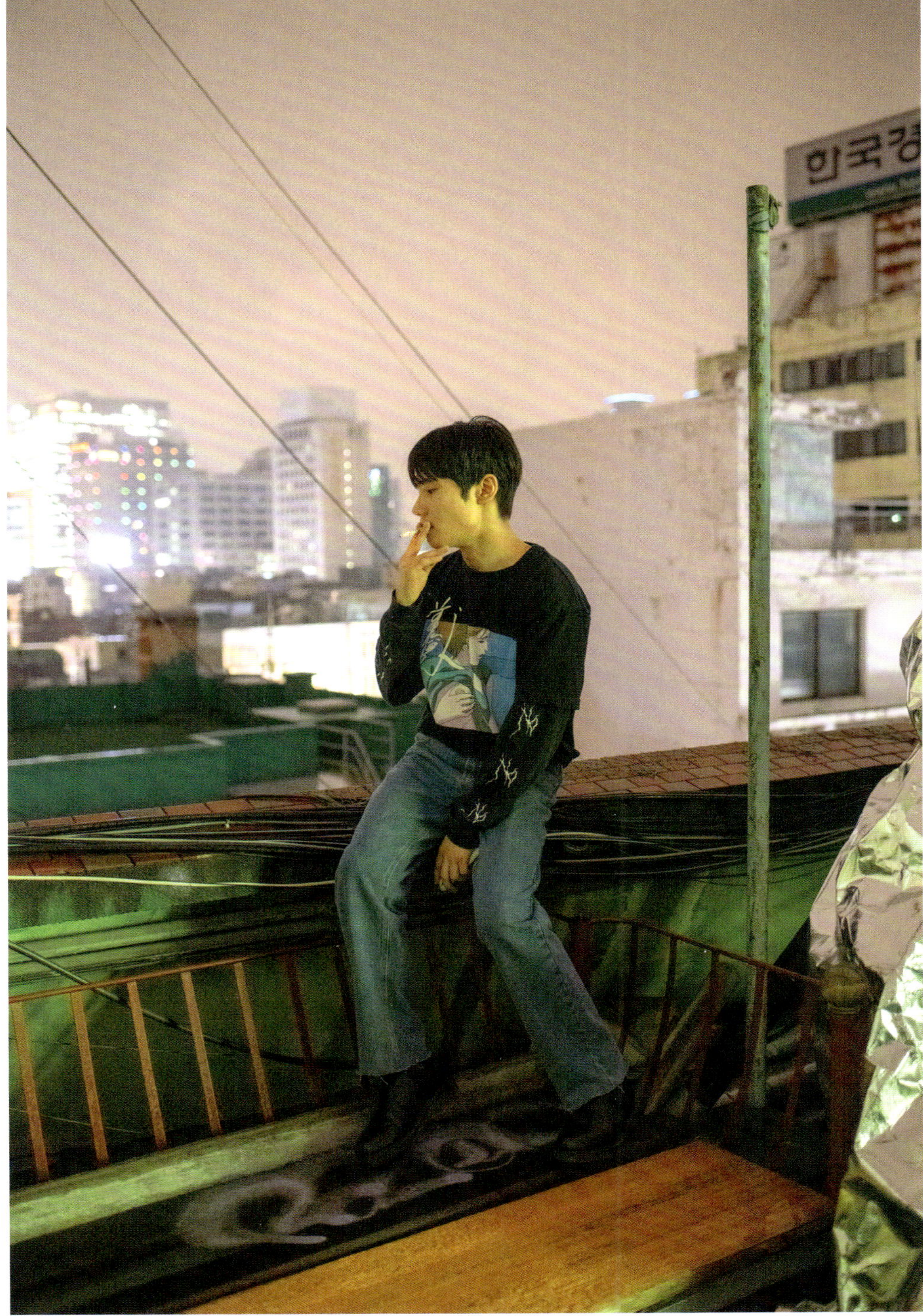

whatever they consider to be liberal. I'm worried about that. I don't even know if it's about democracy: the crisis is more general and democracy is no longer able to pacify large parts of the population. Maybe being here in Poland makes me more worried. The same with the pandemic. Beyond what we think is truth, or what the pandemic is about, we just open the gates to all kinds of fantasies. It's almost like children who don't want to know what's going on.

KB: **I worry, too, but I have moments of optimism in which I see a critical mass building of people who were complacent before. Now, they're activating to not only preserve the better parts**

of democracy but also, and more importantly, to think of new systems that might work better.

TZ: I agree with you. Of course, I'm on the side of the people who think that it is time for a change now more than ever. But I wonder if we are strong enough or radical enough.

KB: **Things are not going to be easy. Can we find other ways to celebrate?**

TZ: There's nothing wrong with celebrating and coming together. I don't even think we always need reasons to do so. I see it more in the social aspect

rather than celebrating one hundred years of this or that. We rely on looking back at our lives, and the lives of our friends—appreciating the things we've been doing together in whatever ways—and working toward a future focusing on care and solidarity.

Kimberly Bradley is an art critic and writer based in Berlin. She is the Berlin correspondent for *Monocle* magazine, and her work has appeared in *ArtReview*, *Frieze*, *PIN-UP*, and the *New York Times*.

Jean Depara
Night Revels of Kinshasa

Yasmina Price

Jean Depara's photographs of nocturnal cosmopolitanism capture the effervescent sense of possibility that preceded and accompanied the Democratic Republic of the Congo's shift from Belgian colony to early years of independence, in the mid-1950s to mid-1960s. A hedonistic night owl roving around the nightclubs and bars of the capital, Depara lived his photography as a participant-observer. Depara's practice began in 1951. His big break came in 1954, when he became the personal photographer for Franco, then the magnetic star of Congolese rumba. Depara opened his own studio, Jean Whisky Depara, two years later, establishing himself in portrait and street photography, often capturing vivacious scenes of Kinshasa's nightlife. From 1975 to 1989, Depara lent his services to the government, retiring soon after and finally gaining international recognition in the 1990s, just before his death in 1997.

These images document the eruptive celebratory atmosphere and exercises in urban self-fashioning during a period of tangled transformations. Independence was declared in 1960, but within months, the Pan-Africanist nationalist Patrice Lumumba—one of the country's key architects of anti-colonial liberation—was assassinated. Photography was also in the expanding stages of being used independently *by* African continentals, instead of against them as a colonial technology. In Depara's hands, photography synthesized how political currents registered on the lived scale of people off the clock—not just from their daytime obligations but also from official time lines. His depictions represent a site of slippage, revealing the scrambled temporalities beneath the definitive aspirations of official proclamations. In one image (ca. 1955–65), a young woman with her hand on the horn of an open convertible casts an annoyed sideways glance; her bejeweled impatience with a tardy paramour also channels a more collective longing for a new social and political order.

Depara's style of sensual anarchy defied the notion of a fixed, stable event to offer, instead, a popular reality that existed in the interstices of colonization and decolonization. This period of pleasure-driven abandon in the urban fulcrum of Kinshasa was fueled by cultural pluralities. The music of Franco and his dapper OK Jazz group—pictured in a staged portrait that vibrates with the unpredictable potential of what their music would unleash that night—were sonic manifestations of such syncretism. The emergence of transnationally influenced "modern" popular music in 1950s Congo was the ambient fabric for Depara's photographs. This music of the night was made for the ephemeral encounters and sticky proximities: Depara shows us three men leaning on each other like fleshy dominoes, sly smiles forecasting the revelry to come; or two *sapeurs* posed with impeccable elegance outside a bar. A remarkable quality in Depara's images, even without picturing musicians, is their musicality, an ebullient tension on the cusp of movement that precisely captures the moments of quiet and ebb that also constitute festivity.

Depara's photographs chronicled forms of living that—while they could never be equivalents to economic and national autonomy for the African continent—survived the demise of political projects and were the embers for their potential renewal. The dynamic habitués of nightlife wove a fabric of regenerative possibility: Depara's subjects danced, flirted, drank, and lingered, providing evidence of the euphoric ripples of a people at a time of rediscovery, and offering a glittery suggestion that avenues for collective self-governance could always be celebrated.

A model at the "Festival des Jolies Filles," a fashion show organized by a women's society, Kinshasa, Saturday, September 5, 1959

Yasmina Price is a PhD student in the departments of African American studies and film and media studies at Yale University.

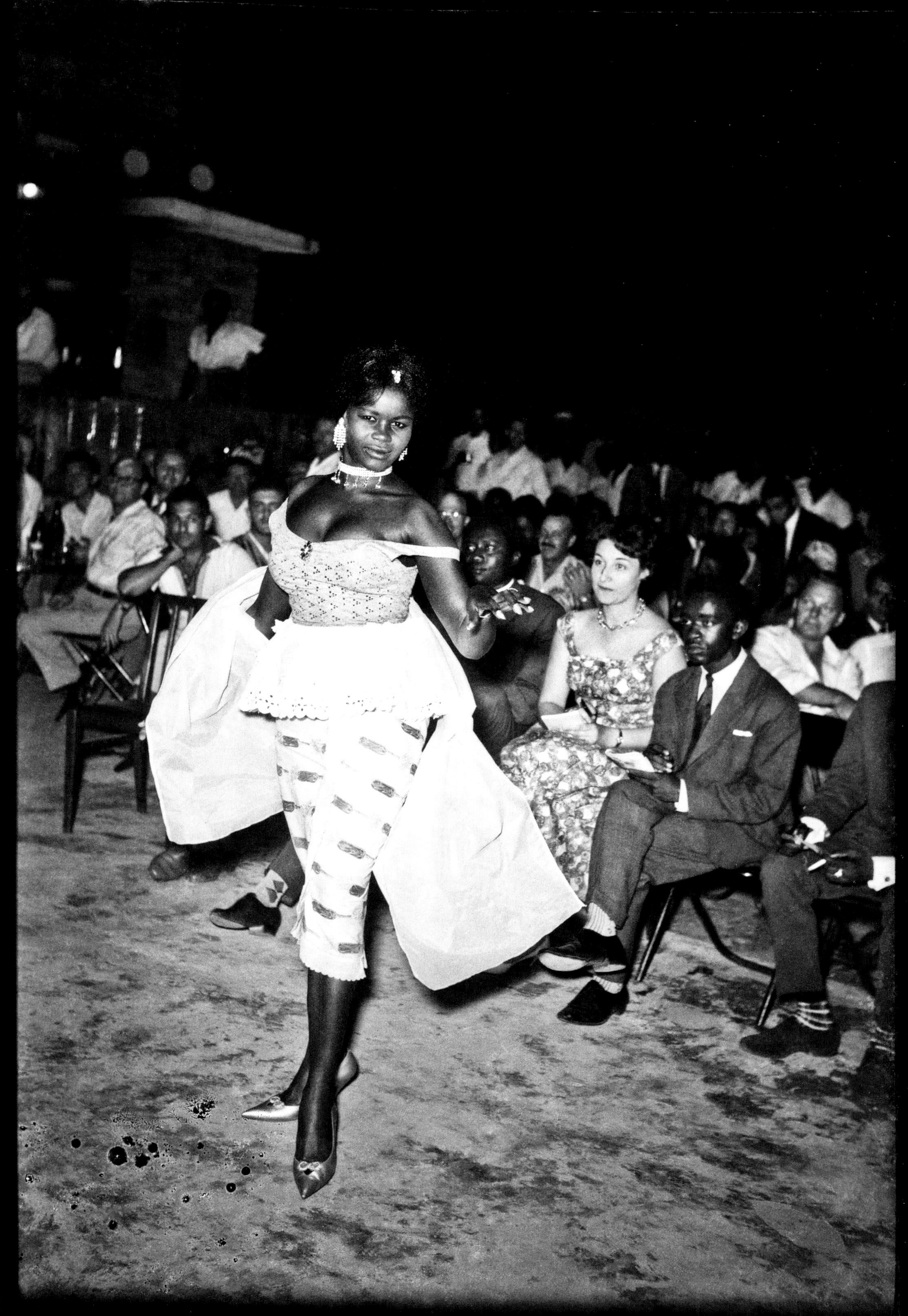

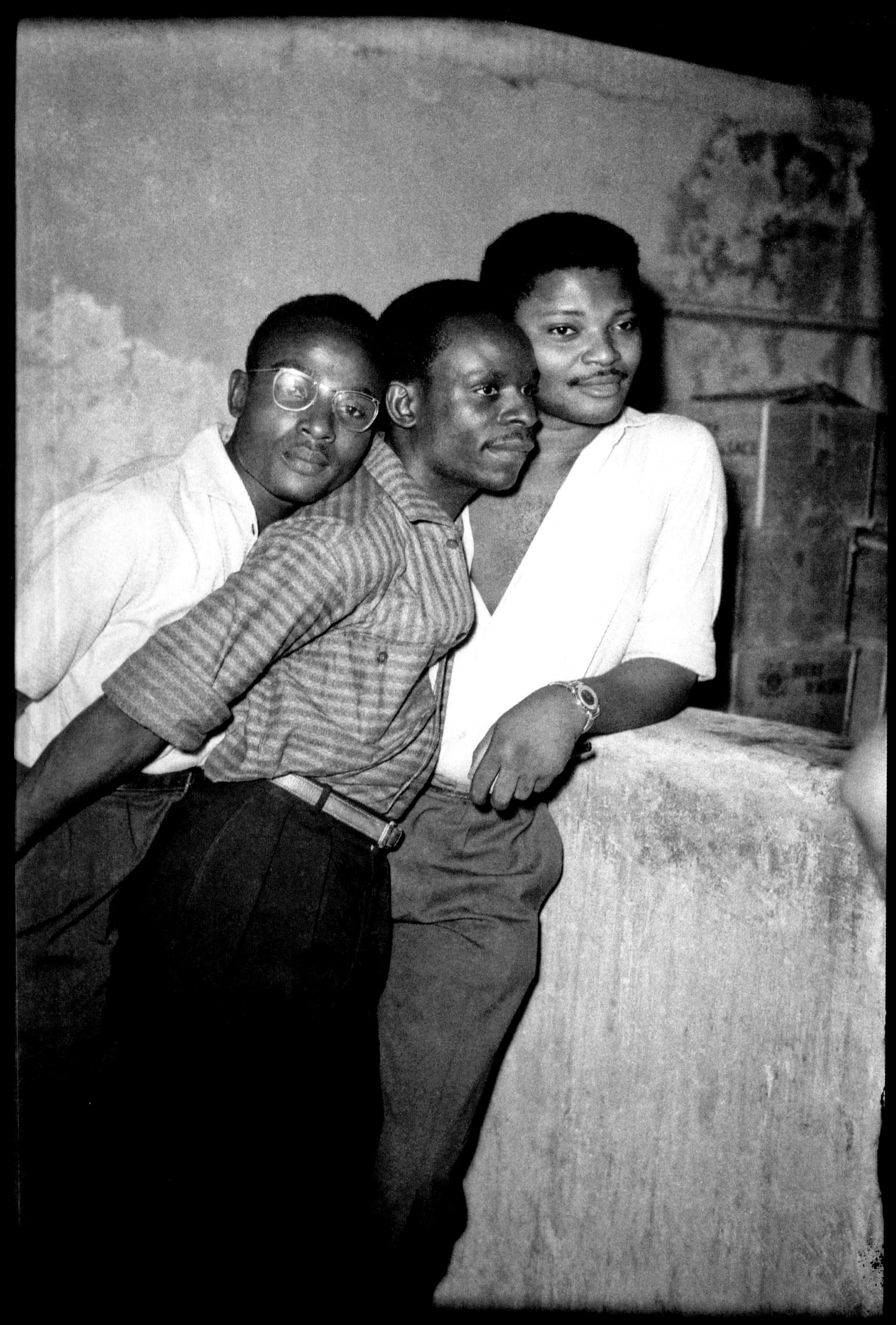

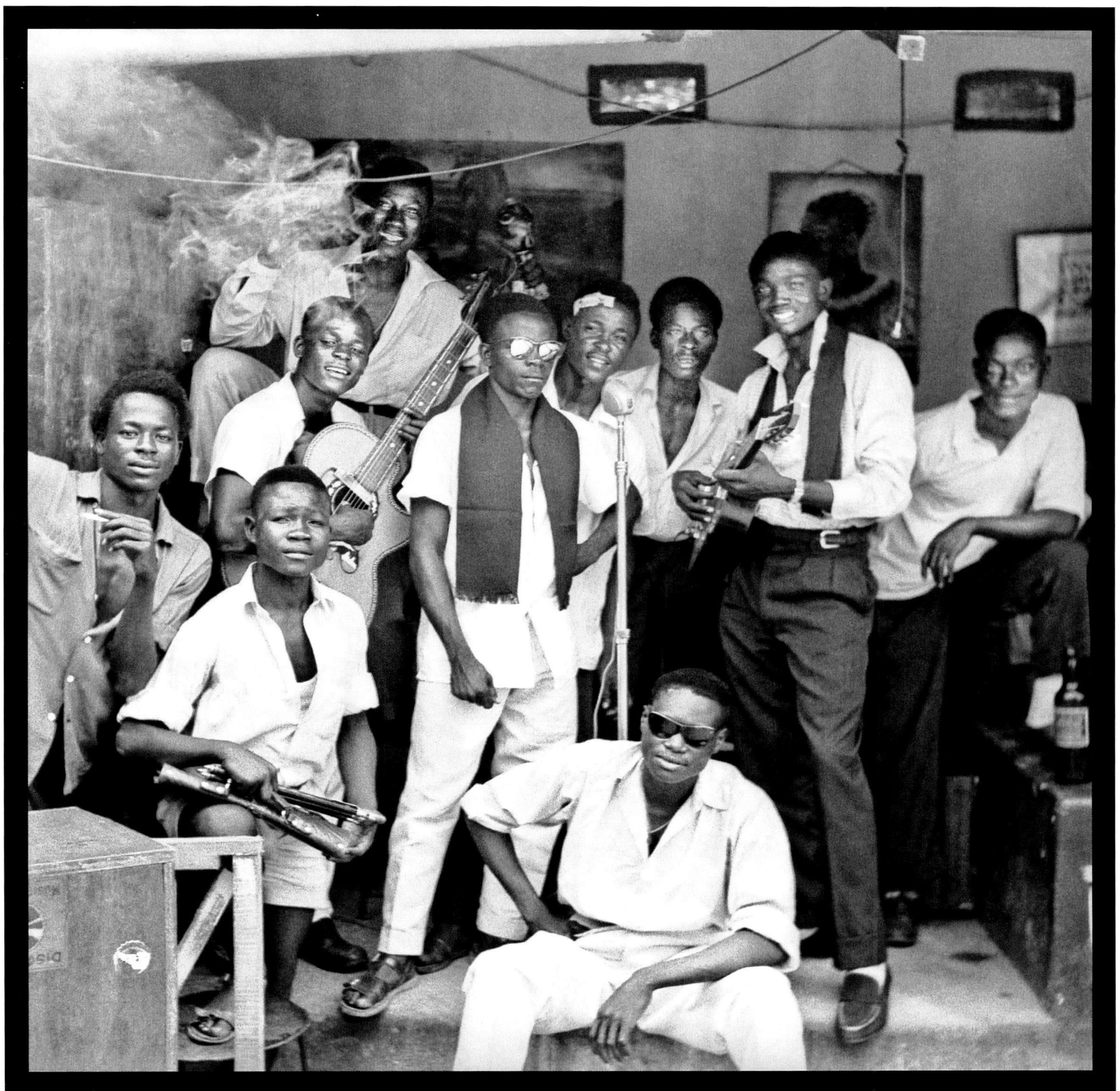

This page:
The musician Franco (right, with guitar) and his group OK Jazz, Kinshasa, 1956; opposite: Three friends on the lookout for a pretty girl in the Kinshasa night, ca. 1955–65

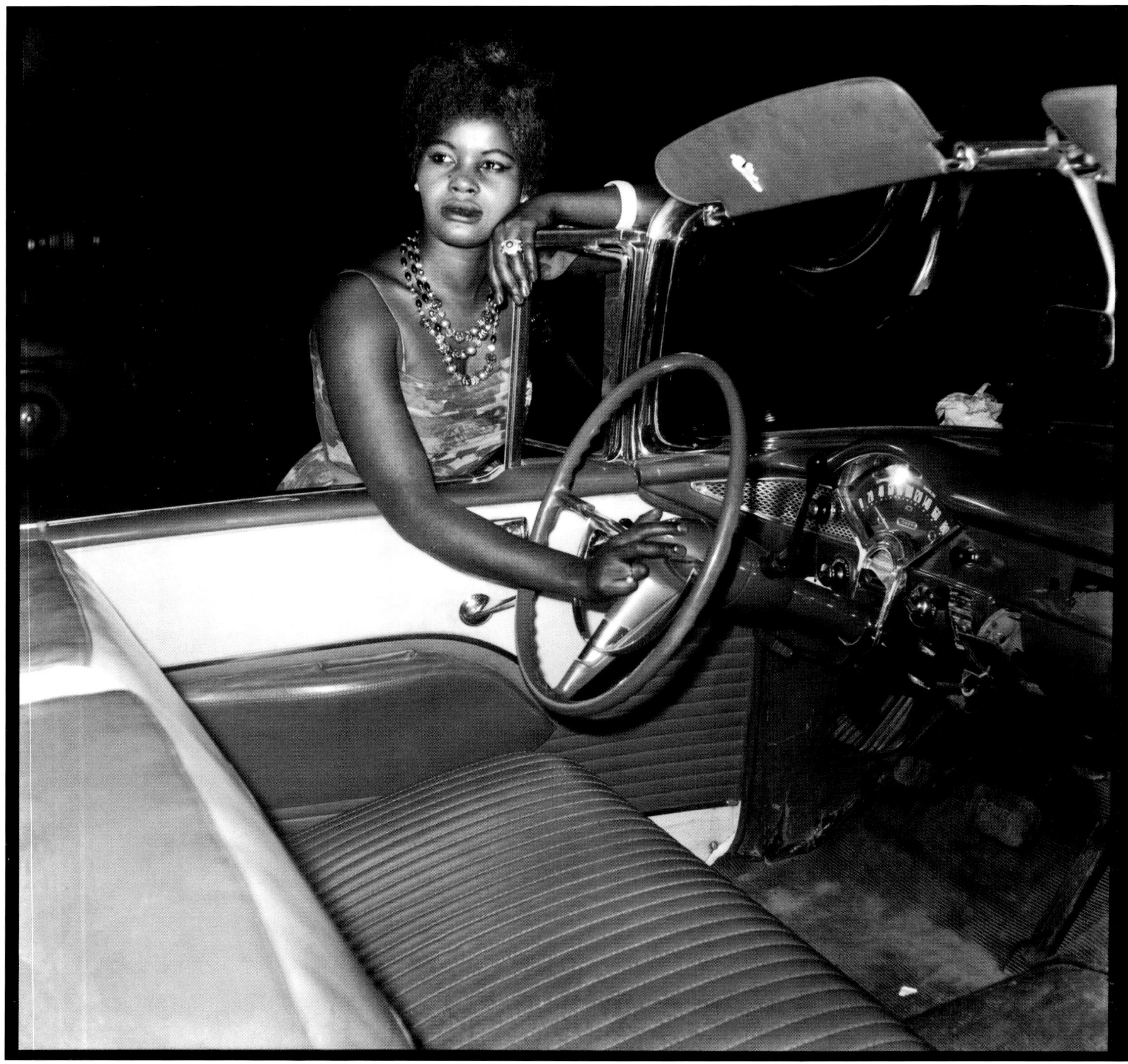

This page:
An impatient young woman honks for her suitor, Kinshasa, ca. 1955–65; **opposite: Two young "sapeurs" seated outside a bar, Kinshasa, ca. 1955–65**
All photographs © Estate of Jean Depara and courtesy Revue Noire, Paris

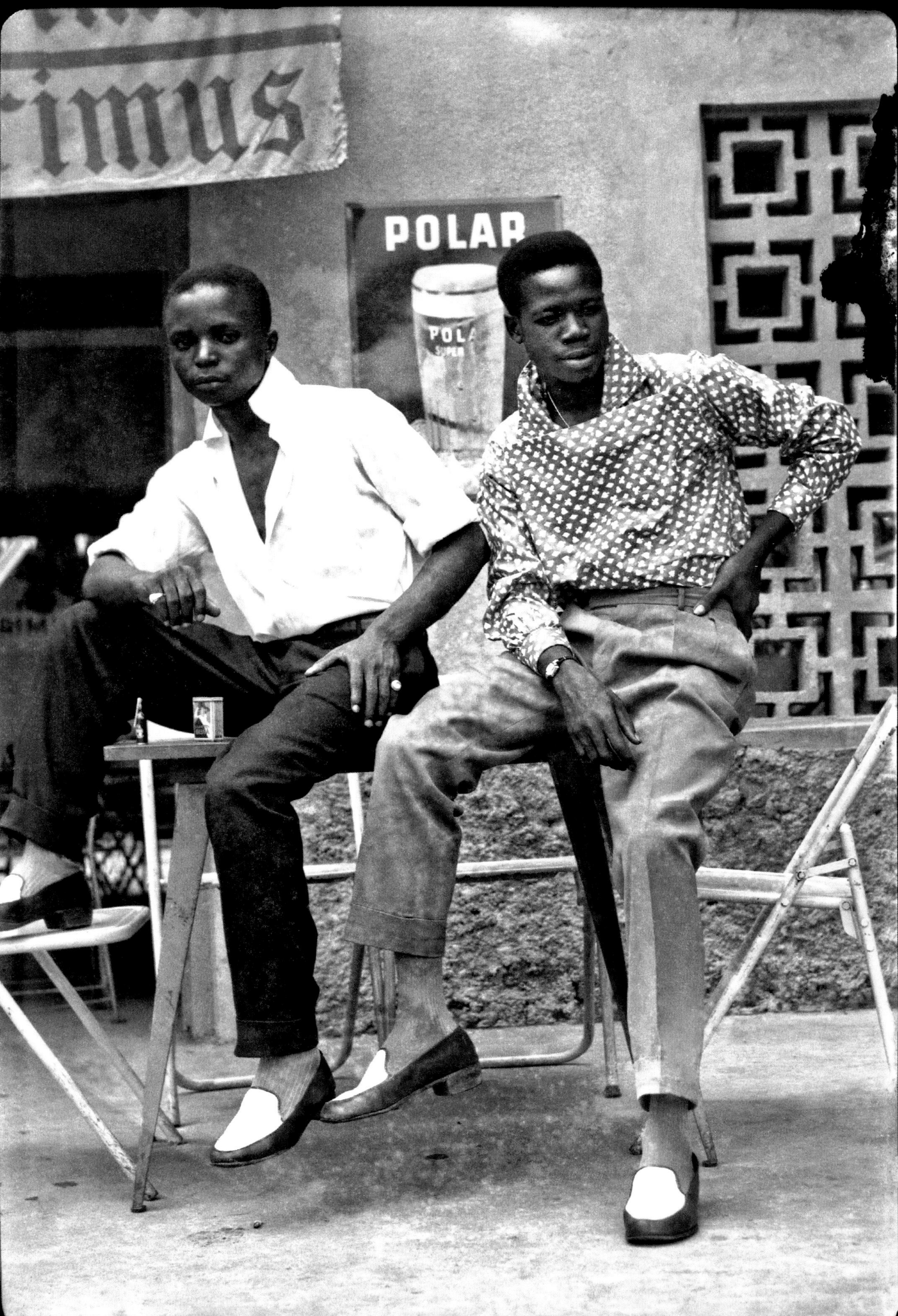
imus
POLAR
POLAR
SUPER

Fabiola Menchelli
Under the Blue Sun

Kate Palmer Albers

Abstractions are generous in their faith: an offering for you, the viewer, to connect with an idea, with an emotion, with consciousness, through an alchemy of form, shape, color, line. With a minimum of descriptive detail from the visible world, abstractions can evoke concepts and dimensions often only accessed indirectly. The artist Fabiola Menchelli draws on this confluence of the material and the cosmic throughout her work. And, descriptive or not, as with any photograph, the conditions of production matter.

Under the Blue Sun No. 2 (2015–17) suggests the movement of a solar flare, and a shifting oculus of indiscernible depth. Menchelli made the series in cyanotype at an observatory at Casa Wabi, a space designed by Tadao Ando along the Oaxacan coast in the artist's native Mexico. From this site, always oriented to the sky, Menchelli tracked the trajectory of the sun—the most elemental component of her medium—in multiple exposures. The effect is one of layered planes, each offering a possible entry into the image. For Menchelli, the mechanical perception of the camera eye adds dimension to the limited capacities of human senses, translating an interpretive realm beyond our own.

Titles, too, connect the observed world with celestial and poetic pathways. *Eclipse* (2020–21), from the *Parallax* series, links the circular forms recorded by discrete objects in the artist's chance experiments with darkroom photograms to an imagined realm of overlapping orbs, cosmic in scope. An eclipse, of course, is an occurrence in which the light of one astronomical body is obscured by the path of another—yet this moment of concealment is also an event of alignment that is always subject to the position of the viewer. Menchelli's *Eclipse* is a scene of abundance, a collective gathering that suggests its own exponential growth.

Yoru (2020–21), from the same series, offers a darker visual puzzle. Here, shadows permeate the image, only punctuated by elements of clarity. The artist traveled to Japan in 2019, finding a Buddhist cosmology rich with interpretive connections. *Yoru* translates into English as *night*, but, phonetically, also reminded Menchelli of the Spanish word *lloro*: "I cry." As with *Eclipse*, the first-person singular is conjured in unexpected ways, grounding the seemingly nonspecific and chance visual imagery with an unfixed, but distinct, sensing body. Menchelli shifts her earlier process of mediating perception via a camera's multiple exposures to a cameraless process of recording multiple times within the photogram. Each process is direct, yet ultimately as abstract as it is literal. These repeated sleights of hand—or, rather, sleights of vision and perception—invite a viewer to consider sensorial interchangeability on a radical scale.

This seeming contraction is furthered even more in Menchelli's most recent abstractions, which have become highly visceral, the product of a deeply sensorial process. In the series *Unfold* (2021), Menchelli works with color photographic paper entirely by hand in complete darkness, folding and unfolding, feeling her way around the edges of the sheets and combining color through multiple exposures. Over the hours in the darkroom spent on this work, "the distance becomes personal, measuring visual space with the tips of the fingers," she says. Mingling perceptions from the intimacy of touch to the scale of a planetary orbit is at the heart of Menchelli's endeavor.

Kate Palmer Albers teaches the history and theory of photography at Whittier College in Los Angeles. She is the author, most recently, of *The Night Albums: Visibility and the Ephemeral Photograph* (2021).

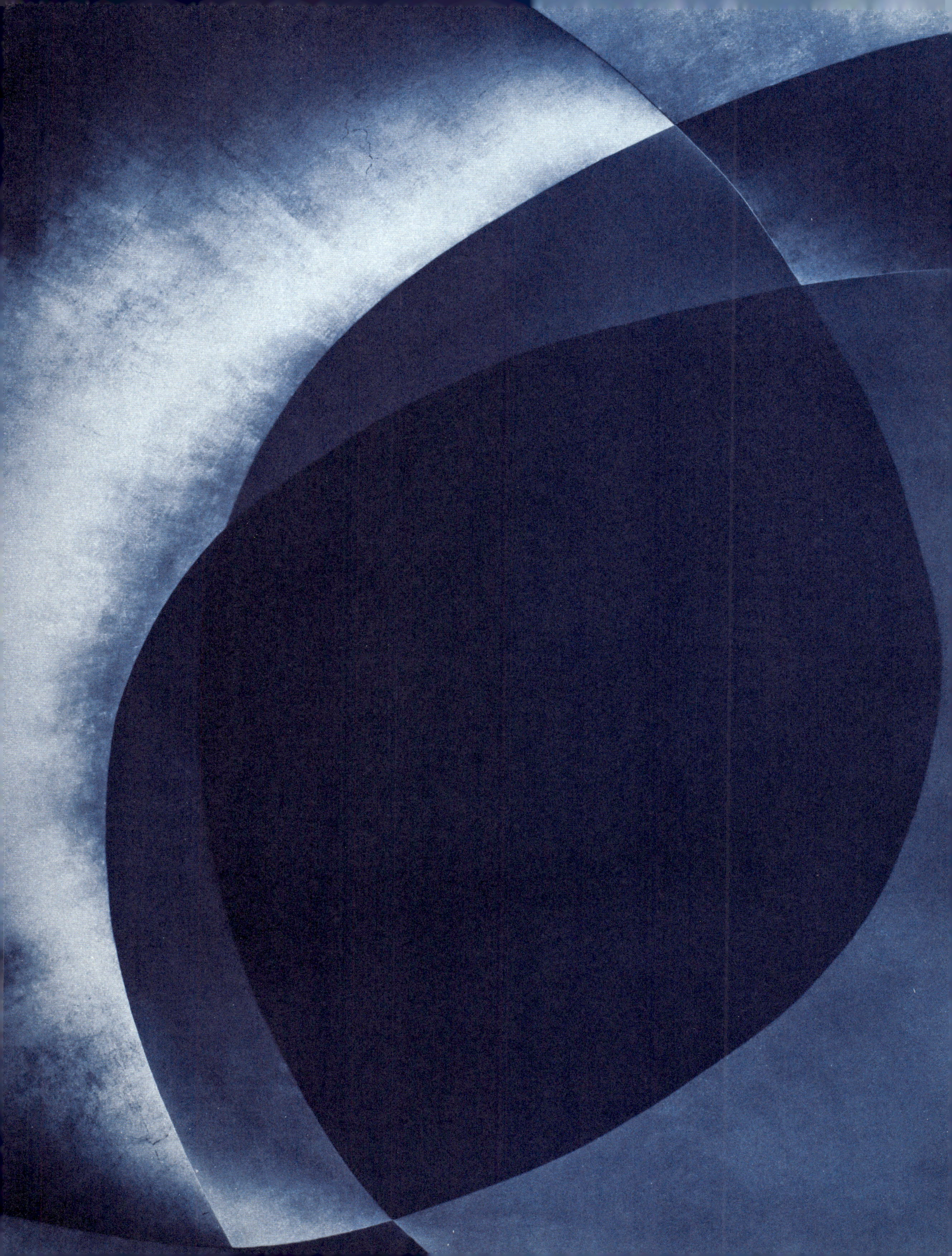

Previous page:
Under the Blue Sun No. 2,
2015–17; this spread:
Tenkai suru VI, 2021,
from the series *Unfold*

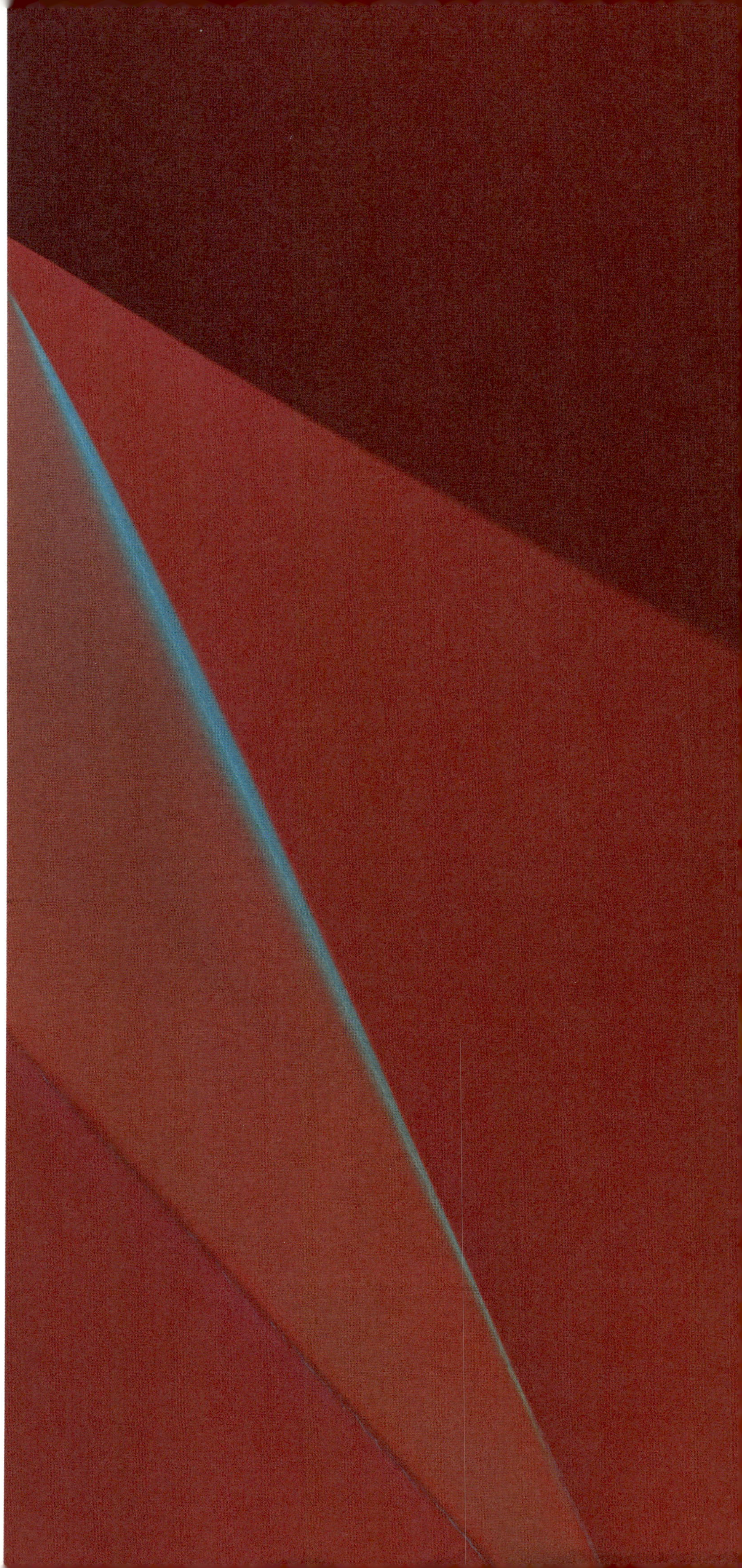

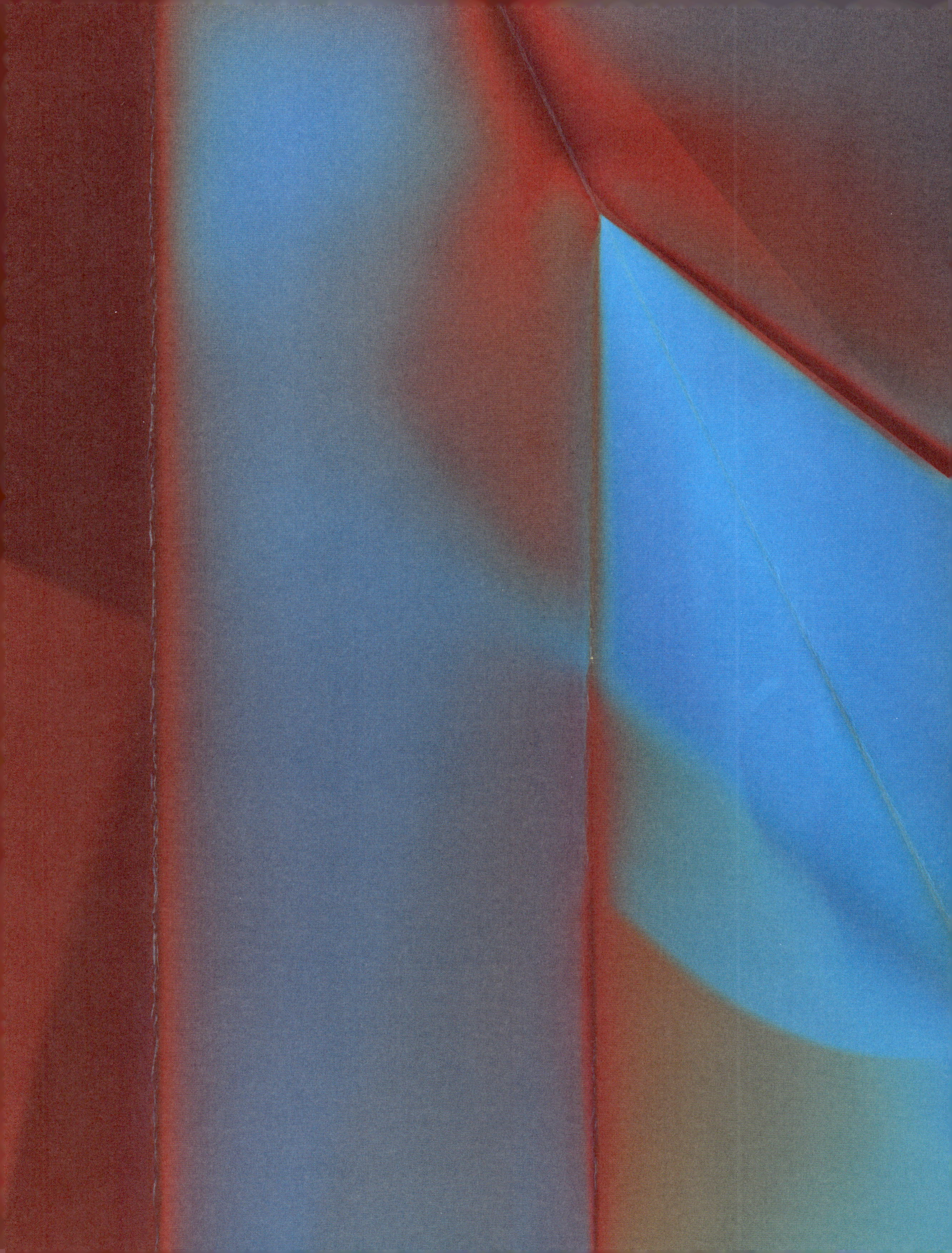

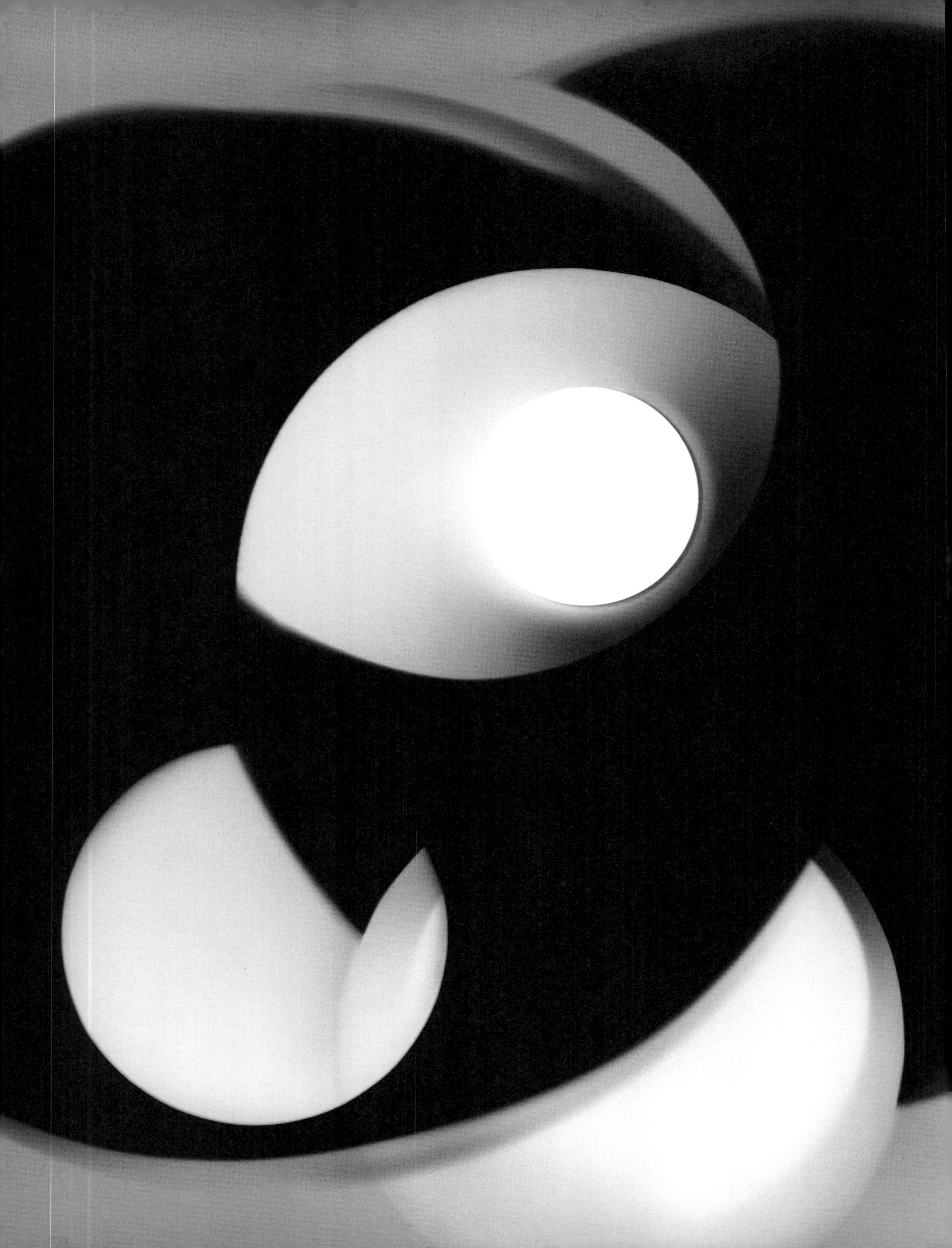

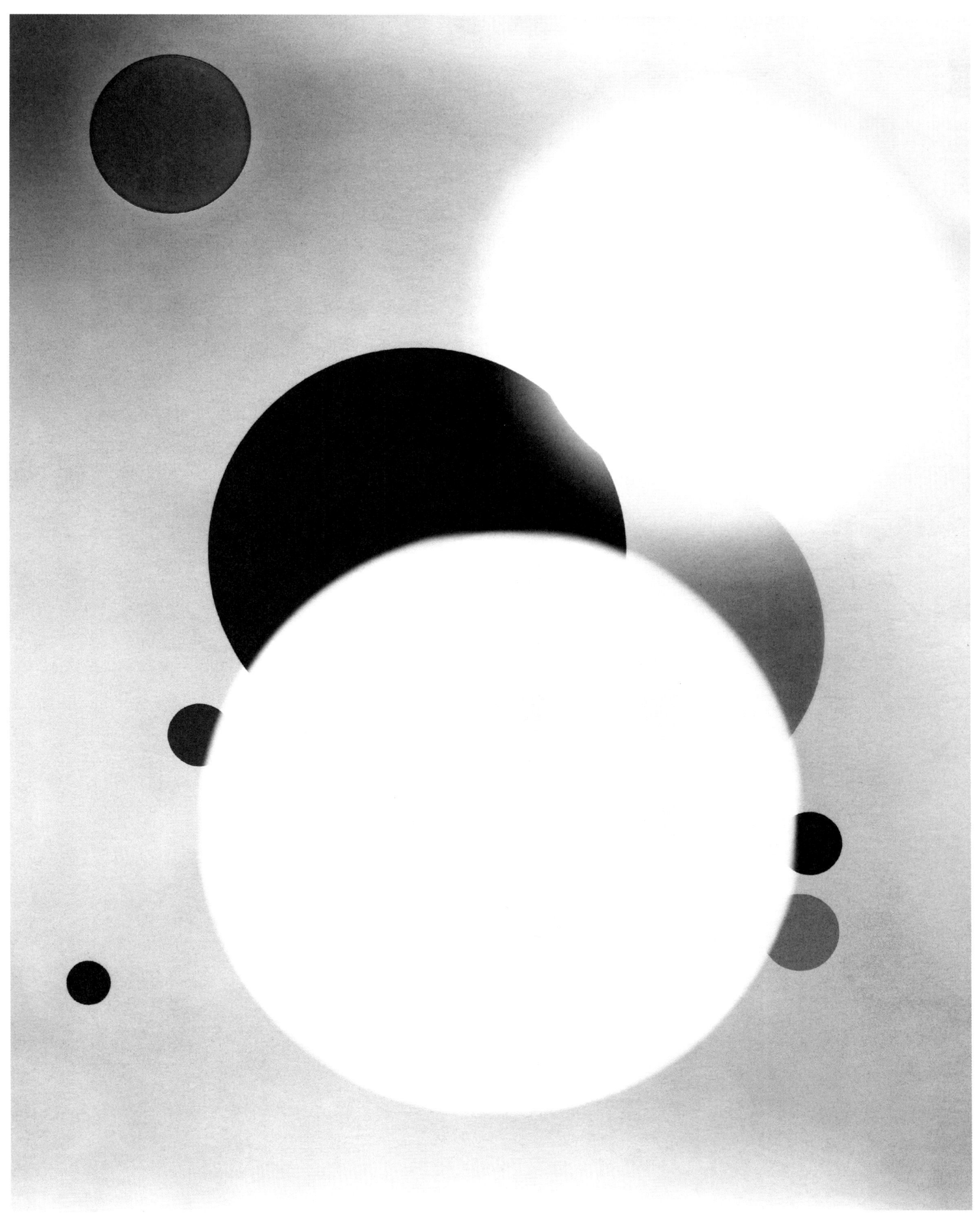

This page:
Eclipse, 2020–21; opposite:
Okami, 2020–21. Both works
from the series *Parallax*

Tenkai suru IV, 2021,
from the series *Unfold*
All works courtesy the artist
and PROXYCO Gallery,
New York

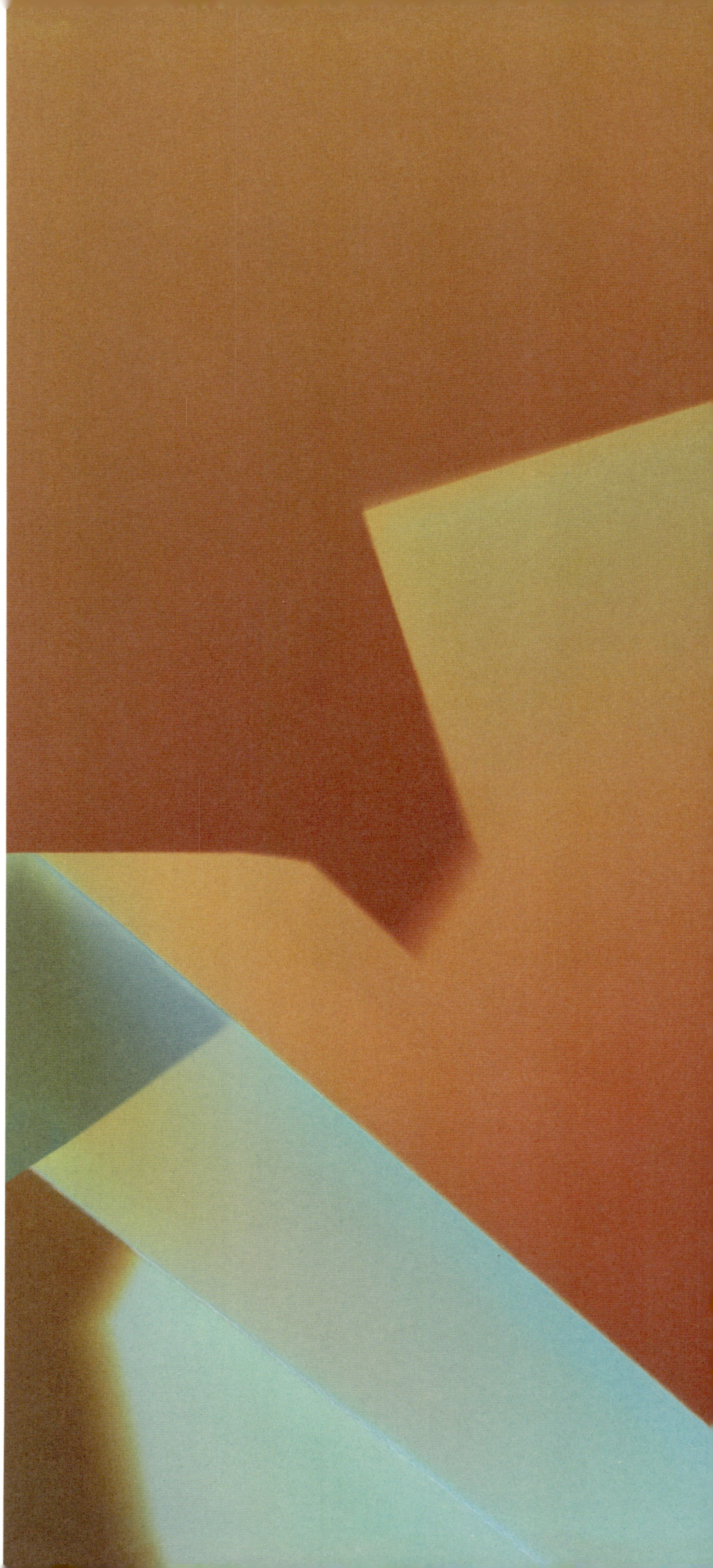

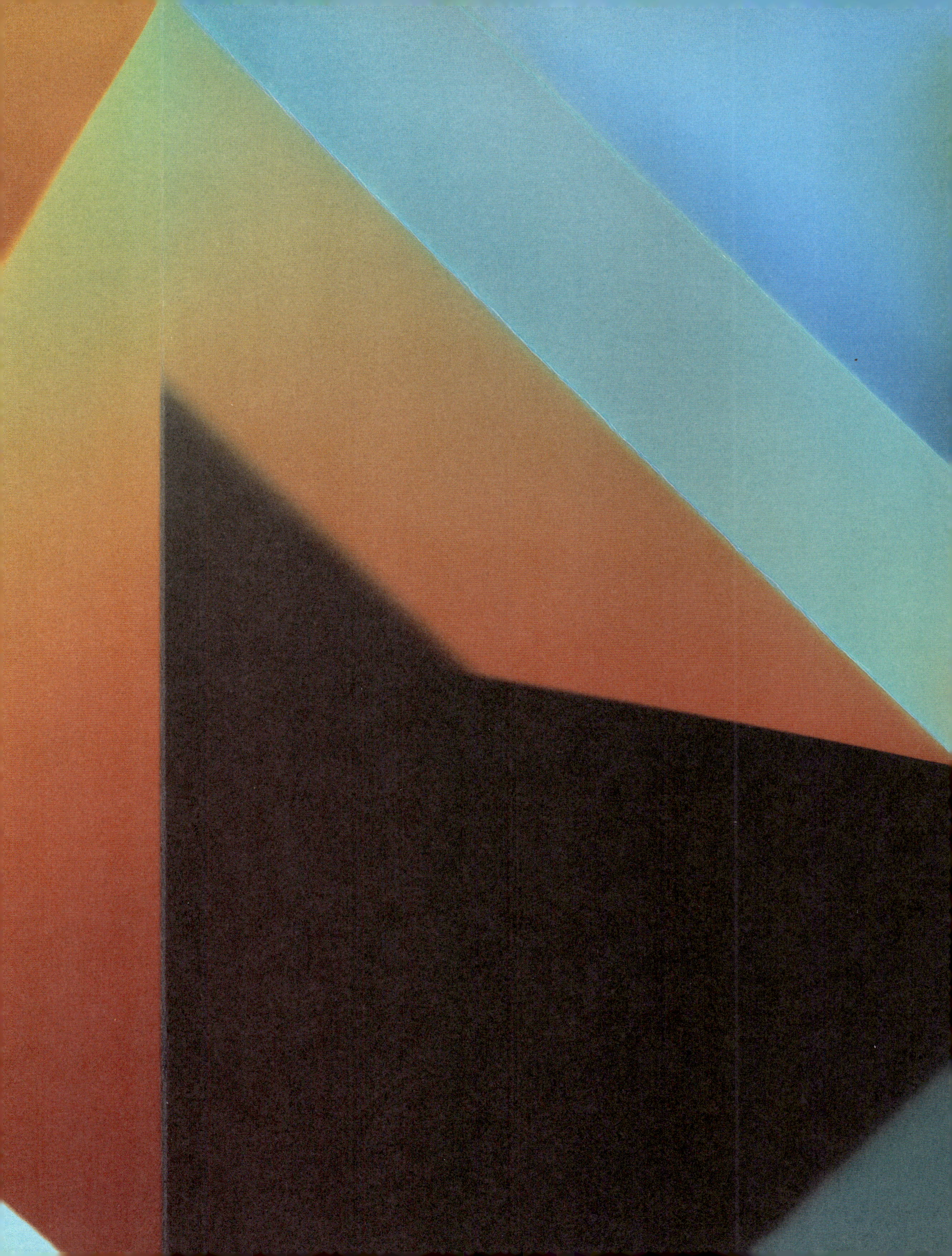

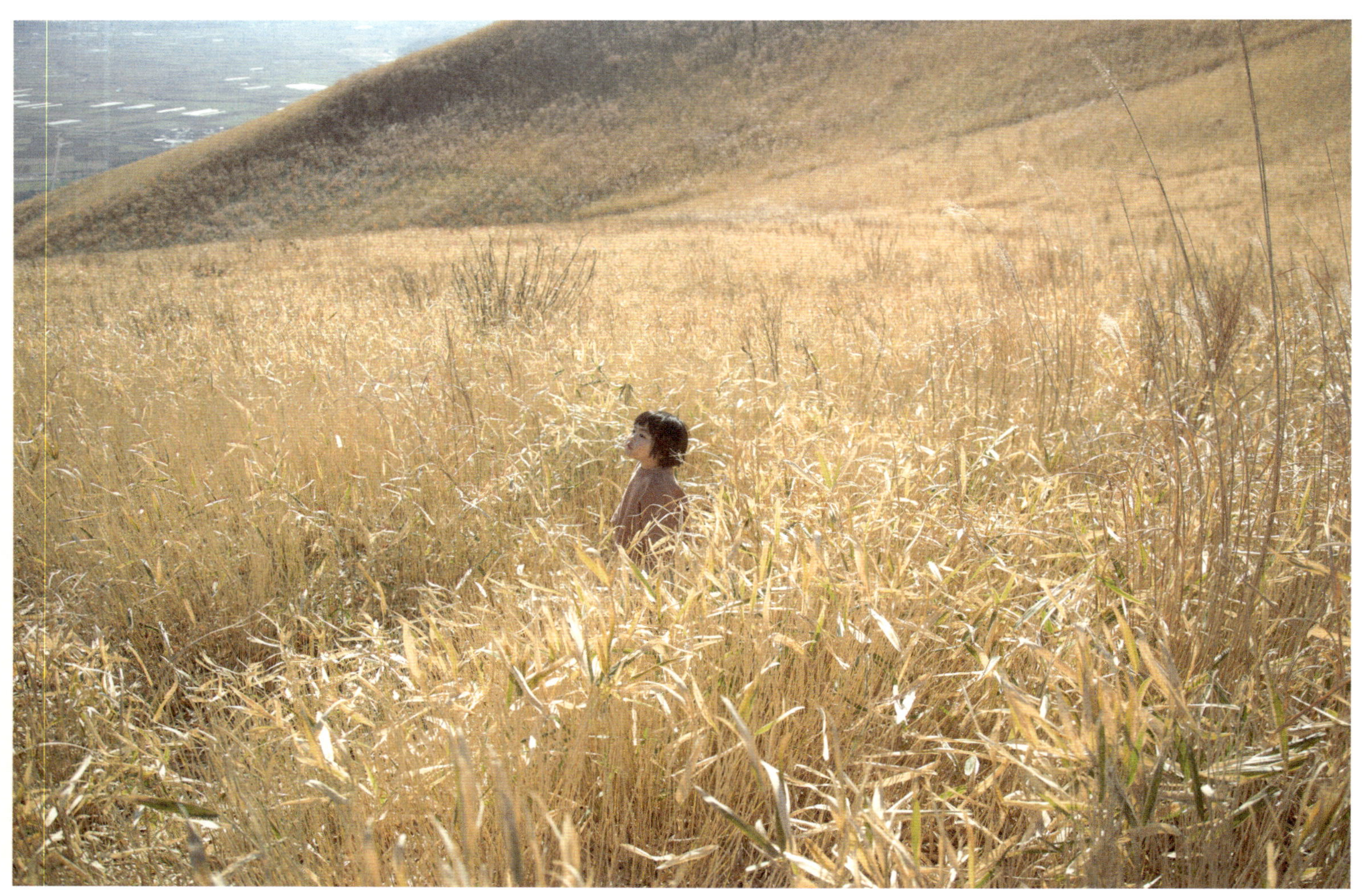

Rinko Kawauchi
The Shape of Things

Through her recent projects, Kawauchi's light touch
melds the everyday with the cosmic.
Moeko Fujii

This page and opposite:
Untitled, 2020, from the
series *as it is*

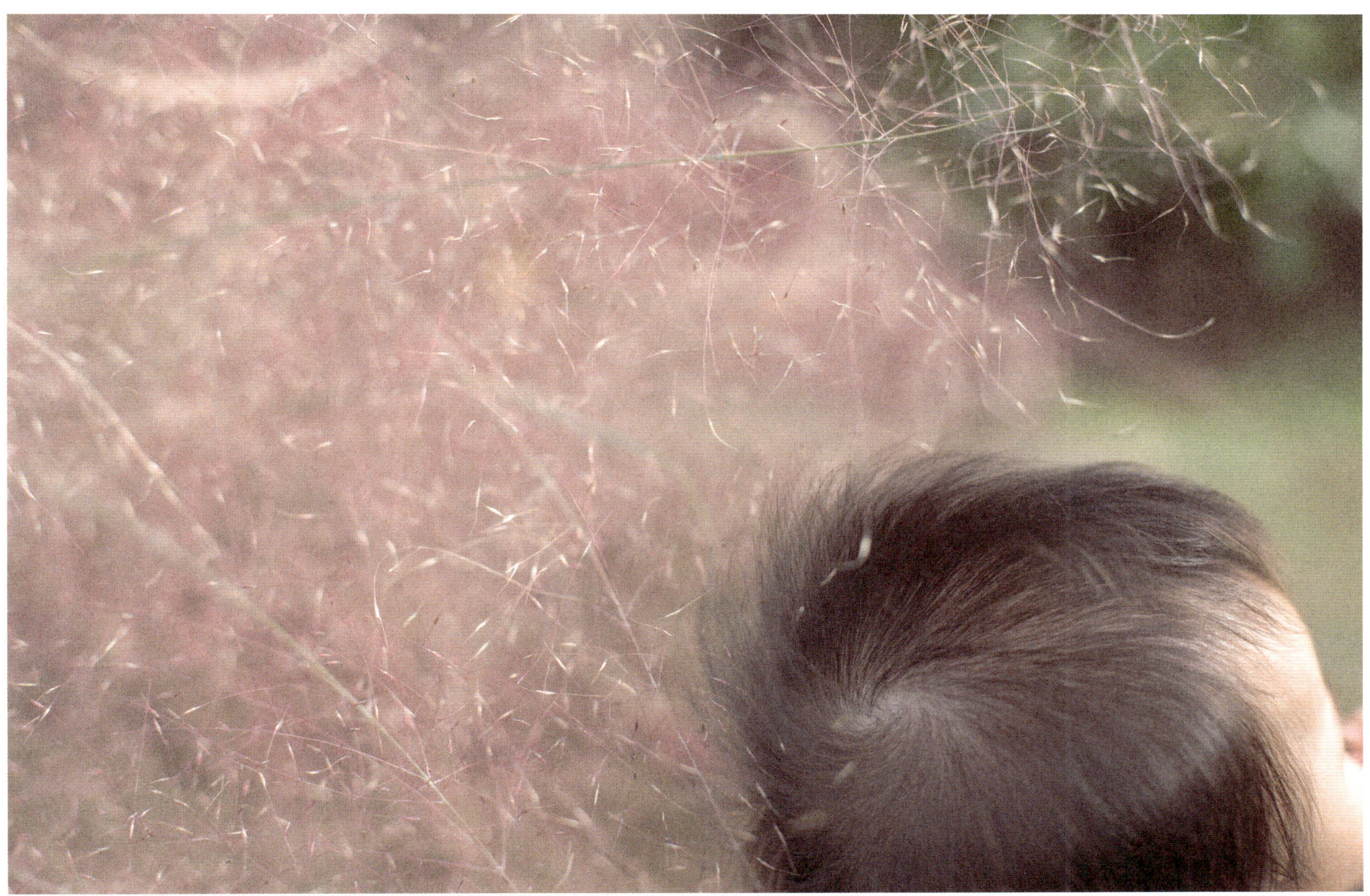

Rinko Kawauchi's book *as it is*, published in 2020, chronicles her daughter's first three years of life. As the baby grows, her actions and movements start to resemble things in the world. She grasps a person's shoulder in a manner that calls to mind a drop of water sticking to a leaf. Her foot acquires the pokiness of a tree branch. Her fists, held in another's older grip, are reminiscent of an insect's clinging. The baby stands, reaches to touch thresholds within and outside the home; she looks at doors, white curtains, the edge of bubbles, the shoreline of a beach. Then she begins grasping for objects: a bowl, an insect, a camera, her grandfather's coffin. The last page of the book features the girl in blue sneakers, holding a length of wheat. She observes it carefully, as though it reminds her of something else: a firework, perhaps, or a memory. Kawauchi writes in the book that her own body during these years was like "a conduit, made for connection." But a conduit to where? "The baby was like having an alien inside of me, conquering me, as though someone else besides myself had control," she told me during a conversation last autumn. "Even after birth, I was someone else's food. From my breast, that person was half connected to me. A self connected to someone who is not yourself—this book is a document of that relationship."

"Why are you looking at baby photos?" my partner asks me, and I say, "They're not baby photos," automatically, as though it should be obvious. But his comment has pinpointed something true about Kawauchi's celebrated photographs. Contentwise, they cover similar ground to any new mother's personal photo album: babies and nature, fireworks and skies. The effect of her work—and of the precise sequencing in her many acclaimed photobooks—however, is far less a catalog of daily life and more of a philosophical investigation into the distinction between human and inhuman, skin and surface, caress and corpse. "My conception

of time changed after having her," she tells me. "That duration we have with a child until they're three—it's magical. Fifty centimeters grows to a meter, faces change; humans shift so much during that period. But the flow of time has been a theme in every single one of my works."

From her debut in the art and photography world in 2001, Kawauchi, who lives in Chiba, Japan, has been hailed as a visual poet of the ordinary; she finds "eternity in the everyday," the Japanese photography critic Kotaro Iizawa wrote in a recent review of *as it is*. But I've never quite found this "everyday" to be stable in her work. From her 2001 book *Utatane*, which was more interior ("I started off interested in my surroundings and in inner lives"), Kawauchi explains that she went outward to the birth of animals with *AILA* in 2004 ("I was interested in a human's 'other'"). Then, in 2005, she chronicled her family in *Cui Cui* ("because family is our first society"). For the past few years, Kawauchi says, she was more interested in training her attention on events far from the everyday—such as volcanic eruptions in Aso, Japan, in her 2013 photobook *Ametsuchi*, and murmurations of birds in Brighton, England, or villagers throwing molten iron at walls in Hubei, China, for *Halo* (2017). And now, she's back to the more quotidian—to interiors, with a baby, in a global pandemic. Her most recent collection, *Des oiseaux*, looks at nests of sparrows that made their home in her neighborhood during quarantine. "I guess you can call it a cyclical return," she states. But the thing about cycles, of course, is that a return registers both change and stasis. What has shifted in her early "everyday" photographs? What has remained the same?

Utatane is a craft lesson in dialogic metaphors with surprising contrasts of images that trace the shapes of lines and meditate on the forms of circles: on one spread, the gawping, irregular mouths of carp are juxtaposed with the orange, bubbled yolks of fried eggs. Throughout the book, Kawauchi demonstrates an unerring grasp of how things move—and provides a metaphorical link between the practical and the cosmic, from, say, the similarity of the swirling, downward movement of a washing machine to that of stormy clouds, or the flash of lightning to the ramming needle of a sewing machine. But no particular structure of being is elevated over the other. One of my favorite juxtapositions in *Utatane* features a cracked watermelon opposite a doll's head held on an open palm. When seeing these two photographs together, we learn a sense of fragility: things with innards will split if handled without care.

"I'm drawn to swarms as a metaphor for societies," Kawauchi tells me. "Birds fly in flocks to protect themselves—sometimes that force is positive, but there's always a minus side to it, too, like people swarming against someone on social media. The crowd—there's a disgusting side to it, but there's also hope." In her book *Illuminance* (Aperture, 2011), an image pairing appears that I have returned to many times: a person (a woman?) smoking in a cool blue light on one page, and a plastic bag, low on water, crammed with dozens of goldfish squeezed and fighting for room on the facing page. Solitude on one side, survival on the other. Both pictures are linked by the same shade of a perfect orange: that of the scales of the goldfish and the glow of a cigarette at dawn. But like the watermelon and the doll's head, the diptych is not necessarily a contrast of two opposite poles, say, nature versus human, or the mechanical versus the spontaneous. Instead, the pairings ask us to explore the exhilaration of one image blurring into, and shading, the read of another. Does a goldfish feel lonely among other fish, as humans do in a crowd? Can smoking a cigarette be an act of individual survival within a crowd?

For both the photobook *as it is* and her more recent images, Kawauchi was interested in what it means to *yorisou*—to stand by someone. I asked her if this Japanese verb, with its peculiar connotation of both distance and closeness, is in line with her philosophy of photography (it is further than a nestle but closer than simply standing nearby). Kawauchi answered that she would like for this to be the case but notes that you can't force circumstances: "I like to take photographs of things I can't control." Her favorite things to photograph, she says, are children, bugs, nature, and the weather. You can't tell a rainy day to get sunny, and even if you tell a child to sit still, she may not do as told.

"When you raise your child, you think, I want them to be as themselves as they can be. But what does it mean—to be like yourself?" Kawauchi asks. Her work in progress on Yamanami Kobo, a collective of artists with disabilities, in Shiga Prefecture, expands and explores this question. Kawauchi's involvement started as a commission from the Japanese confectionary company Taneya for images to illustrate a pamphlet highlighting the culture of Shiga, for which she visited the atelier once every two months for a period of two years. "We are able-bodied," she tells me. "But I feel the artists are more free than we are. Each time I went, it was like visiting a temple, like I was being shown what beauty human beings could have."

The *Yamanami* series includes a photograph that Kawauchi took the first time she went to the atelier, one of a hand grasping another. When I asked about it, Kawauchi replied that she noticed that the artists do this gesture every day, whenever they get off or on the bus. It wasn't as if holding hands held any special meaning; they were just comfortable holding each other, sustaining contact, whether it was via hands or linking arms or in an embrace. "They would link arms with me too," she says. "It's a natural flow for them, and I found it very symbolic."

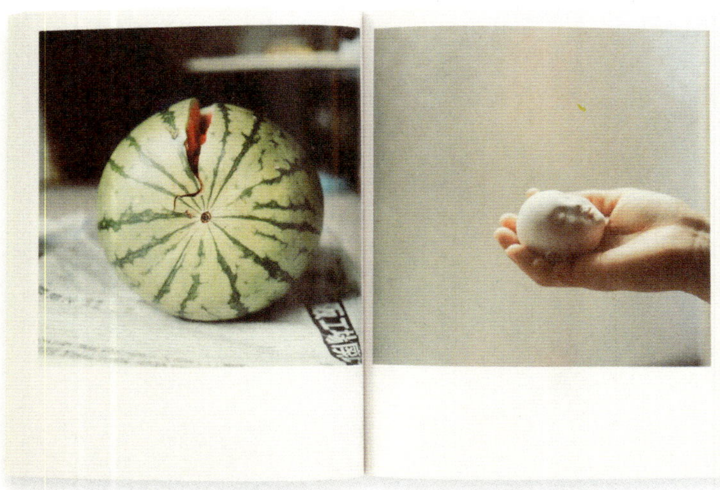

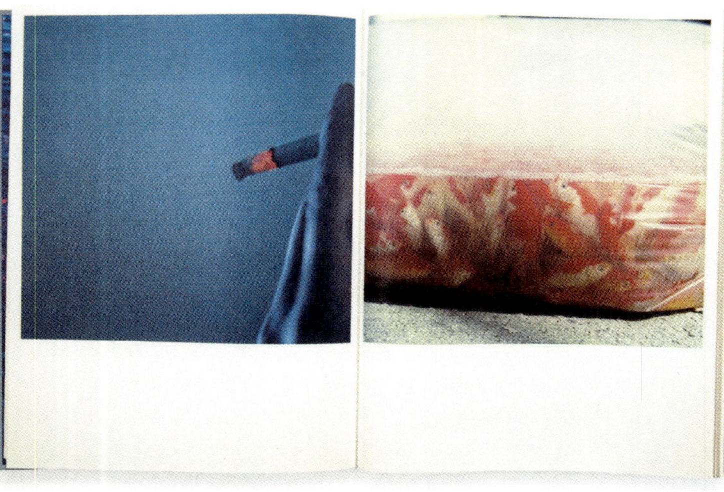

Top:
Spread from *Utatane*
(2001); bottom: Spread
from *Illuminance*
(Aperture, 2011);
opposite: *Untitled*, 2020,
from the series *as it is*

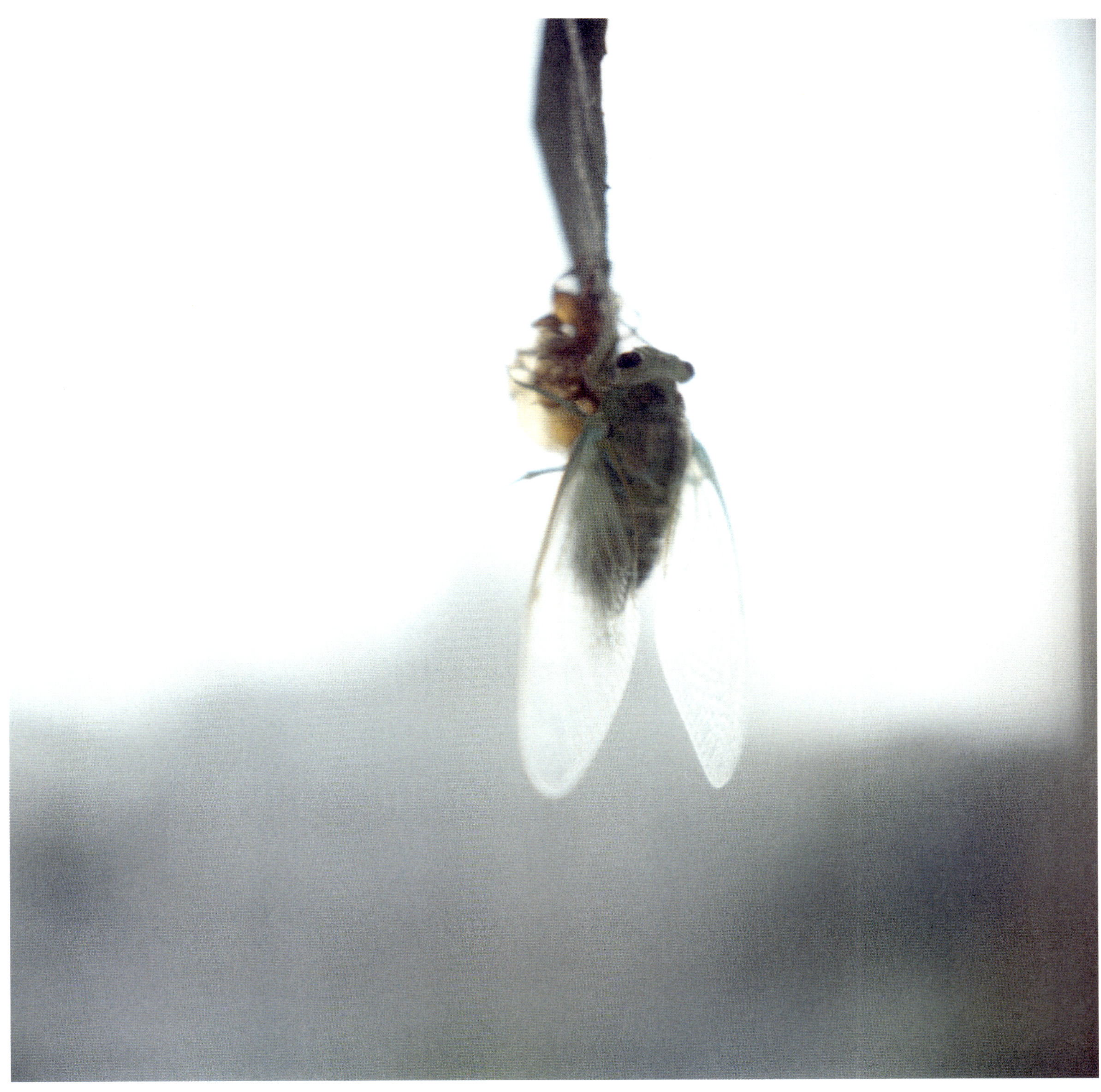

Kawauchi proposes that the sensory experiences of making art and navigating our worlds both take us to a similar place.

The photographs feature artists whose mouths are pursed in concentration as they paint and sculpt. "When you're concentrating, your 'self' isn't there," Kawauchi remarks. Other images show daily routines at the collective: people taking breaks, going about their everyday lives, cleaning the interior spaces, eating lunch. In one, an artist looks somewhere beyond his paintings; in another, a man stands with arms wide-open next to a windblown tree. When we concentrate—on the next line of paint or the feel of wind on our cheeks—where do we go? Kawauchi proposes that the sensory experiences of making art and navigating our worlds both take us to a similar place.

There was a particular artist Kawauchi liked to observe, a man she photographed mid-smile as he folded up some cardboard. "This person is amazing," she says, smiling, and explaining how he creates tiny statues of monks—dozens and dozens of them— but is most known for remembering everyone's birthdays in the

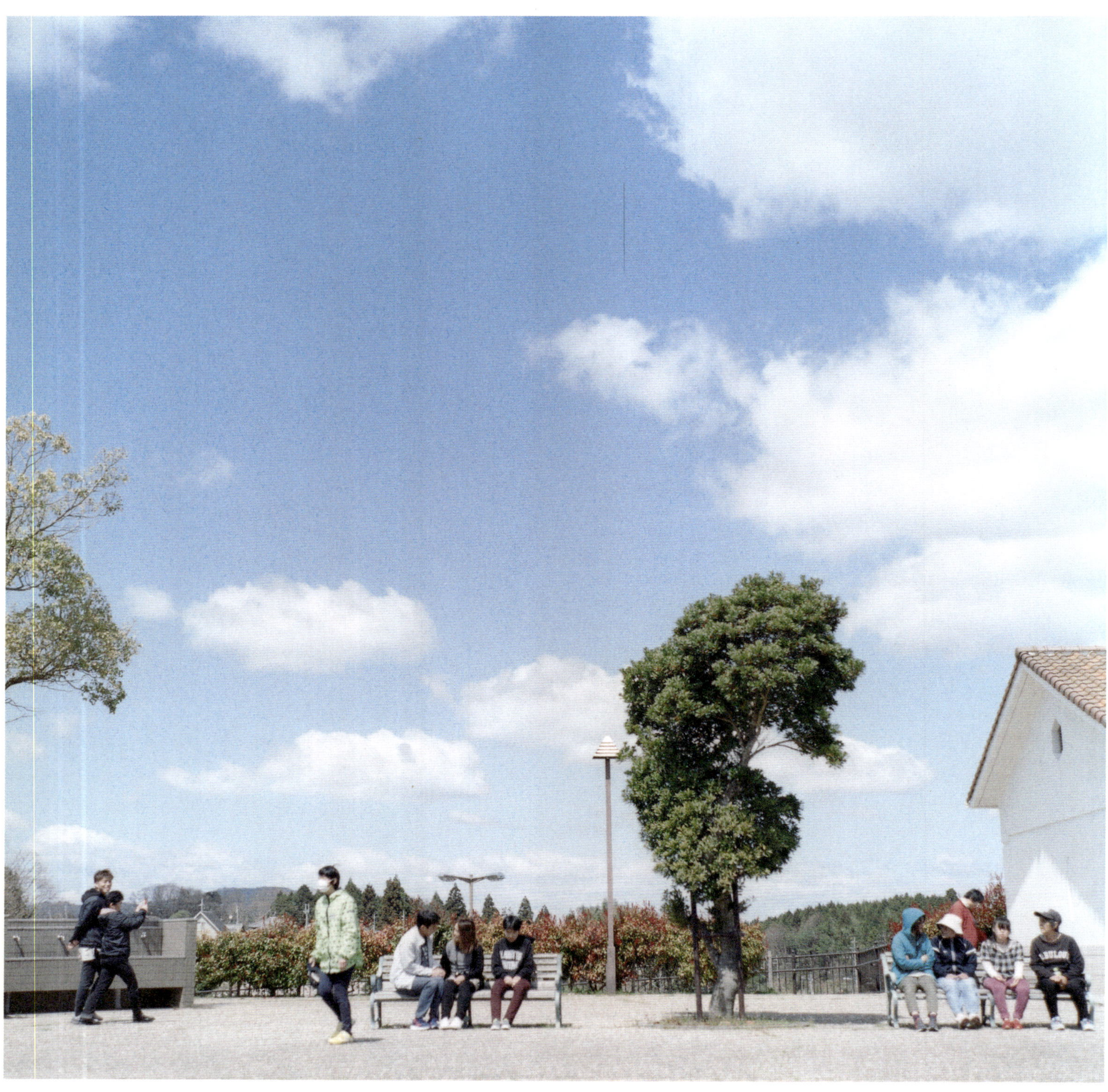

facility, all ninety-something of the people working and living in the collective, and singing to them on their birthday, first thing in the morning. "That person likes folding up cardboard, he likes doing these everyday tasks—and he's doing it because he wants to." As in her other bodies of work, you can hear her pressing on a concept that seems so familiar but turning, through her careful vision, what she sees into something odd and particular. She has observed that material successes don't appear to matter to these artists at all. Some of their art, known worldwide, sells for significant amounts of money, but they have no interest in recognition; they paint, draw, or sculpt in between their daily tasks, and only when they want to. "What does it mean to be like yourself? Questions such as that just fade away. You nap. You do what you want to do. It isn't some idealized place; you live together so, of course, there are problems. But then you solve them, and you move on." Instead of defamiliarizing the familiar, or making the ordinary

extraordinary, Kawauchi has us see—brilliantly—what lines, angles, and movements constitute the everyday, the beauty and care of the practical gestures that make up our world. Sometimes, she gets an urge to go to Shiga just to observe those artists again. "When I watch them work, I feel two feelings at once: that I am such a small being, but also that people contain such possibility."

Moeko Fujii is a writer and critic whose essays have appeared in *Aperture*, *The New Yorker*, the Criterion Collection, and *Orion* magazine.

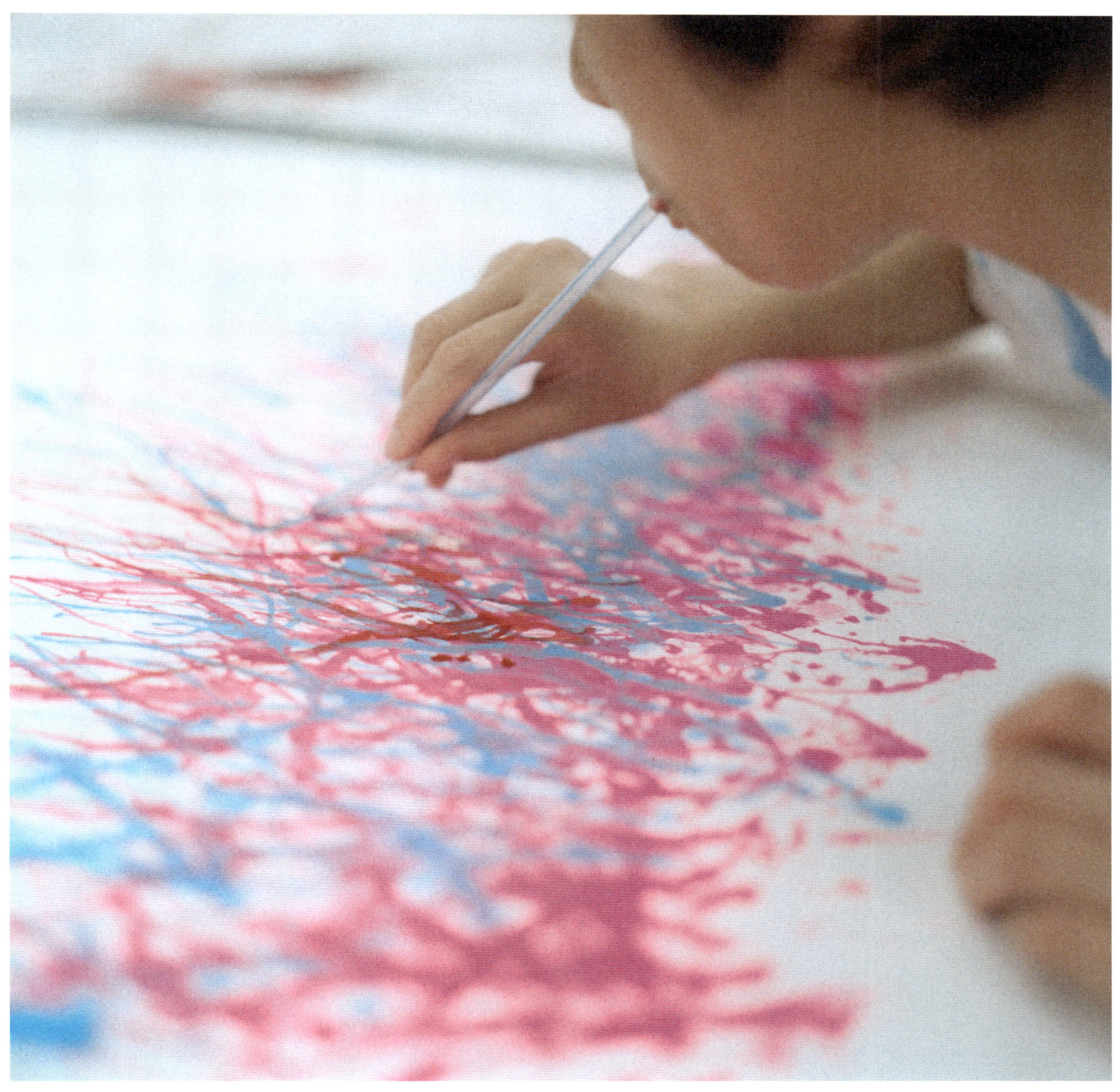

This page and opposite:
Both images *Untitled*,
2021, from the series
Yamanami

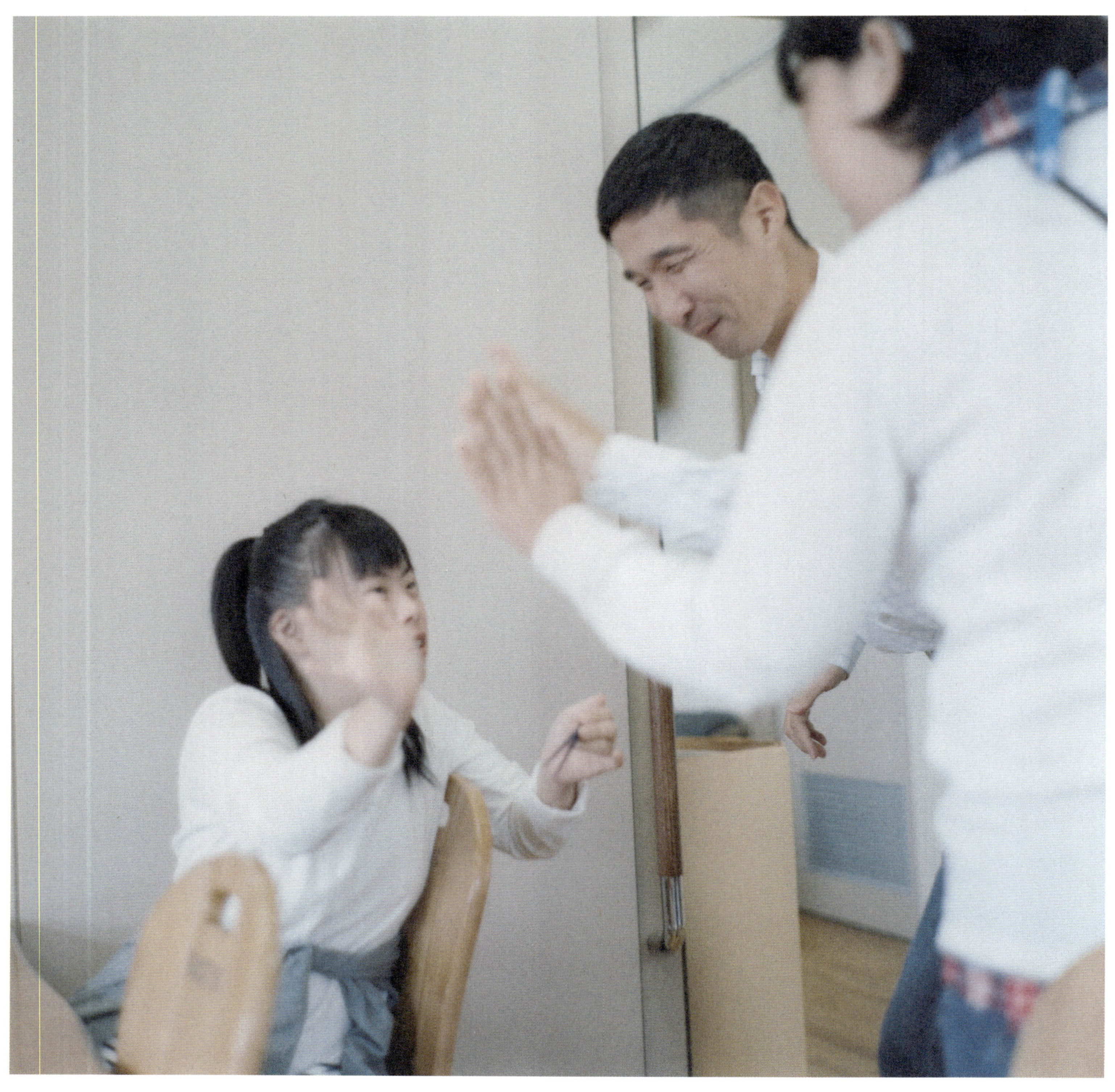

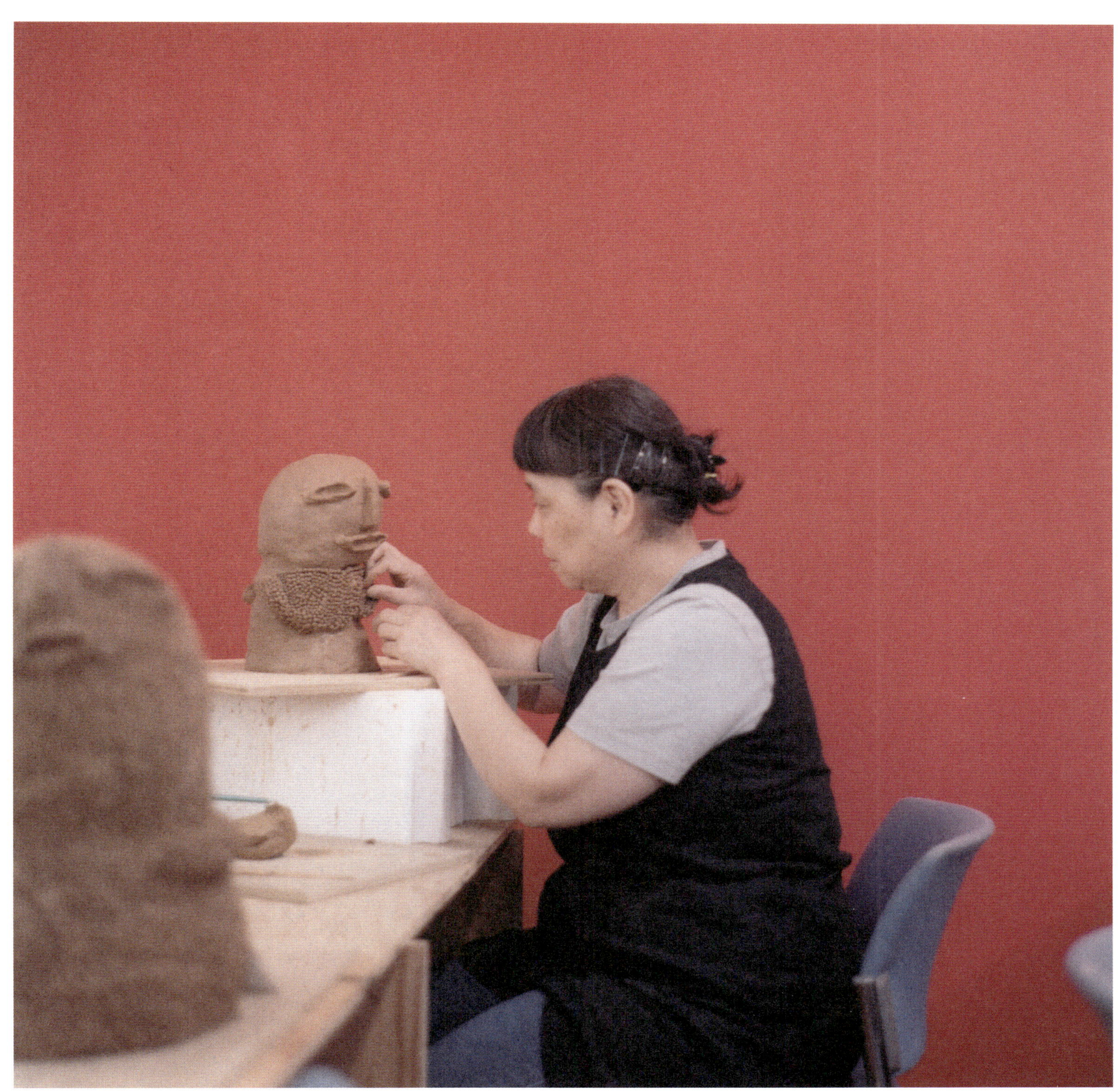

This page and opposite:
Untitled, **2021, from the**
series *Yamanami*
All photographs courtesy
the artist

Will Matsuda
Hanafuda

Lucy Ives

Will Matsuda grew up in Oregon, a state famed for its environmental extremes—dense forest, volcanoes, desert, and Crater Lake, the deepest such body in the United States. Matsuda began to be interested in making images about place when he left home for college and experienced a longing for visual materials that reflect the complexity of the American landscape, with its ambivalent histories of theft, loss, and reinvention.

As *Susuki #2*, an image from his series *Hanafuda* (2020–21), reveals, Matsuda works with a distinct vocabulary, seeming to construct his photographs piece by piece, using simple tools such as on-camera flash to create resonant, nearly aphoristic effects. Similar to *vanitas* paintings of the sixteenth and seventeenth centuries, Matsuda's pictures manipulate elements of the natural world in order to comment on the ultimate artificiality and fleetingness of human mastery. *Susuki #2*, for example, might ask that we question our overly celebratory, frequently acquisitive, Instagram-abetted relationship to images. The hand of the mirror holder, who would appear to have successfully captured the face of the moon and its delicate maria, has, ironically, begun to fade away.

But the *vanitas* connection is merely one reading. *Hanafuda*, or "flower cards," are a Japanese style of playing card developed from Portuguese decks that entered the Asian nation in the seventeenth century. These cards were banned by the Japanese government and then constantly redesigned and recirculated by enterprising gamblers to circumvent the rulings. Matsuda encountered modern-day *hanafuda* during New Year's gatherings in Hawaii with extended family. His paternal grandmother, Amy Matsuda, encouraged him to play. The cards are organized into twelve suits corresponding to the twelve months of the year; their imagery is simple—landscapes, flora, and fauna printed primarily in black, red, and white—yet striking, memorable.

Matsuda's work in this series is, in part, derived from *hanafuda* illustrations. He sometimes titles the photographs after the plants that correspond to the suits—*susuki* (grass), *kiku* (chrysanthemum), *ume* (plum blossom)—or after special cards that bear figures, such as the phoenix. Yet the cards' calendrical structure does not absolutely determine the content of Matsuda's images, which are rather loosely inspired by memories of time spent with family and questions related to place. As he explains, the Japanese ukiyo-e woodblock tradition has also been a primary influence. Matsuda is drawn to the stylized flatness of ukiyo-e (literally, "floating-world pictures") as well as the virtuosic manipulation of colored ink seen in these patently commercial images, which became popular in urban centers during the Edo period. The term *uki* (浮) refers to a "floating" lifestyle of consumerist hedonism that grew up in the context of sumptuary laws that prevented wealthy nonaristocratic city dwellers from purchasing some items, including but not limited to land.

According to the photographer Ricardo Nagaoka, a friend of Matsuda's who is depicted in *Ricardo* (2021), even Matsuda's portraits "feel connected to the landscape"—human figures seem intimately mingled with, rather than set above or against, natural elements. Given present-day environmental disasters, along with housing shortages and astronomical real-estate prices in the United States and beyond, Matsuda's *hanafuda* are a reminder that, although we may all be experiencing a certain floating feeling, it is possible to come back down to Earth. Just follow the stark and strangely joyful outline of a chicken held aloft, for example. Viewed in a particular light, it is, in fact, a phoenix being reborn.

Lucy Ives is a novelist and critic and a contributor to magazines including *Artforum*, *Art in America*, and *Frieze*.

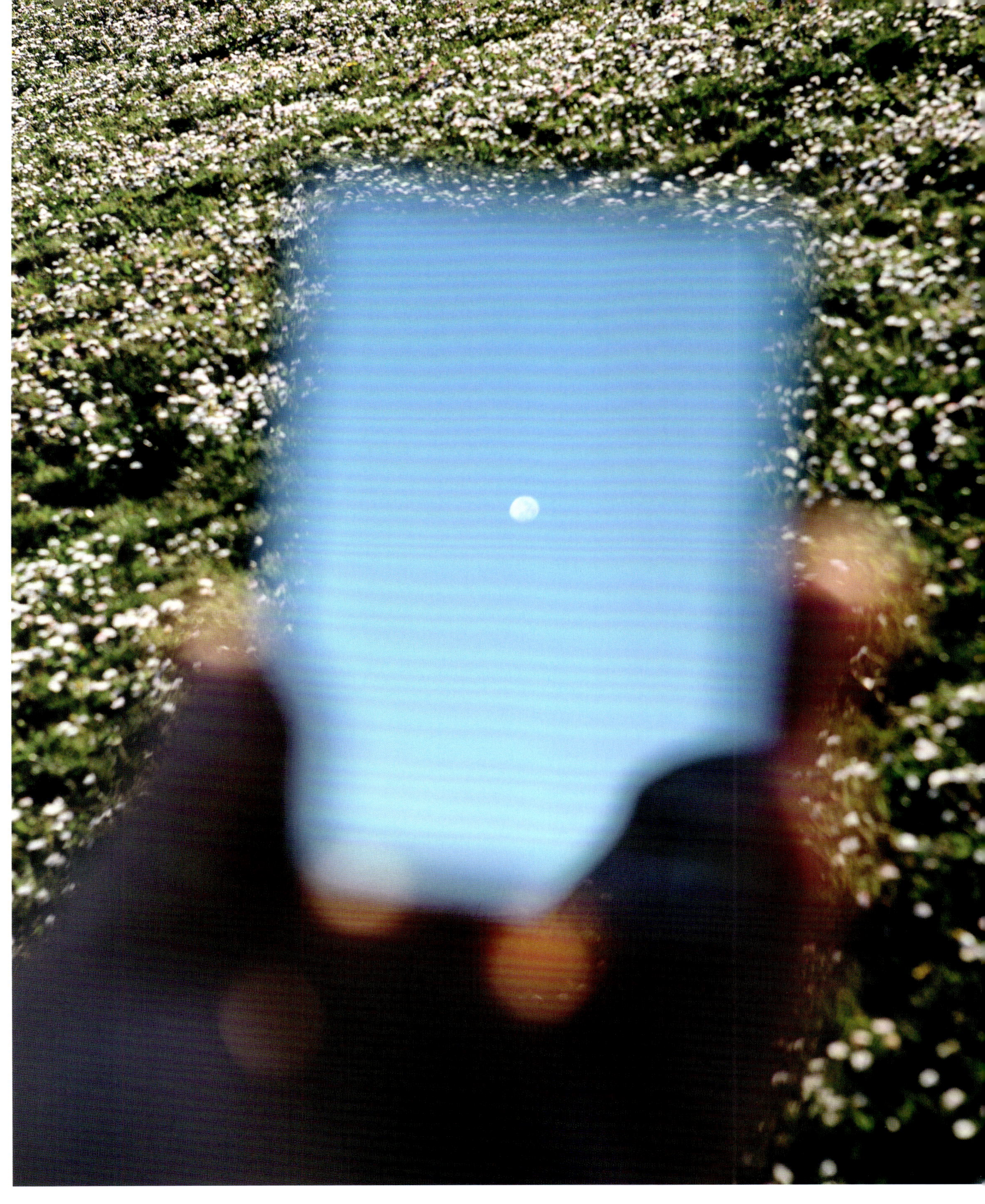

Susuki #2, 2020

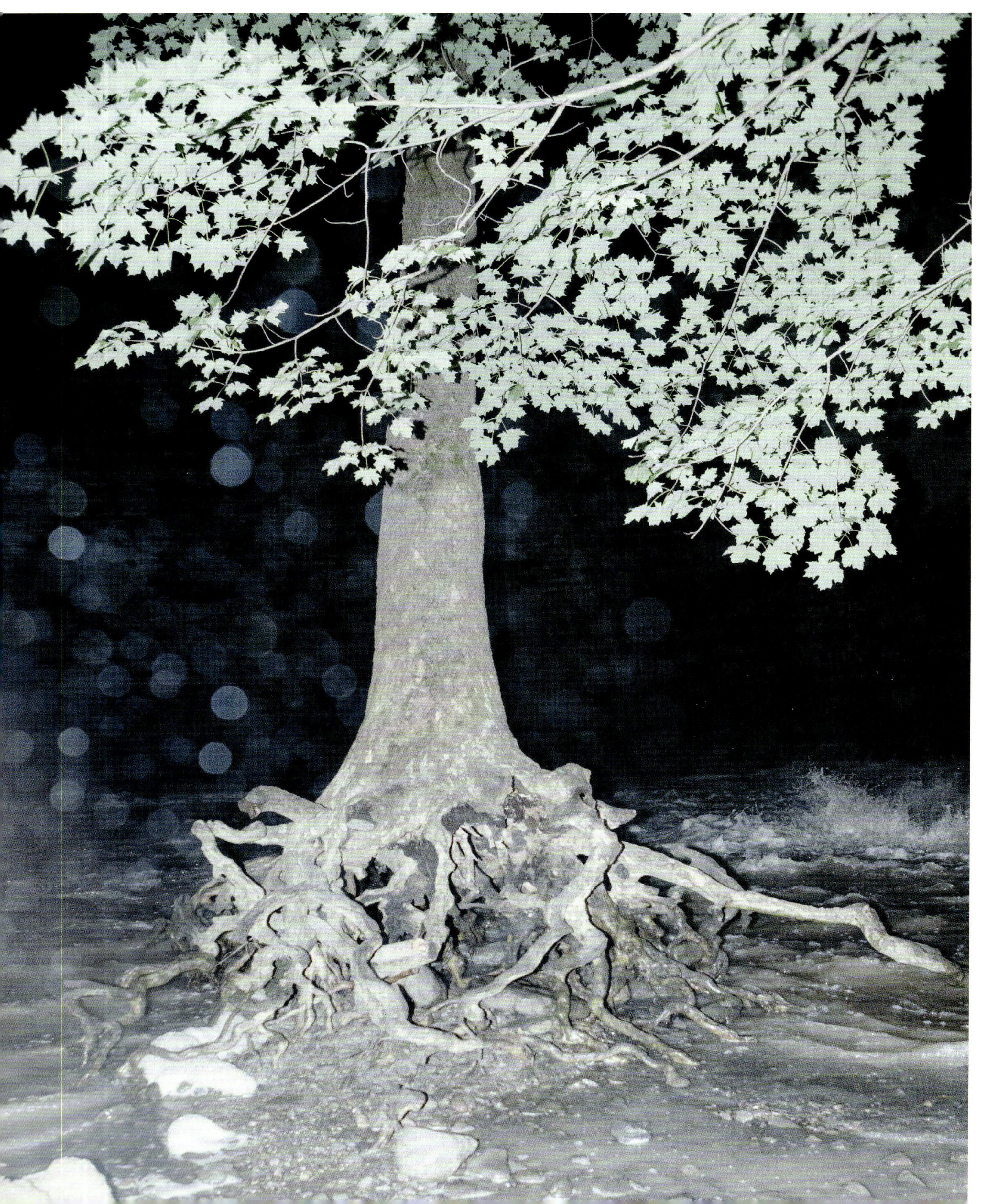

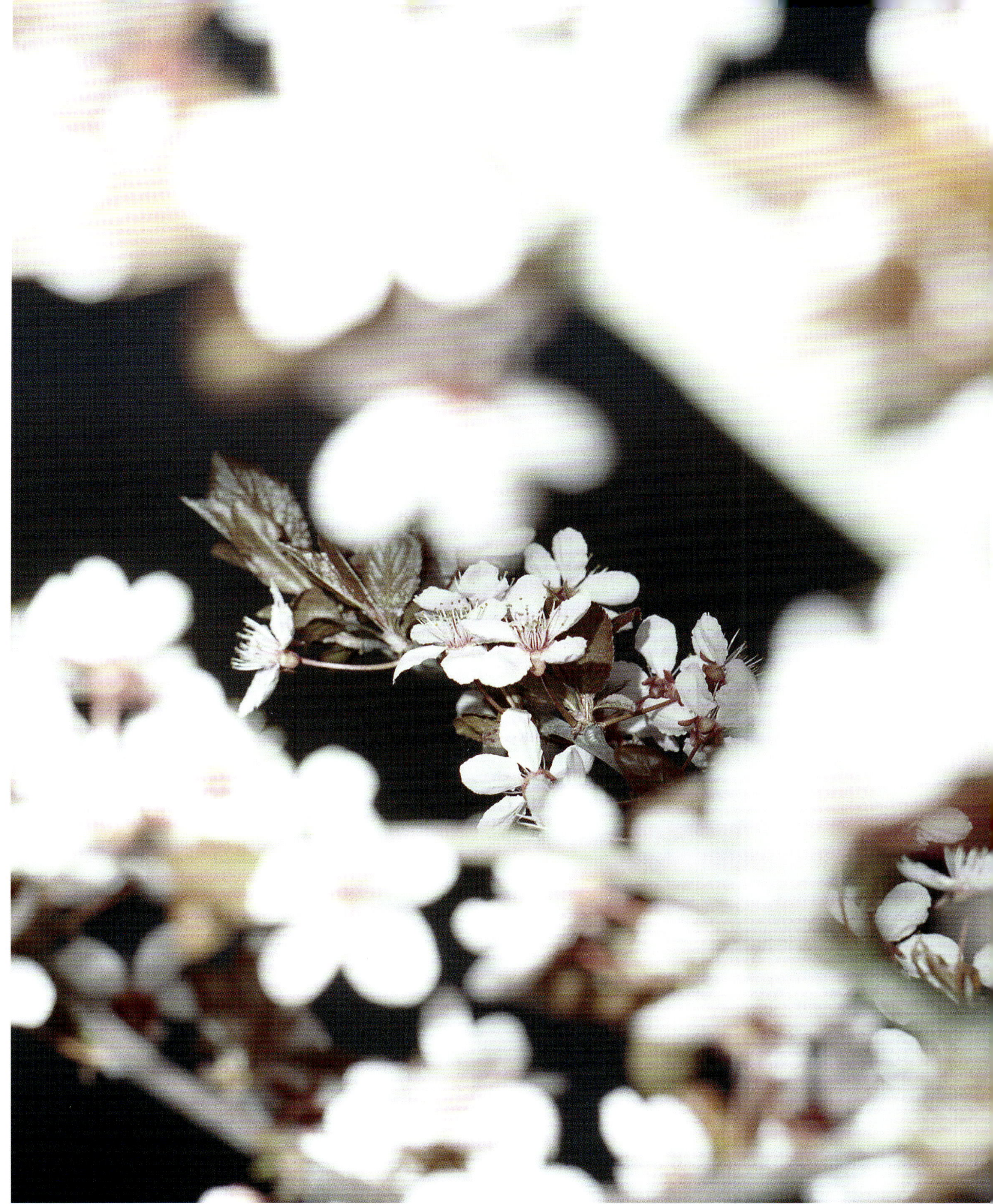

Ume #1, 2021

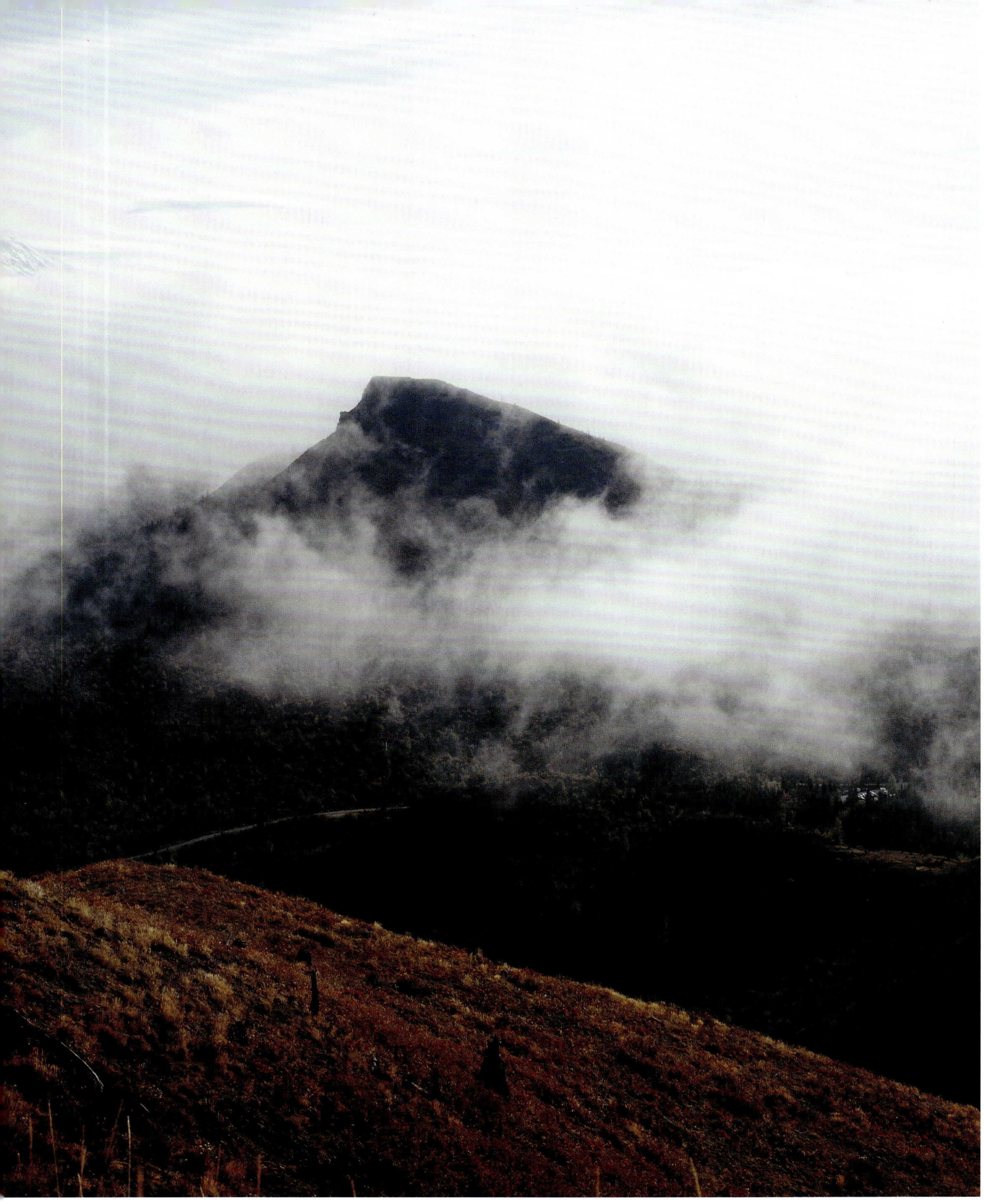

Susuki #3, **2020**

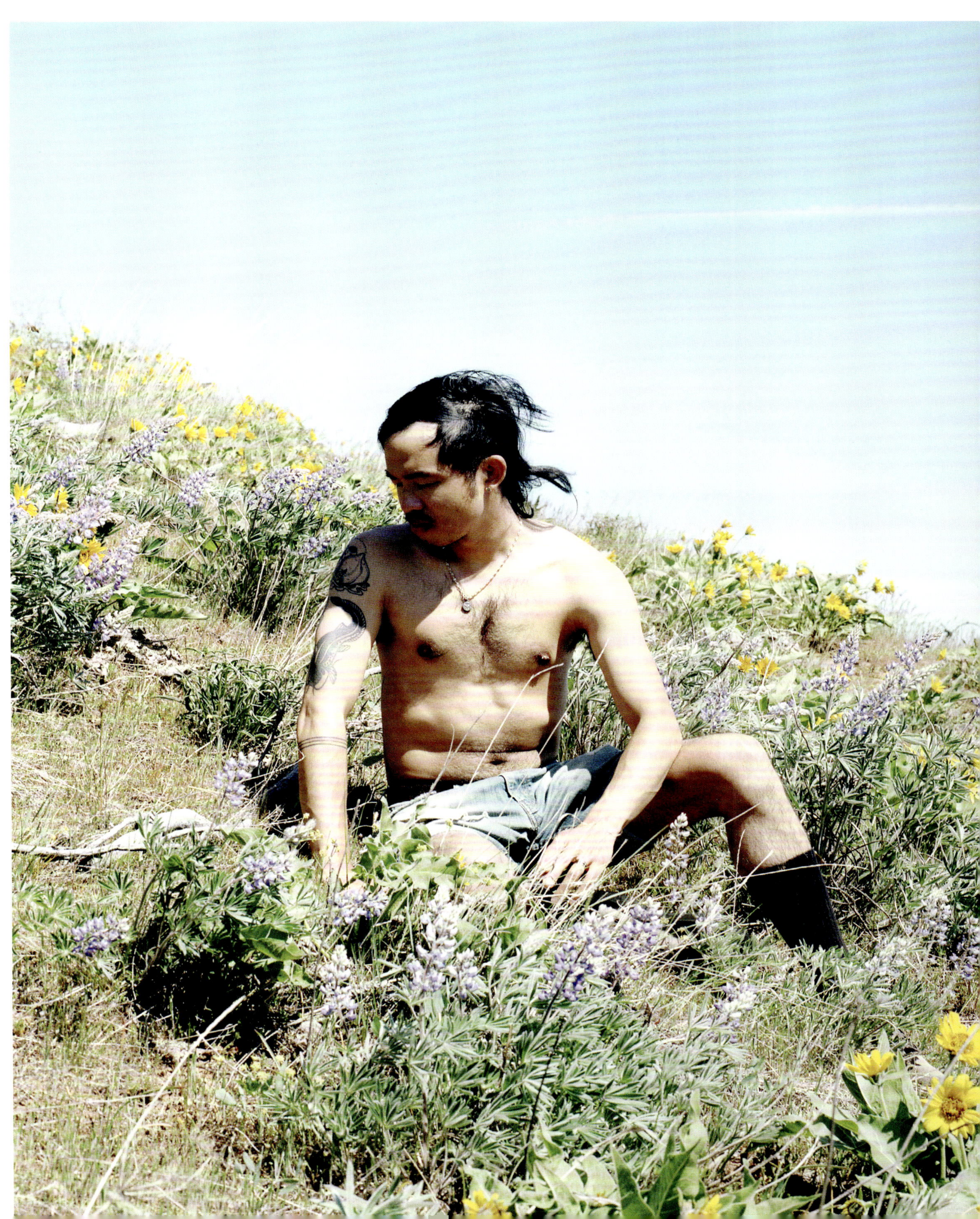

Ricardo, 2021

Untitled, 2020

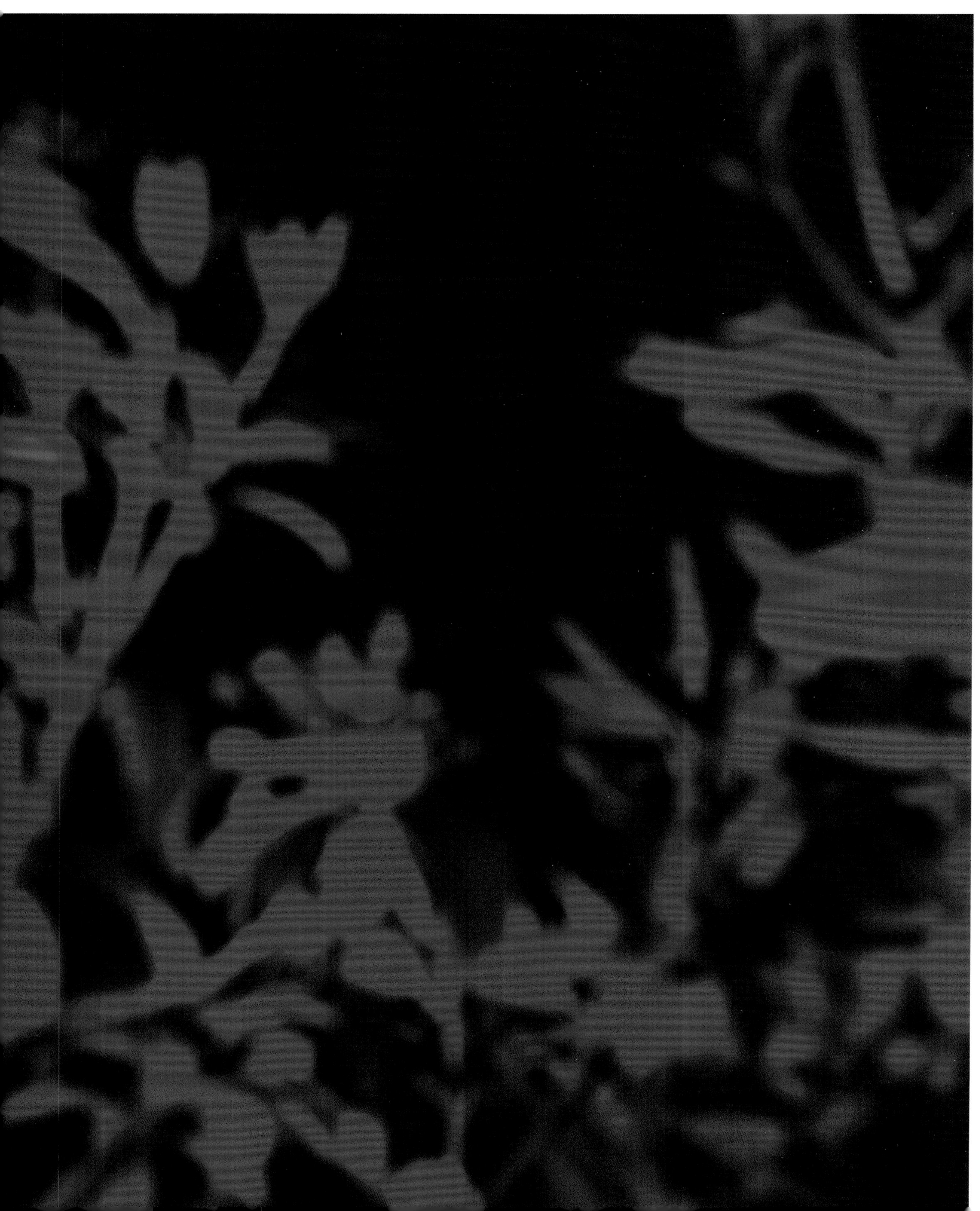

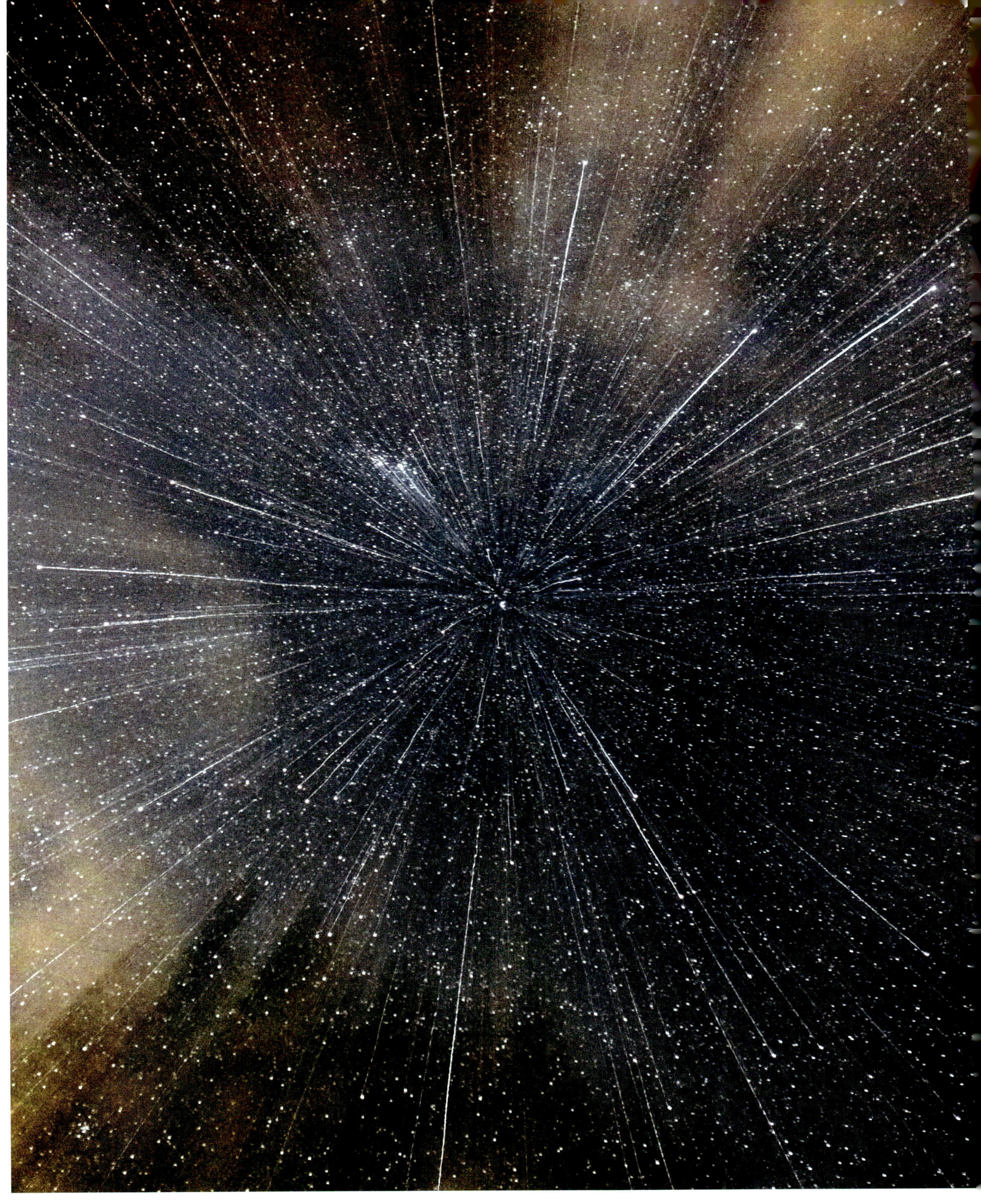

Kiku #3, 2021

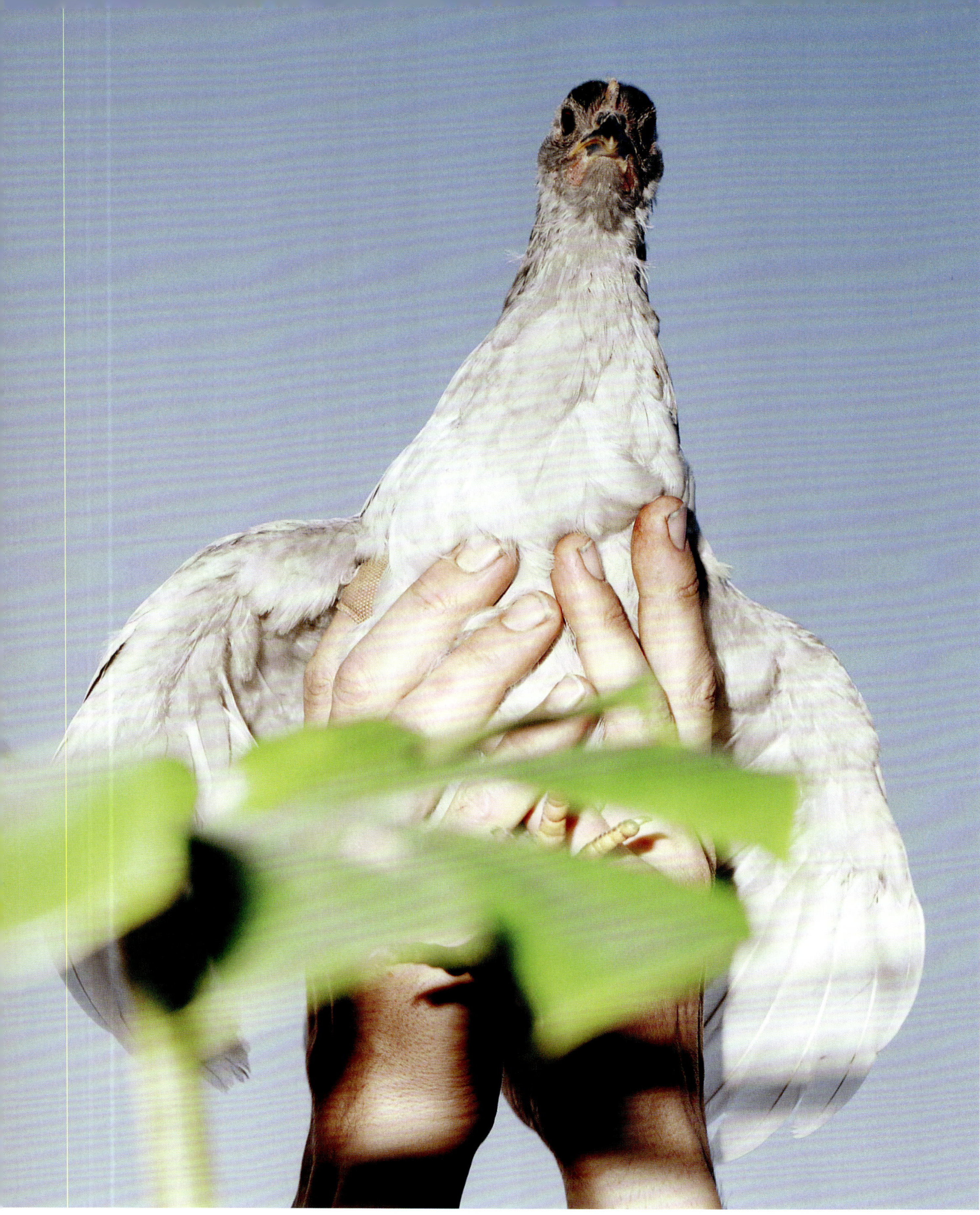

Phoenix, 2021

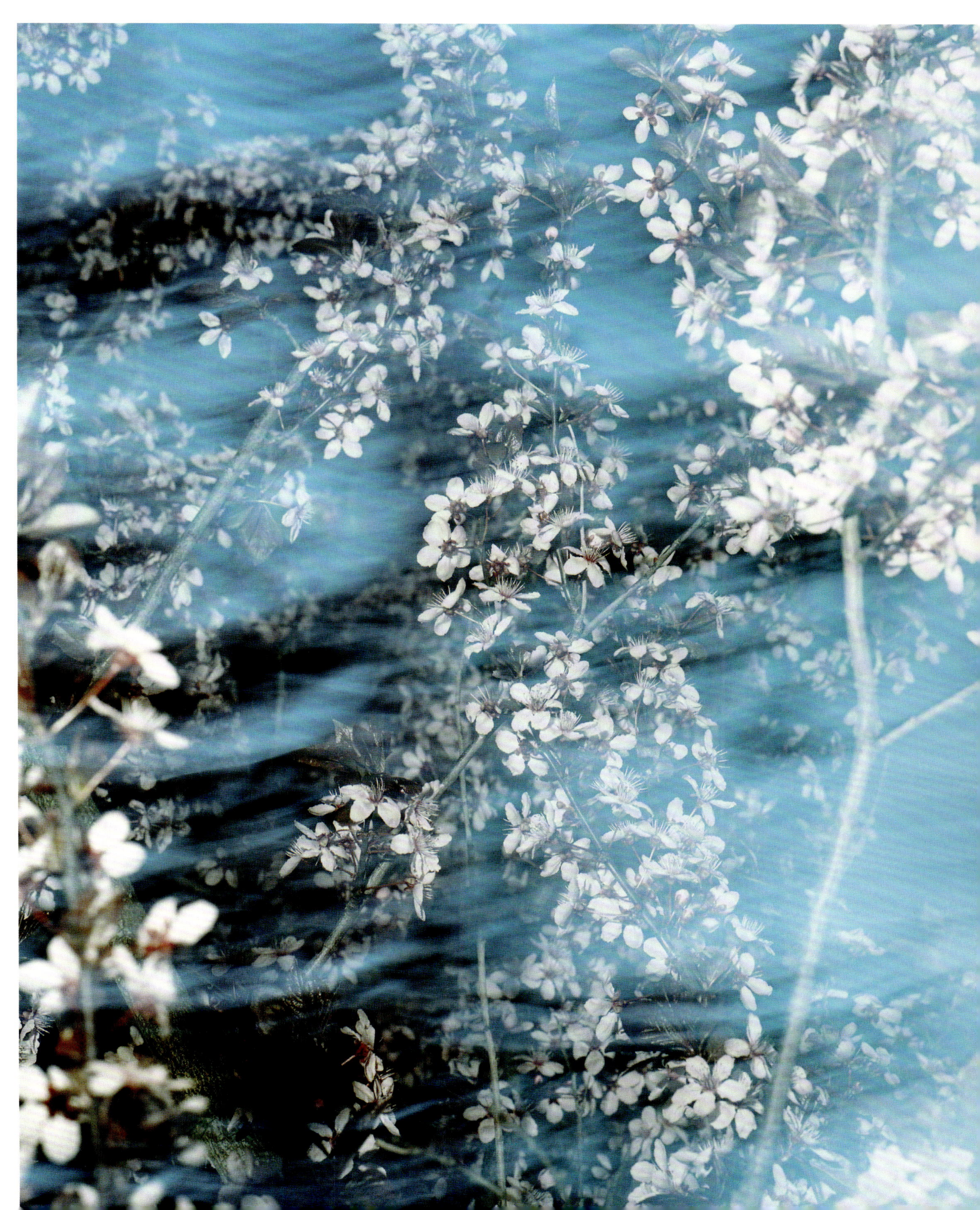

Ume #2, 2021
All photographs courtesy
the artist

Spring 2022 Books

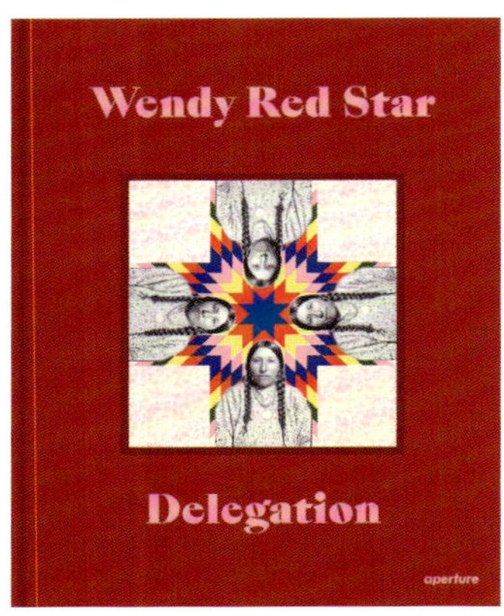

Wendy Red Star: Delegation
Delegation is the first comprehensive monograph by Apsáalooke artist Wendy Red Star, whose lens-based multimedia work recasts historical narratives with wit, candor, and a feminist, Indigenous perspective.
$65.00

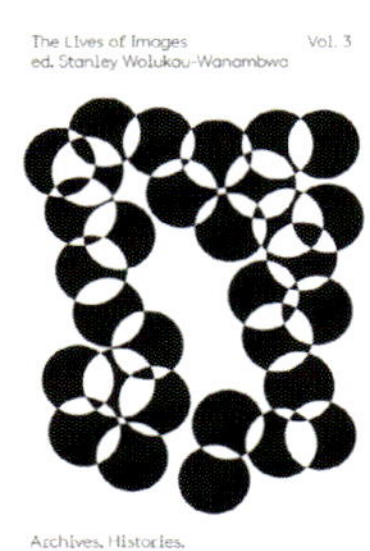

The Lives of Images, Vol. 3: Archives, Histories, and Memory
The Lives of Images series, edited by Stanley Wolukau-Wanambwa, gathers essays and interviews by essential voices in the field. Vol. 3 probes the necessity and limits of history, the politics of preservation and collective memory, and inquires as to what strategies centered in the archive might tell us about our present moment.
$24.95

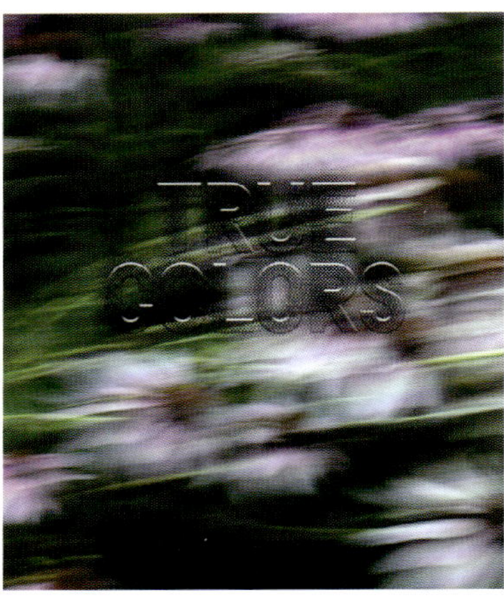

Zora J Murff: True Colors (or, Affirmations in a Crisis)
In *True Colors (or, Affirmations in a Crisis)*, trailblazing artist Zora J Murff constructs an incisive, autobiographical retelling of the struggles and epiphanies of a young Black artist working to make space for himself and his community.
$65.00

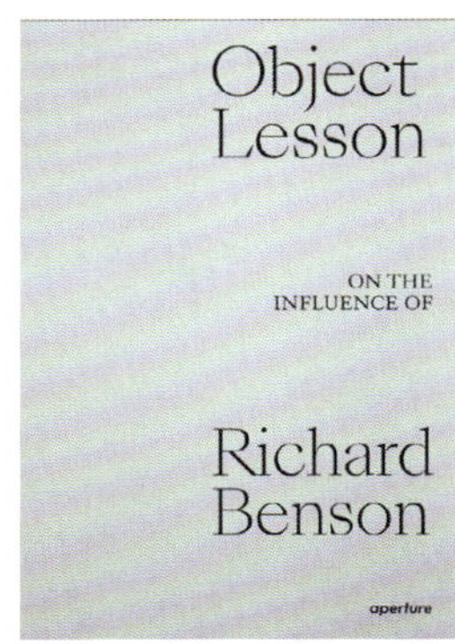

Object Lesson: On the Influence of Richard Benson
Through engaging interviews, testimonials, and anecdotes from photographers, curators, printers, and colleagues, *Object Lesson: On the Influence of Richard Benson* pays homage to this legendary Renaissance man and his lasting impact on generations of photography educators and practitioners.
$50.00

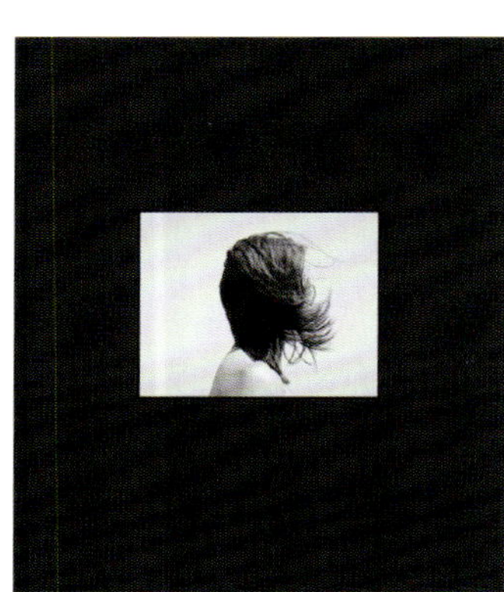

Tom Sandberg: Photographs
This monograph, produced in close collaboration with the Tom Sandberg Foundation in Oslo, is a long-overdue celebration of the late Norwegian photographer.
$75.00

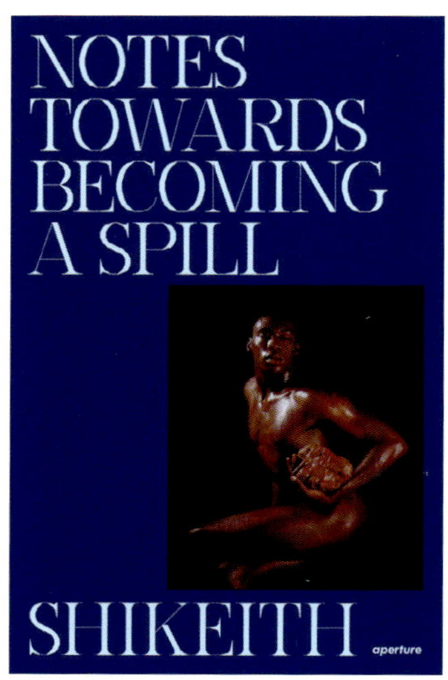

Shikeith: Notes towards Becoming a Spill
The first monograph by artist, filmmaker, and photographer Shikeith, *Notes towards Becoming a Spill* brings together a series of striking studio portraits of Black male subjects as they inhabit various states of meditation, prayer, and ecstasy.
$75.00

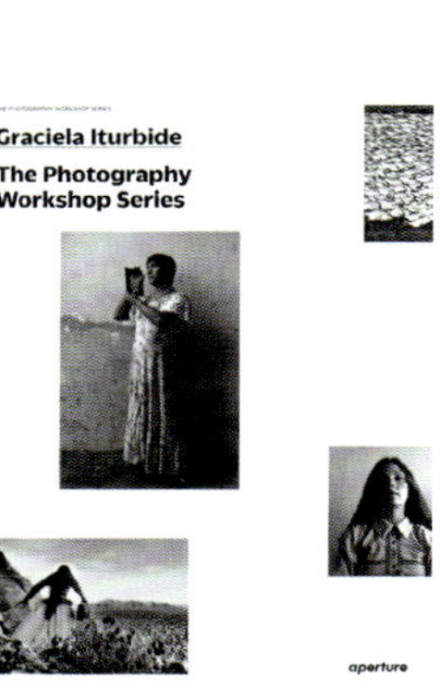

Graciela Iturbide: The Photography Workshop Series
In this volume of *The Photography Workshop Series*, Graciela Iturbide—known for her portraits and landscapes imbued with poetic ambiguity and documentary truth—explores photographing in ways that employ a deeply personal vision, while also reflecting subjects' rich cultural backgrounds.
$29.95

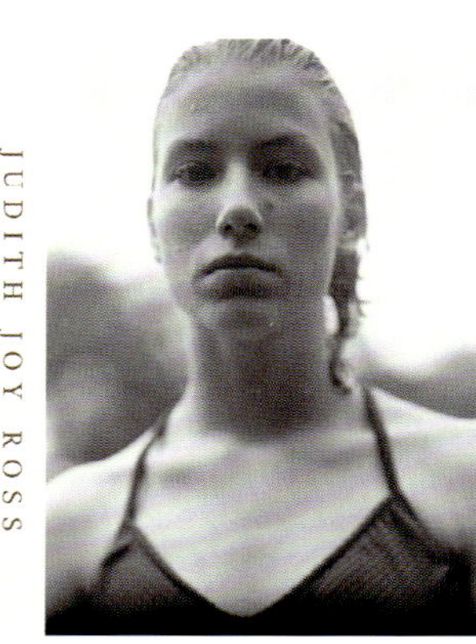

Judith Joy Ross: Photographs 1978–2015
Judith Joy Ross: Photographs 1978–2015 is an illuminating retrospective that explores the life and career of a revered American photographer illustrated by two hundred of her images, many never before seen or published.
$65.00

"

Twenty years ago, a then-unknown Ryan McGinley published a modest book of his early, ecstatic photographs that chronicled, with unvarnished intimacy and vibrancy, the lives of his close-knit friend group in downtown New York. The book would mark a pivotal crossroads in his emerging career.

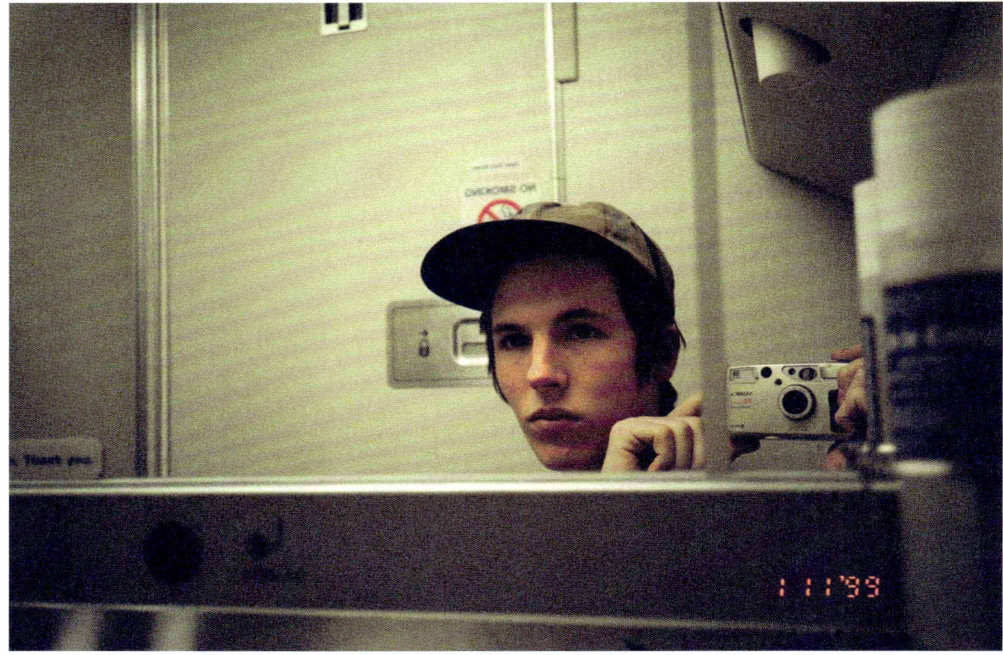

Ryan McGinley, Self-portrait, 1999
Courtesy the artist

You found your way to photography via a circuitous path but then quickly managed to produce a book. How did this come about?

I was in school at Parsons School of Design, and I was bopping around all the departments—painting, poetry, graphic design—and then I discovered photography. I was sneaking into the darkroom to enlarge and print poster-sized images. George Pitts saw them and hunted me down, basically, and asked me to switch to photography and study with him. He had a class called "Nudity, Sexuality, and Beauty in Photography" that he taught at *Vibe* magazine, in their back office.

Since I had just entered the department and wasn't a four-year photography student, I wasn't allowed a show like the rest of the students. I was bummed. So, I did my own photography show. A friend had a space on West Broadway that was empty. I made all these large prints and covered the whole space—and we had a big blowout. It was between an exhibition and a nightclub.

At this point, were you already making zines of your work?

I'd really been into zine making my whole life. Every few months, I'd make a zine at Kinko's, pumping out stuff on their copiers.

That show was pre-Internet. I went to 1-800 Postcards and made invitations and gave them to cool people on the street. I had done party promotion for Limelight and the Tunnel, so I was versed in that. A lot of people showed up, including some *Index* magazine staff. They got a zine I'd made and showed it to Peter Halley [the publisher]. Peter really looked up to Warhol, and *Index* was similar to early *Interview*. Peter wanted to publish artists' books and said, "Since you have all this work no one has seen, why don't we publish a book?"

What was the response to the book, which is simply titled *Ryan McGinley*?

The people who read *Index* were in art, fashion, or literature—so they were exposed to my work. Agnès b. was the first person to reach out to me. She wanted to do a show in Paris. A young curatorial assistant named Chris Perez was working at the Whitney. He bought one of the books for Sylvia Wolf, the curator, and she called me, and we started to have studio visits, in my apartment, over a number of months. And then, she asked me if I'd be interested in having a show at the Whitney—so the book was the catalyst for that happening.

What was in your zines before you started working with photographs?

I was into BMXing when I was younger, and I'd make all these zines, always at Kinko's. They were just about BMX culture, and bands I listened to, with both my drawings and clippings from magazines. I was really into shrinking and enlarging on a photocopier.

So it must have come naturally for you to make that first book.

Books are still the most important thing to me. They are beautiful and democratic. You can give a book to someone. And books don't get thrown out. They are always circulating. A lot of people don't make it to galleries or museums—and I want them to see my work too.

What do you feel when you look back on those early days?

It was so great. The *Index* team took a chance on me. I remember the smell of the ink on the paper when the boxes of books arrived. And I had to hustle to get them out into the world myself. I rode my bike to take them to bookstores like Spoonbill & Sugartown and St. Mark's Books. I remember driving to deliver them to Arcana in LA. It was a cool moment in time.